Grade 3

Lisa Lord

Helen G. Cappleman, Series Editor

With grateful acknowledgment to the late Anne H. Adams,
the originator of *SUCCESS in Reading and Writing*.

GoodYearBooks

An Imprint of ScottForesman
A Division of HarperCollins*Publishers*

Cover illustration by William Johnson.
Cover design by Amy O'Brien Krupp.
Book design by Carolyn McHenry.

Good Year Books

are available for preschool through grade 6 and for every basic curriculum subject plus many enrichment areas. For more Good Year Books, contact your local bookseller or educational dealer. For a complete catalog with information about other Good Year Books, please write:

Good Year Books
Scott, Foresman and Company
1900 East Lake Avenue
Glenview, Illinois 60025

Lord, Lisa
    Success in reading and writing. Grade 3 / Lisa Lord. — 2nd ed.
      p. cm.
    Anne Adams and Mary S. Johnson were the authors of the 1st ed.
    Includes index.
    ISBN 0-673-36003-2
    1. Reading (Elementary)—United States—Handbooks, manuals, etc.   2. Language arts (Elementary)—United States—Handbooks, manuals, etc.   3. Teaching—Aids and devices—Handbooks, manuals, etc.
I. Adams, Anne H. Success in writing. Grade 3.
II. Title   91-12873
LB1525.L72 1992   CIP
372.4'1—dc20

ISBN 0-673-36003-2

    4 5 6 7 8 9 10 - VHJ - 99 98 97 96 95 94 93

▶ Preface

Lisa Lord, author

SUCCESS in Reading and Writing is a student-centered integrated reading and writing program that is based on a belief in the capabilities of students and the professionalism of teachers. The instructional materials in this exciting program are library books and everyday materials, such as newspapers, magazines, and other materials from our print-rich world. Students of all abilities are routinely involved in individual and cooperative problem-solving activities that ask them to make decisions and take risks, without the necessity of placing them in ability groups. The flexible structure of the 180 lesson plans insures a balanced curriculum and a daily routine, but at the same time these lessons continually ask both teacher and student to make choices in the reading and writing taking place in the classroom.

Developed in the mid-1970s by the late Anne H. Adams, *SUCCESS in Reading and Writing* has stood the test of time. For more than twelve years, in all kinds of settings, *SUCCESS in Reading and Writing* has proven that valuing literacy and thinking results in literate, thinking students and teachers.

This second edition of *SUCCESS in Reading and Writing* follows in its philosophy and intent the first edition. In the years since *SUCCESS in Reading and Writing* was first developed, we have learned much about process teaching and learning, and a great deal of what Dr. Adams knew instinctively has been researched and proven true. She was able, even then, to outline a structure that insured balanced teaching but was flexible enough that teachers could adapt it to their teaching styles, curricular demands, and, most importantly, their students.

Our goal with this new edition of *SUCCESS in Reading and Writing* was to make the philosophy of the program clearer and even easier to implement. Now the procedures are clearer; the Writing module has been updated; we have placed an even greater emphasis on the importance of students reading and otherwise experiencing good books; and we have provided more information assisting teachers in making decisions within the framework of *SUCCESS in Reading and Writing*. These decisions range from integrating content-area themes and incorporating more children's books throughout the curriculum to assessing and meeting the needs of all students.

Perhaps the most apparent change comes in the names of the modules. In an effort to make the module names consistent across all grade levels, Research Practicum has been changed to Research; Composition to Writing; and Decoding in Context to Word Study.

The process of revision is ongoing. Learning about learning does not stop.

▶ Acknowledgments

SUCCESS in Reading and Writing workshop leaders, who have helped shape SUCCESS as it has developed in classrooms across the country:

Mary Armstrong	Becky Haseltine	Cam Newman
Peggy Bahr	Debby Head	Kathy Newport
Jean Becker	Paula Hertel	Ola Pickels
Patti Bell	Bridget Hill	Libby Pollett
Jean Bernholz	Tina Hinchliff	Karen Powell
Barbara Blackford	Robbie Ivers	Susan Quick
Jill Board	Connie John	Donna Rea
Elaine Bowie	Shae Johnson	Cathy Reasor
Ann Bryan	Delores P. Jones	Patty Redland
Jacqueline Buckmaster	Joanne Jumper	Mary B. Reeves
Helen Cappleman	Janice Keegan	Carole Reindl
Stacey Carmichael	Nancy Kerr	Pat Reinheimer
Kathi Caulley	Dana Kersey	Marilyn Renfro
Betty Cramer	Annie Kinegak	Janice Reynolds
Donna Croft	Barbara Krieger	Marlene Rotter
Suzie Desilet	Esther Lee	Pat Scherler
Bobbi Donnell	Sue Lippincott	Janet Schneider
Marilyn Enger	Lisa Lord	Shirley T. Scruggs
Betty S. English	Kathy Malick	Celeste Singletary
Sandra Fain	Judy Mansfield	Kathleen Smith
Debra Fetner	Howard Martin	Patty B. Smith
Neita Frank	Judy Martin	Pat Sumner
Carol George	Lila Martin	Pam Tate
Randy Gill	Nancy J. Mayhall	Donnye Theerman
Lynn Gori-Bjerkness	Becky Miller	Shirley A. Thompson
Letha Gressley	Debbie I. Miller	Jean Weaver
Andra Gwydir	Debby Miller	Beth Whitford
Carol Hall	Paul Moller	Pat Wong
Mary Harris	Cinda Lee Moon	Michael Wong
Roberta Harrison	Avril Moore	Kristin Zeaser-Sydow

Special thanks to Mike Wong, Jean Becker, Debbi Fetner, Paula Hertel, and Barbara Krieger for their help in writing this book. Also, thanks to Betty Cheeley, a *Math Their Way* instructor from Coeur d'Alene, Idaho, for her careful reading of the manuscript in its early stages. Thank you to Sharon Pearce, a third-grade teacher at Cainhoy Elementary School in Berkeley, County, South Carolina, for her thoughtful planning of the third-grade curriculum themes. Above all, thanks to my students at Cainhoy Elementary School, who taught me everything I know about third-graders and their reading, writing, and learning.

▶ Art Acknowledgments

The following young artists have contributed to this edition of *SUCCESS in Reading and Writing,* Grade 3:

Erin P. Johnson, Richmond, Virginia
J. R. Zufelt, Soldotna, Alaska
Michael B. Sellman, Richmond, Virginia
Cheever Farley, Richmond, Virginia
Aleishia Dobbins, Washington, D.C.
Jacob Barron, Soldotna, Alaska
Andy Giesbrecht, Soldotna, Alaska
Jessica Myers, Richmond, Virginia
Sarah Whitten, Masdens, Virginia
Ann-Sydney Harden, Richmond, Virginia
Jim Conant, Seward, Alaska
Deleshia Williams, Huger, South Carolina
William Johnson, Seward, Alaska
Josh Demske, Soldotna, Alaska
Shea Hutchings, Soldotna, Alaska
Sheena Manigault, Huger, South Carolina
Desiree Jordan, Seward, Alaska
Ann Schnell, Richmond, Virginia
Kevin VanKleeck, Seward, Alaska
Bethany Davidson, Soldotna, Alaska

▶ Contents

Grade 3

Chapter 1 SUCCESS: An Invitation to Learning

Learners are welcome in a SUCCESS classroom, where hundreds of the best books for children, as well as stacks of local newspapers, baskets of magazines, and boxes of maps, brochures, and catalogs line the shelves. Learners of all kinds, from every ability group, are invited to read, write, and learn with friends in this place where everyone can succeed. The teacher here creates a safe structure within which learners make choices every day. Learners enter this place as members of a literary community, knowing what to expect, not waiting to be told what the teacher wants, but ready to act like full-fledged readers and writers.

What an impressive and exciting invitation! Is it pie in the sky? Is it idealistic? Over the past decade, SUCCESS teachers have found that such an invitation to learning is in easy reach of students everywhere if their teachers can envision how much students *want* to read, write, and learn.

This book explains how teachers go about issuing this generous invitation to learning; in addition, the last 180 pages are outlines of lesson plans that might be used in a third-grade class. A quick glance at those pages reveals that every day's plan is similar to every other day's plan. For such a grand invitation, the plans *look* fairly monotonous.

It's true: procedures in a SUCCESS class don't change much throughout the year. *It is the children who change.* The sameness of the teacher's lesson plans allows for true child-centered instruction, along with time for the teacher to help children individually and in small groups.

For a teacher who intends to invite all children to learn, SUCCESS becomes a way of organizing time for language arts instruction. Given a consistent schedule of times for reading, writing, and seeking information, students rapidly develop these abilities using all kinds of everyday materials, including the best literature for children. Students work with partners and student-selected groups and are allowed to make many choices about their own reading and writing.

The consistent schedule comprises four main, daily activities, which are called modules: Research, Recreational Reading, Writing, and Word Study. Each module should last for at least thirty minutes every day. Possibilities for extending the amount of time for the modules are explained later in this chapter.

Within this consistent daily schedule of four main activities, essentially the same things happen every day. Again, teachers find that rather than changing procedures and programs all the time, they can watch their students change! These are the basic procedures:

Erin P. Johnson

Here's how!

1. Research:
   a. The teacher conducts a brief lead-in activity (5 minutes).
   b. The students search for information in a variety of real-world materials and take notes (20 minutes).
   c. The students share what they learned (5 minutes).
2. Recreational Reading:
   a. The students read books they choose (30 minutes or more).
   b. The teacher confers with the students.
3. Writing:
   a. The teacher leads a brief mini-lesson (5 minutes).
   b. The students write (20 minutes or more).
   c. The students share their writing (5 minutes).
4. Word Study:
   This is a time for investigating spelling patterns and new vocabulary in meaningful context.
   a. The teacher leads chart-making (10 minutes).
   b. The students write (15 minutes).
   c. The students take a partner spelling test (5 minutes).

In addition to these four activities, SUCCESS teachers *read aloud* to their students for fifteen to twenty minutes a day.

The modules are not independent, isolated activities. Sometimes teachers may plan to emphasize materials or topics in more than one module. More often, the skills a student is developing in one part of the day's work are involved in what he or she does in another module. Students marvel when something they learned in one module coincidentally appears in other material later in the day. Because students make many choices about their work in SUCCESS, they can choose to extend the work they do in one module into their work in another activity. In many ways the four modules are interrelated and dependent upon each other.

Same schedule every day. Same procedures every day. A language arts program needs more excitement, some would say. Maybe that would be true if the growth of children as learners was not exciting, or if the availability of a great variety of children's literature was not exciting, or if a teacher's enthusiasm for learning was not exciting. The secret of SUCCESS is in the wonders of learning as experienced by a single child, compounded by the joy of a whole community of children learning, and celebrated by a teacher who loves to learn. Same schedule. Same procedures. The children are changing every day.

Many educators seem to believe that children learn because of a perfect presentation by the teacher, a perfect choice of examples and materials for activities, and the right questions asked at the right time. But, more important, children need time for learning and the teacher's trust in them as learners. Teachers need time to work with the learners in their classroom and trust in the appeal of real reading and writing and

SUCCESS 562 PX

22A 23 ▼23

SUCCESS has given me more opportunities to be flexible and creative in all areas. I feel I can use a greater variety of materials than before I used the program. SUCCESS provides opportunities for all children to participate at their own levels and, as a result, they feel good about themselves.

Isabel B. Hernandez, teacher

learning. SUCCESS provides the *time* and *trust* for learning that children and teachers need.

SUCCESS teachers work to establish the routine of consistent times and activities for reading and writing beginning on the first day of school. Once they and the students know the procedures of SUCCESS, learning begins in earnest, in an atmosphere of freedom and trust. Teachers find themselves so confident of the lesson plans that they only need to glance at a few key words in the plan each day: perhaps the topics, the materials, or the skills emphasis. The words describing the routine procedures remain on every lesson plan page for the sake of substitute teachers, principals, supervisors, and anyone else who may not be totally familiar with SUCCESS. After a quick glance at the lesson plan, the teacher is ready to focus intently on the children in his or her classroom.

A sample outline for a day's SUCCESS lesson appears on page 6. Where there are blank lines, teachers are encouraged to choose topics, skills, and materials that are most appropriate for their classes.

Lesson **23**

Research

LEAD-IN
Teacher introduces the Project Idea.
Topic: Land forms or _____
Material: Social studies textbook or
_____
Comprehension Skill: Classification
or _____

SEARCH & RECORD
Group Size: 4 or _____
Project Idea: After getting ideas from
pictures in the textbook, draw pictures to
show hot, dry, and wet places in the
world or _____.

SHARING
Display pictures or _____.
　Papers are dated and filed.

Recreational Reading

All students read books for approximately
30 minutes.

CONVERSATIONS
The teacher also reads silently. The
teacher has some short conversations with
readers. When appropriate, the main
focus of these conversations is decoding
skills.

CLIPBOARD NOTES
Teacher notes students' selections of
books and their ability to decode well
enough to sustain attention to a story.

READ-ALOUD BOOK
White Dynamite and Curly Kidd by Bill
Martin, Jr., and John Archambault or
_____

Writing

Theme: Places or _____

MINI-LESSON
Teacher demonstrates ideas for writing
descriptions of places or _____.

COMPOSING
Write a description of a place or
_____.

SHARING
Volunteers read their descriptions to the
whole group or _____.
　Papers are dated and filed.

Word Study

CHART DEVELOPMENT
Spelling Emphasis: *e* or _____
Other Emphasis:
■ adjective with noun
■ land forms or _____
　On the chart, the teacher lists phrases
volunteered by students using:
■ *e* words
■ adjective/noun phrases
■ land form vocabulary or _____.

WRITING
On their papers, students write their
favorite words from the chart or other

words, phrases, or sentences that would
be appropriate for the chart.

SPELLING
Partners call out words for each other to
spell aloud.
　Papers are dated and filed.

HOMEWORK
Write sentences with adjectives/nouns
containing the letter *e* that describe items
you would find in a department store.

It is possible to extend the amount of time spent on some of the modules when teachers integrate other content-area objectives into the language arts curriculum. Integrating content-area information seems to enhance instruction in all areas of the curriculum; nevertheless, *language arts* objectives can be met by conducting daily the four thirty-minute modules described earlier. This book can be used as a guide for language arts instruction equally well by teachers who are limited to a two-hour period for language arts separate from the rest of the curriculum, and by teachers who can extend language arts time by incorporating content-area objectives into their students' reading, writing, and learning.

Beyond the minimum two hours needed for language arts instruction, teachers who choose to integrate content-area objectives into the SUCCESS format will spend longer than thirty minutes on the Recreational Reading module and on the Writing module. For example, a teacher who chooses to incorporate social studies information into the Research module can add the time scheduled for social studies class to the Recreational Reading module. Children benefit from having more than thirty minutes to read. A teacher who incorporates science and health topics into the Word Study module will be able to increase the time scheduled for Writing, another beneficial change for children.

The SUCCESS format uses no worksheets, textbooks, teacher's guides, or other teaching aides. Instruction in each SUCCESS classroom is unique because teachers, students, and the decisions they make differ from class to class. One of the major strengths of SUCCESS is its reliance upon teacher professionalism and decision making. For this reason, SUCCESS is not recommended for teachers who don't like to make decisions!

▶ Which Teachers Could Use SUCCESS?

All SUCCESS teachers are literate decision makers who believe children want to read, write, and learn. By making decisions that allow children to be part of a literary community at school, they know that children can enjoy the same built-in rewards of literacy that adults do.

They truly believe that reading, writing, and learning are pleasurable, worthwhile, and even essential for a satisfying life.

They are not adults who have "received" or "completed" an education; they are lifelong learners who are enthusiastic about sharing their ongoing education with younger learners.

They believe that reading, writing, and learning are so rewarding in themselves that the role of teacher becomes one of facilitator, not director.

▶ The Big Decisions

Any teacher who recognizes the characteristics of a SUCCESS teacher in himself or herself will want to know more about what SUCCESS teachers do every day to carry out this language arts program. It is, after all, only a framework for instruction, and any SUCCESS teacher will need to make decisions constantly. What are those decisions all about?

DECIDING TO FOCUS ON STUDENTS

Because SUCCESS teachers believe children like to learn and are rewarded by what they learn, they choose to center instruction on their students. They want their children to read and learn more than could ever be included in the textbooks for one grade in school. In addition, they don't believe that any body of information is so valuable that it should be "covered," or that there are essential lessons, questions, or answers that should be controlled by the teacher and merely received by the student.

SUCCESS teachers choose to focus on their students, the learners who are in the process of developing their knowledge and abilities. They must constantly observe each student to determine his or her needs, interests, budding abilities, and development as a member of the literary community. Many of the decisions SUCCESS teachers make are based on what they learn from their observations.

SUCCESS emphasizes the processes of learning rather than the products of the students' work, or the contents of a particular textbook. The emphasis is on the person more than on the subject matter or skills. The human beings who comprise the literary communities of SUCCESS classrooms are the center of the teaching. Those human beings can learn much more than what is generally expected to be covered in textbooks.

J. R. Zufelt

SUCCESS teachers realize that they cannot give students full attention if a textbook, a teacher's guide, or the teacher is the center of instruction in the class. Even many literature-based, whole language programs suffer from directing students' attention to the teacher, to find out what is planned for them that day. SUCCESS teachers, on the other hand, invite students to know exactly what to expect every day and to be active in anticipating and planning their own learning activities. A child may choose to read about Jerry Rice and the NFL and write about the Teenage Mutant Ninja Turtles instead of reading the teacher's favorite book and writing something for the teacher's publishing project. SUCCESS students know their teacher's preferences, but these students believe that their own choices are valued and not controlled by the teacher.

DECIDING TO DEVELOP A COMMUNITY OF LEARNERS

SUCCESS teachers decide to think of their classes as communities of learners, where students can help each other and share what they are discovering. Motivation and an increase in thinking come along with all the talking and cooperating that students do daily as parts of their work. There is little competition and little lonely work. There is lots of explaining and suggesting. The words "What if we . . ." are heard often. Students consider many possible ways to go about their work and know that there is rarely only one right answer.

This community of cooperating learners differs from the ability groups found in many language arts classes. Test scores and textbooks do not control what students learn in SUCCESS classrooms. Because of the routine activities they lead and the wealth of everyday reading materials in their classrooms, teachers don't have to group the students by their abilities to match their "levels" with the demands of a particular textbook. Instead, in structured, open-ended daily activities, students are expected to do the best work possible for them. In order to do so, they make choices about their own learning.

Perhaps because of the community spirit in SUCCESS classes, SUCCESS students are willing to take risks as learners. Students take the initiative because they know that the limits in SUCCESS classrooms have more to do with available time than with a right answer. Many choices are not only acceptable, but valuable; when there is more emphasis on process than on product, students are not preoccupied with how the teacher judges them. Because of the cooperative approach to learning in a SUCCESS community, students do not feel threatened or afraid. How could they fear failure in SUCCESS classes? With the routine use of everyday reading materials, the initiative students take in the classroom in their reading and writing is more likely to show up at home, to be shared with parents, and to become a lifelong habit.

DECIDING ON A SCHEDULE

SUCCESS teachers are committed to a routine that gives children time they can count on for reading, for writing, and for seeking new information. Scheduling all of the SUCCESS modules and establishing routines for the regular SUCCESS activities teaches students that each day they will have sizable periods of time for various literary endeavors.

The teacher's decision about the schedule conveys priorities to the students: reading, writing, and learning new things must be the most valuable activities of the school day. This structured schedule is extremely important in a SUCCESS classroom.

A SUCCESS teacher first needs to determine the time that is available for language arts instruction each day and choose four thirty-minute periods of time when all, or most, of the students are in the class. SUCCESS is intended for all third-graders, so the schedule should include those who go to resource classes for part of the day, those who leave for gifted and talented programs, and those who attend remedial reading and math classes. Ideally, teachers are able to integrate many content areas into the SUCCESS framework; in those cases, more than two hours will be used to complete the SUCCESS modules every day. For teachers who are limited to two hours of language arts instruction time, the four thirty-minute periods of time need not be consecutive. Special-area classes, lunch, recess, math, social studies, science, health, resource classes, and so on can be interspersed among the four SUCCESS modules.

Michael B. Sellman

One module might be taught first thing in the morning, and the fourth one might not be scheduled until the last thing in the day.

Teachers choose to teach the modules in various orders. Many teachers begin with the Writing module and follow that with Word Study. Then, for many teachers, comes Research. Many teachers manage to schedule Recreational Reading right after lunch. For some, Word Study is a good way to start the day.

What matters is that all four modules, plus read-aloud time, are scheduled to happen every day. Ideally, the same schedule is followed every day. Once the schedule has been determined, the teacher should make a poster listing the names of the modules and the time each is taught. Mounted on the wall by the classroom door, the poster helps the teacher and the students get accustomed to the schedule at the beginning of the year. Before long, the schedule becomes second nature to everyone in the class, and the poster is then helpful to visitors.

Teachers who try to use "some" of SUCCESS as a supplement to another program will have trouble finding time for all of the modules. Those who think of themselves as SUCCESS teachers do all four modules every day, realizing that the four different activities complement and reinforce each other. SUCCESS teachers know that they would not see the same good results if they compromised the amount of time that is recommended for all four modules.

Extra time is available for reading, writing, and learning in SUCCESS classrooms because the teacher spends no time telling the class what is going to happen next. Students can dive right into their reading, writing, and learning without being confused about directions.

DECIDING TO MAKE MORE DECISIONS

SUCCESS teachers have made three big decisions already—to think of instruction as student-centered, not teacher- or textbook-centered; to create a community of learners; and to create a framework of time that students depend on for their reading, writing, and learning. Now they prepare to make even more decisions that will enhance students' learning. Day by day, they decide what topics and materials to make available and when to include skills instruction or new information. They decide when it is appropriate to integrate content-area topics with language arts class and when certain pieces of literature are important for the class. They decide when to ask questions and how to evaluate students' progress. They decide when to pursue the teachable moments that constantly arise. Many of their decisions differ from year to year because they are learning from different students each year, and their decisions aren't the same as those of other SUCCESS teachers because each teacher and class is unique.

▶ Is It Hard to Teach SUCCESS?

All these decisions! Why would anyone deliberately give up prepared assignments and a textbook teacher's guide? Three things about SUCCESS make the decision-making teacher's work easier:

1. Lesson plans for SUCCESS classes are virtually the same every day. The teacher and the students learn the basic procedures for the four modules very quickly, and everyone knows what to do next.

Boring? No, because the topics, skills, and reading materials frequently change. Because the procedures are dependable, the exciting things in class are the new books people choose to read, the new information they learn and share, and the writing they produce.

Teachers don't spend time duplicating materials, checking papers, or listening to the same stories being read over and over. They don't spend long hours developing activities to accompany the trade books they would like their students to read.

2. Individualizing instruction usually means extra work for the teacher. SUCCESS has helped many students with special needs, both gifted students and students who have problems, because of the large amount of individualized instruction that takes place every day. Special needs are met partly because of all the choices students can make, and partly because the teacher is able to spend more time helping students in class.

In the Recreational Reading module, the teacher spends thirty minutes, or 100 percent of the time, responding to individual needs. After leading the mini-lesson in the Writing module, the teacher is available to give individual assistance for twenty-five minutes, including the time for sharing. After conducting the lead-in activity in the Research module, the teacher is available to help individuals until time for sharing, for a total of twenty minutes. In the Word Study module, the teacher leads class discussion for up to fifteen minutes, leaving at least fifteen minutes for individual help.

This individual help is the main teaching that is done in SUCCESS; it isn't squeezed in when the teacher has time. Neither does it embarrass students who need extra help; everyone gets individual attention routinely! That is the SUCCESS teacher's job for at least ninety minutes every day in language arts class alone. For only 25 percent of language

*I*t is more of a lifestyle teaching—a way of thinking that permeates the entire school day. I have seen my students gain an absolute passion for reading and writing with SUCCESS.

Debbie Miller, teacher

arts class is the teacher away from individuals and demanding everyone's attention at once.

3. It is easier to make all these decisions knowing that recent research supports SUCCESS. The most convincing research is what each SUCCESS teacher is able to report about each of his or her students: how each student learns best, exactly what he or she is able to read and write, what his or her interests are, and so forth. Standardized test results of SUCCESS students are acceptable, and sometimes outstanding, and have never been reported as the reason a teacher stopped using the program. But SUCCESS teachers believe that standardized test scores don't come close to showing all that their students have learned.

Educational literature of the 1990s is filled with reports of how little time students actually spend reading real books at school and how few minutes each day they take to write anything longer than fill-in-the-blanks. Newspapers report alarming illiteracy rates and sad stories about poor teaching. The good news is what professional journals report about literature-based instruction, whole language, cooperative learning, process writing, and many other ideas that are integral parts of SUCCESS. In places where educational practices have not changed to keep up with the trends reported in educational literature, it is encouraging to see SUCCESS professionals making the kinds of decisions that are supported by research.

▶ The History of SUCCESS

In 1976, years before terms such as "whole language" and "cooperative learning" were used, SUCCESS was begun by Anne H. Adams to provide an alternative to basal textbook instruction. At that time it was popular to point out all the things that were wrong with basals, since the public was becoming aware of the illiteracy problem in the United States. Teachers attending professional conferences heard speakers criticize traditional reading instruction but offer few substitutes.

Anne Adams joined the best of them in trying to persuade people that basals were certainly not solving the problem of illiteracy. She suggested that assigning one more skills worksheet might do more harm than good. Most significantly, she gave teachers a structured, but flexible, daily plan to replace the basals. She reminded educators that teachers are professionals and should make many decisions every day about how to teach their students.

SUCCESS was used first in Durham, North Carolina. Children who had not succeeded in learning to read and write were indeed successful in SUCCESS classes, and the word began to spread around the country. Anne Adams taught teachers in other states how to use SUCCESS, and more children benefited from this new way of organizing language arts instruction time. Although she died in 1980 before all of the original SUCCESS books had been published, the work she had begun flourished as teachers told their colleagues about what was happening in their SUCCESS classrooms.

▶ SUCCESS in the 1990s

These days, teachers can advocate SUCCESS because of all the things that are right about it, not because it is simply an alternative to basals. Among basals, some of the old problems still exist, but many publishers at least pay lip service to the complaints of teachers. Some basals even incorporate a whole language approach. Many teachers have abandoned the basal anyway and substituted instruction that centers around children's books, a welcome improvement.

Whatever the case may be with the basals of the 1990s and various forms of literature-based instruction, SUCCESS is a way of organizing language arts instruction that truly helps students. Even though every class is different, after more than a decade of using the SUCCESS framework, teachers can examine the characteristics that SUCCESS classes have in common.

1. Students make many decisions, not only about the substance of their reading and writing, but also about who their partners and committee members will be.

2. Students understand that there is rarely just one right answer, and they know they can work with each other to solve problems and seek information; therefore, they are more willing to take risks as learners.

3. The teacher makes many decisions about topics, materials, skills, and the social dynamics of students sharing and working together.

4. Students and teachers focus more on the processes of learning than on the final products.

5. A daily schedule of reading, writing, and learning allows students extended periods of time for making choices about the books they read, the types of writing they do, and so on.

6. The teacher strongly emphasizes the importance of communication among students.

7. The teacher's role is to establish the framework within which students can read, write, and learn. Being a creative, energetic teacher in a SUCCESS classroom means observing the strengths and needs of the students and being open to the endless possibilities of what they might learn as literate people working together. A creative SUCCESS teacher learns much from and with the students.

SUCCESS is not meant to be used by all teachers. It is recommended for teachers who appreciate the characteristics that make the program work. They must believe that reading and writing are wonderful and that students really do wish to join in the fun of learning and developing as literate human beings. Those who have read this far understand the main decisions a teacher must make in order to organize language arts instruction this way. The next four chapters explain more about each of the four modules. Chapter 6 covers relatively minor decisions the teacher must make: how to get materials; how to evaluate; how to adapt SUCCESS to special situations; and how to acquaint administrators, parents, and others with SUCCESS. Finally, in the second part of this book, 180 lesson plan outlines are suggested for use within the framework of SUCCESS.

Chapter 2 The Research Module

In the Research module, SUCCESS students have at least thirty minutes every day to search for information in a variety of written materials. In the process, they gain knowledge about all kinds of subjects, and their competence in using reading skills increases. In their search for information, they have the opportunity to work with other students and to let others know what they have learned.

Students work during the Research module with the enthusiasm of a child who has been turned loose with a copy of the *Guinness Book of World Records*. Who could possibly prevent that child from seeking information as long as that book is within his or her grasp? The only thing that can intensify this insatiable thirst for knowledge is an audience. If there is an unsuspecting person nearby, the child cannot resist divulging what he or she is learning. At first, the telling sounds more like a question: "Do you know who has the longest beard in the world?" The audience doesn't know, of course, but will soon be told.

Educator Frank Smith believes that humans cannot resist learning. He says that only boredom and confusion can stop children from learning in our classrooms. So, in SUCCESS, teachers do what they can to avoid the things that cause boredom and confusion. They don't use boring skill sheets that often have confusing directions. They eliminate the boredom that often follows when a child finishes an assignment by making assignments open-ended. They lessen the chance of confusion by keeping the directions consistent, by following the same schedule every day, and by encouraging cooperation so that individuals can seek help from many learners.

What does the teacher do while the students are searching for information and sharing what they have learned? After introducing the activity with a very short lead-in, he or she teaches a considerable number of reading comprehension skills, all in the context of the meaningful information students find during their search through various materials. Most of this teaching is done with individuals and small groups. Finally, when it is time for the students to share what they have found out, the teacher decides on the best sharing technique to use.

▶ How to Lead the Research Module

Only three things happen during the Research module every day. First, the teacher does a short lead-in, which is usually a demonstration of a new source of information or even some simple instructions for the students' work. Second, the students use most of the module time for searching for information. Third, the teacher and students have a chance to learn what other members of the class found during the searching time.

S u c c e s **S** u c c e s **S** u c c e s **S** u c c e s **S** u c c e s **S** u c c e s **S** u c c e s **S** u c c e s **S**

Chapter

Cheever Farley

Lesson **37**

Research

?

LEAD-IN
Teacher introduces the Project Idea.
Topic: People in the news or
_____.

Material: Magazines or _____.
Comprehension Skill: Classification
or _____.

SEARCH & RECORD
Group Size: 3 or 4
Project Idea: Cut out pictures of
people. Paste them on poster in groups
according to where they live: in cities, in
cold places, etc. or _____.

SHARING
Display posters or _____.
Papers are dated and filed.

The Lessons include daily outlines of suggestions for this module, such as the one above.

As in the other modules, blank lines indicate where teachers should consider other topics, skills, materials, group arrangements, project ideas, and sharing methods. The topic of this sample lesson corresponds to the theme of the Writing module in Lesson 3. The rest of this chapter explains how to interpret the lesson outlines and what teachers should consider as they make decisions about the best way to teach the Research module in their classes.

In the Research module, lesson plans are organized to insure the regular use of a wide range of materials, to relate reading skills to many content areas of the curriculum, and to build and develop students' expertise in a long list of reading comprehension skills. By following the lesson plans as they are written, teachers balance their attention to various materials, skills, and topics. Just as in other SUCCESS modules, however, the teacher is encouraged to make many decisions throughout the Research module to tailor each lesson to his or her students. Materials, skills, and topics can all be changed. What isn't flexible? The principles of effective instruction described on pages 21–24 should govern the teacher's decisions, and the procedures described here should form the framework of each Research lesson, even when topics, materials, and skills are changed.

SHORT LEAD-IN (5 MINUTES)

First, the teacher tells the students what materials they will be using. Much of the motivation for third-graders in this module comes from the materials themselves. They may not have been privileged to use road maps, or encyclopedias, or real dictionaries; they may not have been turned loose with all kinds of music textbooks so that they can look at any page they choose; they may have thought the newspaper too hard for them to read. They appreciate the teacher's confidence that they can read these materials.

Most of the time the teacher's lead-in sounds like the instructions for a treasure hunt: "Look in your magazines and see how many animals you can find," or, "Look in the encyclopedia and see how much you can find out about big cities." Sometimes that is enough said, and wild horses can't hold third-graders back from beginning the search!

Sometimes, however, the teacher may wish to give directions that are a little more specific. The lead-in might need to remind students of some information they need related to a content area theme. If a teacher conducts a Research lesson with the topic "machines," which many third-graders study in science, the lead-in dialogue might go like this:

"Today we're going to be looking for machines in our magazines. Who can think of a machine you might be able to find?"

"Cars."

"We'll find lots of those, I think. Would you classify a car as a simple machine or a complicated machine?" (This question can also lead to a brief example of the reading comprehension skill for that day.)

"It's very complicated," or, "I think they're pretty simple. All you do is turn the key to make it go."

"What is an example of a simple machine?"

"What about those pulleys you see in places where they're building tall buildings?"

"Good idea. Now, after you cut out the machines you find, work with your group to arrange the pictures in stacks, one for the simple machines and one for the complicated. Now you may begin."

The teacher circulates, handing out the materials to the students at their desks. Students work with partners on many of these activities. Sometimes the teacher asks students to work in larger groups of usually three, four, or five students each. It is extremely important for students to be allowed to work with other students, and it helps if the students are allowed to choose their fellow committee members. The committees in most third-grade classes are very informal, partly because students work in committees regularly. Because of various kinds of desks and limited classroom space, many groups gather on the floor. That way people can be in their groups working very quickly with no time wasted moving furniture.

SEARCHING TIME (20 MINUTES)

Students search   As soon as students have their materials and find a place in a group, they begin searching. Usually, soon after they begin searching, some students start to realize they don't know what they are searching for. As the teacher moves around the room, he or she points out examples in the materials students are using, asking questions about choices and helping when someone is sure that "My magazine doesn't have any machines." Many of these discussions are happening all around the room at the same time as students answer the same kinds of ques-

SUCCESS promotes creativity and active learning while encouraging higher levels of thinking. The sky is the limit!

Karen B. Williams, teacher

tions for each other and question each other about their discoveries and choices.

Procedures for the teacher during searching time

1. *Content conferences.* The teacher often becomes involved in interesting conversations about the content of materials that students choose. Most of these conversations would be inappropriate for the entire class, and none of them could have been planned ahead of time. They are quintessential teachable moments about history, science, inventions, people, ethics, and much more!

2. *Skill conferences.* The teacher often becomes involved in reading skill instruction as individuals struggle to decipher the print they need. In addition, the teacher can initiate conferences with questions that pertain to the reading comprehension skill that is highlighted that day.

In the example described above, students are classifying the machines that they cut out of magazines. The classification is based upon the students' decisions about the simplicity or complexity of the machines. The teacher will ask many groups, "Which is your stack of simple machines?" "How did you decide to put that lawn mower in the complicated category?" "What is this third group you've made, an in-between group?"

3. *Audience.* The teacher also serves as a sounding board, "Did you know that . . ." and as a checker, "Is this right?"

4. *Evaluation.* The teacher keeps notes on a clipboard during searching time. This may be a checklist of which students are successfully demonstrating the skill that is emphasized in the lesson, or of which students are able to locate the kind of information that is needed. For his or her own information about who is accomplishing what, the teacher makes notes about individual progress. The chapter about evaluation explains more about clipboard notes.

Students record Students usually do a little bit of writing during searching time. The searching is always much more important than any written product; however, writing is sometimes necessary to record things that a group located in its search. At other times, students may "record" what they find by pasting pictures on a poster and writing some labels.

It helps if the students are more focused on the search than they are on what they are to write down. The objectives for this module have much more to do with getting information than with recording it.

If what the students need to record wasn't obvious from the lead-in instructions, the teacher writes the directions for the recording on the chalkboard: "Make a list of the animals you found."

SHARING TIME (5 MINUTES)

In the final five minutes of the module, students have to clean up and put materials away properly, and depending on the lesson, the teacher may need to orchestrate a sharing time. Much sharing of information happens spontaneously throughout the searching time, but if the teacher wishes to emphasize a particular comprehension skill using information the students have found, he or she can direct a sharing activity. Here are several examples of sharing techniques:

1. Make a chart on the chalkboard about the topic. For example, to emphasize cause and effect on a day when students found information about electricity, the teacher might ask, "What is something you found that uses electricity?"

"A lightbulb?"

The teacher writes "lightbulb lights up" on the chart under "effect" and then asks, "What causes the lightbulb to light up?"

"You turn on the switch." The teacher writes this response under "cause."

Figure 2-1

CLIPBOARD NOTES

Andy
Dominic
Jerome
? Jason concentrated on poor conservation
Timothy
Tawanna
X Cedric more interested in styles of cars than the topic
Tiffany
Thaddeus - found picture of car with only the driver, no passengers
Shannon - helped her group get organized
Deadra
Hayley
Sheena
V+ David - his group noticed trees providing shade to home
Jamie
? Anthony - off the subject
Carla - noticed storm windows in a picture
Scott
Terrence (David's partner)
Al
Dee Dee
? Otis excited about collecting lots of pictures - incomplete explanation
? Sam

Jan. 12
Research

Topic: Energy
Skill: Comparison

Which picture shows best conservation of energy? Worst?

Magazines

V = student could explain why one picture showed better conservation

2. When various committees have located different kinds of information that is important from a curriculum standpoint, such as information about Native Americans that they need to know in social studies, the teacher can record major findings from each committee on a piece of chart paper to share with the entire class. For example, if the students looked in their social studies books and in trade books for tools used by Native Americans, each committee may tell the class about its favorite tool and the teacher records the names of the tools on a piece of chart paper.

3. Another reason for a more formal, orchestrated sharing time might be that committees have produced something with the information they found, such as a song based on headlines in the newspaper. In that case, they certainly need a chance to present their work to the rest of the class. Later in the year it becomes more and more important to provide presentation opportunities for the committees.

4. The fastest way to send students out to share what they learned is to say, "Searching time is over. Go get a partner and tell him or her what you found out."

5. If the Research activity was the treasure-hunt type, the teacher can say, "Time is up. Put away your materials. Raise your hand if you found at least ten businesses named in your newspaper. Who found at least twenty?" Then the teacher can call on someone to read his or her list, and the class can challenge if it thinks something on the list isn't a business.

6. Some Research activities result in a group project. For example, in one activity, groups assemble as many pictures of people as they can cut

Figure 2-2

STUDENT WRITING

Chris E,   10/8/9   Research
Down Long Grassy Slopes
What theyre doing is skiing on
grass. Your using ground
when you go skiing.
It's about people using
grass skis. And what
the popularity is, In U.S
it's not done very much.
In Europe it's done alot.

out of magazines. They then arrange the pictures in order, according to how old they think the people are. This is a perfect opportunity to assign each group to a partner group. The two groups show each other the posters they made and question each other about their decisions concerning the ages of the people in the pictures. (The teacher will certainly have some questions about how the students decided on the arrangement of the pictures!)

7. Other group projects need to be displayed on the wall. Putting posters up for display is a way to extend the sharing over a longer period of time.

▶ Principles of Effective Instruction

1. *Students need to work in groups and these groups should not be ability groups.* Group work is good. "Friend" groups are much more helpful than ability groups. Ability groups are not needed for meeting individual needs in SUCCESS because individualized instruction takes place through committee work and many teacher-student conferences.

Traditional ability groups handicap all kinds of students, not just those who feel that they are not as good as the other students. Former members of the "top" group sometimes have the most difficulty learning what it means to do one's best; those students have to be reminded more often than others that "There is no such thing as being finished." So, in SUCCESS, when teachers ask students to work in groups, they are not labeling or limiting the students according to their expectations for their abilities or achievements. Instead, teachers are asking students to learn all they can, knowing that people are more motivated to learn when they are establishing goals themselves, not just complying with someone else's wishes.

Unless he or she has a special reason, the teacher always lets students choose their own groups. Naturally, he or she intervenes when inappropriate choices are made. Teachers will see the most progress in reading when students work in groups that students choose.

2. *The teacher shouldn't know all the answers or locate all the materials.* It is important for teachers to learn along with their students. This calls for a new definition of the teacher's role in the classroom, and it calls for the teacher to make a statement not often heard from the teacher in traditional classrooms: "I don't know. Let's find out." SUCCESS teachers need to be prepared to tell their students that they don't know the answers to many questions.

If a teacher thought he or she had to locate all the materials students would read in a Research activity, or that he or she had to know all the information students would learn through one of these activities, very few Research activities would be done in that classroom! It isn't that SUCCESS teachers are lazy, or even practical; they say, "I don't know," in order to provide better instruction. They do not limit what their students will learn to what they happen to know already, nor do they give

Figure 2-3

STUDENT WRITING

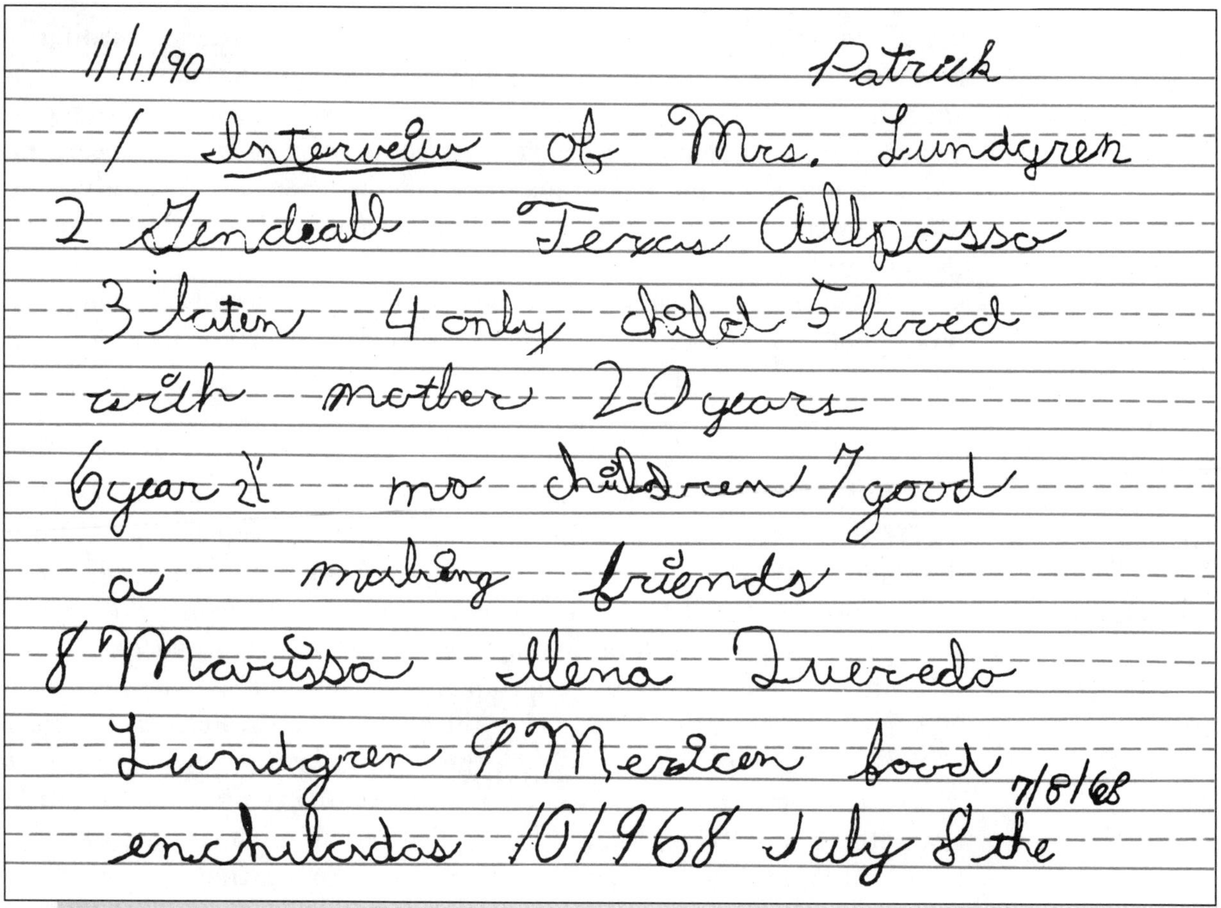

11/1/90   Patrick

1 Interview of Mrs. Lundgren

2 Gendeall Texas Allpasso

3 later 4 only child 5 lived

with mother 20 years

6 year 2 — mo children 7 good

a making friends

8 Marissa Mena Quevedo

Lundgren 9 Mexican food

enchiladas 10 1968 July 8 the   7/8/68

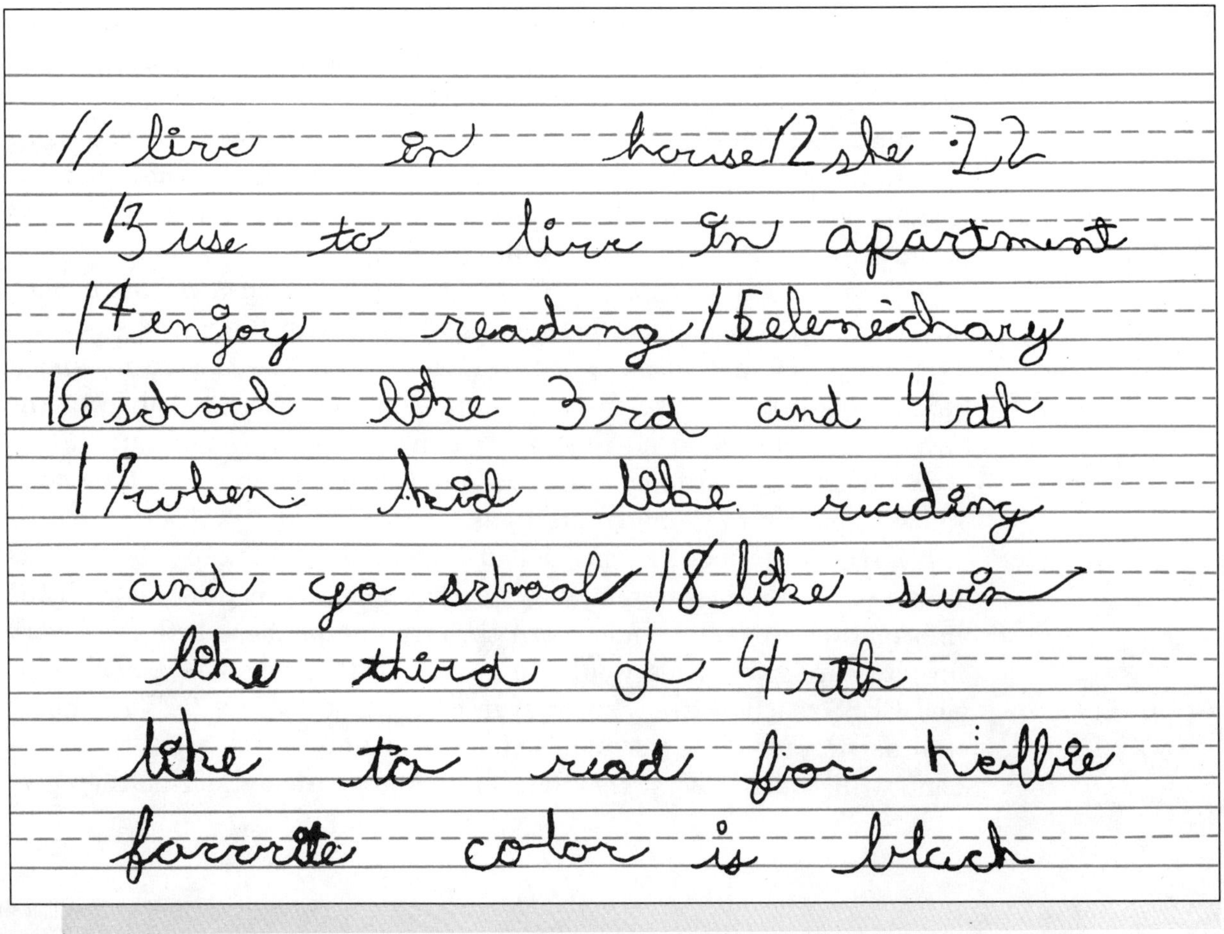

11 live in house 12 she 22

13 use to live in apartment

14 enjoy reading 15 elemenchary

16 school like 3rd and 4rth

17 when kid like reading

and go school 18 like swin

like third & 4rth

like to read for hobbie

favorite color is black

the students the impression that they are playing a game in their research work. These activities are not conducted to see if the students can figure out what the teacher already knows. SUCCESS teachers teach their students that teachers love to learn new things every day.

3. *Reading skills can be taught without worksheets.* More than in any other module in SUCCESS, students will be using a great variety of materials in the Research module. Rarely will two students look at the same page at the same time. The students' choices of reading materials is very important.

How are skills taught in SUCCESS? Skills are taught in the context of the information students locate in all kinds of materials. The major skills necessary to locate information are a part of every day's work in this module. In addition, each day's lesson plan focuses on one reading comprehension skill. The teacher has three methods of teaching that skill, no matter what the topic or material for the lesson might be:

a. The teacher may incorporate some attention to that skill into the lead-in at the beginning of the lesson.

b. In twenty minutes of the students' searching time, the teacher can focus on each student's use of that comprehension skill as he or she circulates among the working students. The students may all be using different materials, but the opportunity to work on the same skill exists for every person.

c. Often, in sharing time at the end of the module, the teacher can draw everyone's attention to the reading comprehension skill again, always in the context of information the students are learning.

4. *Content information can be taught without assigned readings in textbooks.* Textbooks aren't the only source of information, after all. If students are learning about government, for example, they could read the information in their social studies textbook about the president, the White House, and Congress. They can also find out what the president has been doing by looking at recent newspapers, where they might even learn about the president's dog's new puppies, an interesting tidbit that won't be in many textbooks!

5. *Students will locate unexpected information.* In the Research activities, there isn't just one right answer. Open-ended instructions for the students' searching allow students to pursue many avenues in looking for helpful information. Some students may interpret an assigned topic more broadly than others; other students may zero in on a very specific aspect of the topic. Still other students may investigate a topic that at first glance doesn't seem to fit the assigned topic at all.

Teachers spend a lot of time during the searching part of the module asking, "How does this picture (or this story) fit in with our topic today?" "What made you think of looking up this topic today?" The teacher encourages students to make both direct and indirect associations of ideas with the assigned topics.

6. *A wide variety of materials is needed for these activities.* The teacher does not locate specific pieces of information for students to read, but he or she does have the responsibility of collecting a plentiful supply of materials that students can search for the information they need. The teacher should collect the following and store them so that students can use them often:

- newspapers (local and national)
- magazines—some to be cut up (such as *Good Housekeeping, Time,* and *Ebony*), others to be read (such as *Ranger Rick* and *World*)
- dictionaries (a variety of student and college-level editions)
- encyclopedias
- maps
- art books or prints
- music, math, social studies, science, health textbooks for all grades
- nonfiction books

Chapter 6 contains more information about collecting and storing materials.

▶ Another Look at the Three Main Steps

The procedures of the Research module are so plain and simple that they sound dull: lead-in, search and record, share. They would be dull if everyone was paying attention only to the procedures. Actually, the procedures are only an underlying framework of what the students and teacher do in class; attention should always be on the people in the room and the topic under study. To clarify that, a close look at Jamie, a third-grader, will demonstrate the format of a Research lesson again. By focusing on one child and the choices he makes, and imagining twenty or twenty-five more third-graders participating in the same activity, a teacher can get an idea of what this module accomplishes.

My students have gained such a positive sense of themselves. By teaching SUCCESS, all the students succeed and are not held to keeping up with every other student. They have a wonderful sense of pride in themselves and are so excited about learning in this nontraditional and exciting way! What an uplifting experience for a teacher!

Wilma Pittman, teacher

"Word Study time is over; it must be time for Research! I hope we will get to use the art books again. Our teacher told us not to look at the naked people if that bothered us. I still wonder why the artists painted so many pictures of naked people. Oh, well. I looked at some of them. There are plenty of people wearing clothes, too: I've seen lots of pictures of Jesus and other people we hear about at church.

"Yes! She says we're using the art books again! Oh, good, I'm sitting next to Dominic, and we got the book that has pictures from the National Gallery of Art in Washington. Thaddeus had this book yesterday, and he said it was good. Wow! Would you look at that shark! Those men are really trying to spear it. I don't think they can save that man in the water.

"Now what are we supposed to find? Tell words that explain about the people in the pictures? Well, we could start with this shark picture. Dominic says we should put down *brave*. That's true. The teacher just came to our table and asked us what else we could figure out about these people. Dominic said that man in the water is dying. We could write that down. The teacher asked us how we could tell he was dying. Well, just look at all that blood. He could probably drown, too. The other people aren't pulling him out of the water; they're too busy fighting the shark.

"That's enough about that picture. What about this guy? Dominic says he's a bullfighter. Another dead man! Look at all that blood! He was really dressed-up, too. His mama would be mad about how he got his good clothes all messed up. We'll write down, *bullfighter, dead,* and *fancy clothes*. The artist's name is Manet.

"We found some more good pictures, too. We got so busy talking about the pictures that we forgot to write about what we found. The teacher had to remind us. Then, we made our list pretty long.

"Then the teacher interrupted us, right when we found a good picture of George Washington. She says time is up. We have to put our books away, but before we do that, we get to find some partners and show them our favorite painting. We chose David and Scott, and we showed them the shark painting. They liked it, too. We asked them if they thought the guy was dying. They think so, too. They had a book from a museum in Paris. It had some good pictures, too. They showed us a neat battle scene. We put our books back on the shelf and filed our papers in our Research folders."

▶ Teacher Choices and Opportunities

1. The teacher can restrict the scope of the topic for searching time as much as he or she needs to. When students are more advanced at reading the various materials, the teacher can ask them to search for more specific things.

2. The teacher can change the topics that are given in the Lessons. When incorporating science, social studies, or health objectives in language arts class, he or she can steer the search toward particular topics.

Aleisha Dobbins

The topics included in the Lessons are typical third-grade curriculum topics, and there is no reason they cannot be changed to fit a teacher's preferences (see Figure 2-4).

3. The teacher can change the materials that are specified in the Lessons. If he or she is expected to "cover" a content-area textbook, the students can search in that book more often. A teacher should not substitute any kind of worksheet for the materials in the Lessons, nor should everyone in the class use the same pages of the textbook at once.

4. The teacher can change the amount of time devoted to a particular topic, and can link assignments together, rather than using only day-by-day tasks. If he or she needs a product for a particular occasion such as a P.T.A. program, the teacher can stick with the same topic for a longer period of time and have the students prepare projects that are the culmination of several research activities.

5. The teacher can emphasize the aspect of the day's lesson outline that is most appropriate for the students and school. If accountable for a list of comprehension or study skills, the teacher can make certain that those skills are an essential part of the lead-in, the searching, and/or the sharing, and can use clipboard notes to record each student's expertise in demonstrating the skills.

6. The teacher can decide how much the students will move around the room and talk during searching time. If students need to be quiet and sit at their desks more often, he or she can hand out all materials and give students less choice about what they read. He or she can assign partners or have students work with the person sitting next to them. When students are inexperienced in using the materials, giving them a particular item to use helps them get started more quickly, but when they become more expert, choosing their own materials is motivating and educational. The "noise" in this module should always be "constructive sound."

▶ Research: Favorite Module or Skipped Module?

Why do the Research module every day? This module is the most unusual part of SUCCESS; it incorporates all of the principles of reading instruction that are important in SUCCESS. Yet, while teachers who do the Research module daily say it is their favorite activity, there are some SUCCESS teachers who skip this module. Here is a list of reasons the module is sometimes skipped. For doubting teachers, the Research module:

■ demands too many different materials.

True, but all of them are free; and once they are collected, they can be stored in an organized way so that students can use the same ones year after year. Teachers should not locate the exact pieces of information the students will need; finding the information is part of the students' work. Teachers simply supply stacks of newspapers, magazines, and brochures. Students locate the pages that will be useful to them. Just think, photocopied worksheets and expensive workbooks won't be needed!

■ is so different. Teachers have done special activities like these every now and then, but not on a regular basis.

Doing these activities daily makes them easier to lead. Students know what to expect, and they improve daily in their ability to make choices, work well in groups, and use their time well.

■ is too hard to grade. Some days students don't even have individual papers.

Right again, but don't forget how much information the teacher gains about each student's use of reading comprehension skills, knowledge of different subject areas, and expertise in locating information. SUCCESS teachers use checklists to document students' use of skills and clipboard notes to record what they learn about the students.

Figure 2-4

SUGGESTED TOPICS FOR THE RESEARCH MODULE

Lessons	Topics	Lessons	Topics
1–10	Animals	96–105	Music
11–20	School and Home	106–115	Famous Americans
21–30	Land Forms	116–125	Plants
31–40	People in the News	126–135	Weather
41–50	Government	136–145	Cities
51–60	Public Health	146–155	Our State
61–70	Space	156–165	Human Body
71–75	Holidays	166–175	Art
76–85	Energy	176–180	Student Choice
86–95	Transportation		

Sometimes students will follow directions very well and search very enthusiastically, but still not find any information. The student will record, "No information found," on his or her paper. In the real world, there are many times when a scholar searches for something and doesn't find exactly what he or she was looking for.

■ is noisy and messy.

Students do talk a lot in this module, and they also cut things out, use glue, and spread newspapers and maps all over the floor. In this module, they rarely sit alone at their desks and work silently. Research about teaching language arts stresses again and again how important student conversation is. Language arts class should not be quiet all the time.

About the mess: cleaning up well is another habit teachers help their students develop, and good clean-up becomes less of an issue if the students are expected to do it every day.

Here is a list of reasons that this module is the favorite of so many teachers. For the benefit of the students, the Research module is a good way

- ■ to work on reading comprehension skills in context of meaningful material;
- ■ to be expected to think and to explain one's decisions;
- ■ to learn lots of information about many content area topics;
- ■ to gain experience reading real-world materials;
- ■ to apply phonics, context clues, and other decoding skills to unfamiliar vocabulary;
- ■ to relate experiences in the real world to school activities;
- ■ to gain experience working as a member of a group;
- ■ to accomplish the same objectives stated in basal programs with an unlimited selection of materials;

- to accomplish the same objectives stated in basal programs without the detrimental effects of ability grouping;
- to accomplish many objectives that are not even claimed as part of other reading programs;
- to keep the teacher excited about learning new things.
- Last, but not least, the Research module is motivating and fun!
- The format of each day's lesson is simple: lead-in, search, share.

Samples of topics and objectives are in the Lessons. What could be easier?

Chapter 3 The Recreational Reading Module

The teacher said, "Reading time is over. Please put away your books."

A chorus of students groaned, "No-o-o!"

One reader whined, "Can we have just five more minutes?"

The purpose of the Recreational Reading module is being achieved in that class. Students are enjoying their time for reading books so much that they wish they could have more. Maybe that desire will be fulfilled throughout their lifetimes as they seek out opportunities to read books for enjoyment.

One primary activity must take place during the Recreational Reading module every day: students must have thirty minutes to read books that they choose. Meanwhile, the teacher must establish the best atmosphere for encouraging enthusiastic reading by all students. In addition to working to create a community of readers, the teacher conducts conferences with the readers and keeps records of what is accomplished in those conferences. Students also keep records of their daily reading.

At first glance the Recreational Reading module appears to be the simplest part of the SUCCESS program; the procedures for uninterrupted, sustained, silent reading are familiar to teachers and students everywhere. But, contrary to first impressions, SUCCESS teachers have learned that this module is the most complex part of the program. To create the best atmosphere for a community of readers demands expertise from the teacher. He or she must be wildly enthusiastic about all kinds of children's literature, constantly learning about new authors and books and about which authors and genres are the most popular with which groups of students in each class. As in all the SUCCESS modules, he or she must know quite a lot about each student. Most of the decisions the teacher must make in this module focus on individual students, one at a time.

Are comprehension and word recognition skills being taught in the Recreational Reading module? Yes. Through their reading experience every day, the students are developing skills they need for enjoying the books they choose. Teachers monitor the skill development through their observations of the students during reading time, and they sometimes boost growth through their conversations with students about reading.

More direct instruction in comprehension and word recognition skills takes place in the other modules every day. The teacher plans a focus on a particular comprehension skill in the Research module every day. He or she includes a spelling emphasis and perhaps a topic emphasis in the Word Study module every day, thereby addressing word recognition skills in meaningful context. Unavoidable connections between the students' work in the Writing module and their development of comprehension and word recognition skills strengthen reading and writing

Jacob Barron

Lesson **31**

Recreational Reading

All students read books for approximately 30 minutes.

CONVERSATIONS

The teacher also reads silently. The teacher has some short conversations with readers. When appropriate, the main focus of these conversations is what the student is learning about authors.

CLIPBOARD NOTES

Teacher notes students' selections of books and whether they notice who the authors are.

READ-ALOUD BOOK

Shoes from Grandpa by Mem Fox or

———

---

expertise constantly. In fact, a teacher may consider the Research, Writing, and Word Study modules to be "mini-lessons" that enhance the students' work in Recreational Reading.

The outline for a day's work in the Recreational Reading module usually looks like the one above.

This outline reminds the teacher of the major activities that should occur during this part of the school day. The students need time to read books they choose, and the teacher spends some time having conversations with readers and observing what the readers are doing. Some teachers decide before class which students to focus on; others observe the readers first and choose students who seem ready for some conversation with the teacher. The outlines in the Lessons suggest some biweekly areas of emphasis for the conversations and observations; most teachers will tailor their conversations to fit the individual needs of students. Chapter 6 includes examples of record-keeping the teacher does during this module based upon conversations and observations. Throughout this module, the teacher makes many decisions!

▶ The Signs of a Classroom Reading Community

1. *The teachers love to read.* Teachers do everything possible to make it clear that they love to read. They read in front of students. They ask students if they can borrow books from them that look good. They talk about their own reading with other teachers in earshot of students. They use "spending money" for the purchase of books. They speak of "getting" to read instead of "having" to read. They make the privilege of being the first person to check out a new book an important reward in their classrooms.

2. *Recreational Reading "counts."* Teachers do everything possible to make it clear that this is the "reading" that counts. If they are required to include elements of basal series instruction, they are careful not to inadvertently give them more importance than Recreational Reading by assigning worksheet or textbook grades that are averaged and become the report-card grades for reading. They avoid having the report card communicate to parents and students that reading books is less important than completing exercises correctly. Chapter 6 includes more information about grades and report cards.

3. *The teachers have important responsibilities.* They don't do anything that gives the impression that the Recreational Reading module is a free period for them. Yes, it should be obvious that the teacher is having fun, but all of the enjoyment is due to the books and interaction with students about books. They don't correct papers, fill out forms for the office, or talk to adults. They read. They talk to children about reading.

4. *The room is full of great books.* Teachers check out dozens of books from the library. They buy cheap ones from garage sales. They beg for donations. They help students order from book clubs so that they get bonus books for the class. They seek out the newest and best books and make them available to students as prized possessions of the class. How many adults would be excited about reading if it didn't include the possibility of being familiar with current bestsellers?

5. *Conversations with students are not inquisitions.* Teachers learn much about students and their reading progress in individual conversations, but the overall impression students get about conferences is that they are times for teacher and student to enjoy reading together, not times for the teacher to judge the student or for the student to show off for the teacher. Teachers don't stick so rigidly to a list of skills to be covered in conversations that they make the students feel as if they are being tested.

6. *Appropriate emphasis is given to record-keeping.* Teachers don't emphasize record-keeping and conversations so much that they seem more important than the simple commitment of time for reading. The record-keeping is important and it does help, but students make progress largely because they have time for enjoyable reading.

▶ How to Lead the Recreational Reading Module

INTRODUCE BOOKS AND AUTHORS THROUGH READING ALOUD

At the beginning of the year, especially, many teachers read something to the class prior to beginning Recreational Reading. In this way, they begin to introduce the class to certain authors and types of books they would like students to read independently. They might read a picture book or one chapter from a novel. There is more information about reading aloud to students on page 44.

DECIDE ON THE RULES FOR READING TIME

Where will students sit? Some teachers allow students to sit wherever they choose as long as they are reading, and others prefer the students to stay in their seats. No one is allowed to take a book from someone else's desk during reading time.

Will students read alone or with a friend? Some teachers allow students to read with a friend; others ask students to read alone. They may experiment with both arrangements all the time. The goal is for all students to be able to read so well that they can tune out everyone else and be totally absorbed in a book that is enjoyable to them. To arrive at that goal, some students need camaraderie at first to experience the pleasure that can come from reading. Others need a sounding board as they test out their word attack skills on new vocabulary. Still other readers have such difficulty reading that they need a buddy to help dig out some meaning from the print.

Orchestrating a classroom to provide for individual needs can be difficult. One teacher says that sometimes her students sit in their seats and read alone. At other times, she *asks* them to do that and then she notices that neighbors are sliding in next to each other, listening and pointing at print together. At still other times, when she simply asks everyone to read, some of them read with groups and others read alone.

What about students who aren't reading? Teachers observe their students carefully during this module. If they see someone who is being unproductive, by neither reading nor listening to someone else read, they first ask themselves why the child isn't reading. Then, they may ask that person to go to his or her desk and read alone. They also redouble their efforts to help that student become more successful in his or her own choices of books and reading companions. If they observe that a student always depends on someone else's reading for his or her enjoyment of books, they know that they need to help that student become more independent. Allowing students to read with each other actually reveals much about each student's problems and progress.

Is it quiet during reading time? In many third-grade classes, especially at the beginning of the year, it is not practical to make a rule about silence during the Recreational Reading module. Whether reading alone

I have a low-ability group, and they are reading what is meaningful to them. They felt immediate success from day one. They hadn't been SUCCESSful before. The students have gained self-esteem and writing confidence. They especially like to read what they have written and have people listen to them.

Cindy M. Beach, teacher

or with a friend, many beginning readers read aloud. So, while there is no loud talking, it is not necessarily quiet during this module.

MAKE CERTAIN EVERYONE HAS SOMETHING TO READ

The teacher's next job, one that continues for the entire module, is to make certain everyone has something to read. To do this, he or she thinks about two things: how to make the best books available and how to help every student find the best book for her or him.

At the beginning of the year, most third-graders will need several books every day during this module. Even with access to an excellent library, students also need a good collection of books in the classroom. These books are important when a teacher needs to recommend several selections to a reluctant reader. Teachers divide the classroom collection into several sections and place groups of books all over the room instead of keeping all the books in one place. That way students who need to change books during the module time will not all need to congregate on the same side of the room.

Some teachers keep a special box of books that for various reasons cannot be checked out and taken home. Usually, these books are new to the class collection, are in especially high demand, or are appropriate during a given season. For example, soon after one teacher finished reading *Danny the Champion of the World* by Roald Dahl, everyone was eager to read the book themselves, so the teacher kept copies in her special box. One teacher heard Anthony Browne speak and got autographed copies of his books, which her students love dearly, so those books are in the special box for safekeeping. Around holiday times, the books that pertain to the holiday are in the special box.

At the beginning of the Recreational Reading module, some teachers take a minute to "auction off" some of the books in the special box. "Who wants *Willy the Wimp?*" "Who wants *The True Story of the Three Little Pigs?*" "Who wants *Ghost-Eye Tree?*" When lots of hands go up for a particular title, the teacher chooses the person for whom the book is most appropriate and/or the person who needs some special attention that day. Teachers find that handing out several books this way accomplishes two things: it expedites the everybody-get-a-book process, and it feels like a pep rally for books.

BE A MODEL

It is also important, especially at the beginning of the year, for the teacher to be a model during Recreational Reading time, sitting at a desk and intently reading a book he or she enjoys. During most days of the year, the teacher uses the module time for having short conversations and conferences with students, but never forgets how powerful he or she is as a role model. Throughout the year, students see the teacher reading at every opportunity. The teacher always carries around a book he or she is excited about reading.

BEGIN HAVING CONVERSATIONS

Teachers help readers during Recreational Reading time by guaranteeing them a daily time to read. They also help by providing plenty of great books and by modeling. Another way they help is by holding various types of conversations.

With all of this said, however, conversations should not be considered until the main activity of this module has begun: everyone should be reading, or at least going through the motions of reading. Teachers should postpone their conversations until the atmosphere of the reading community is what they want it to be. To help readers get started, teachers may choose to walk around the room conducting mini-conferences, just to check with individuals about their book choices and their plans for using the reading time, instead of having extended conversations. As the year goes on, many teachers plan to include some short conversations and some group conversations, as well as some longer, individual conversations. Examples of these conversations are given on pages 39–41.

Teachers always spend part of the module observing the class. Much can be learned about a student's achievement and progress by watching the student's actions in this module. Sometimes teachers use their clipboard notes to record what they see people reading. (See Figure 3-1 on page 37.) Sometimes they note how many times a student changes books, how many days a student chooses to read the same book, or what author becomes a particular student's favorite. The plans in the Lessons suggest some particular kinds of observations teachers can make. The questions students ask the teacher during reading time also reveal something about their needs. For example, a beginning reader in one class asked, "Which side of the page do I read first, this side or that side?"

ESTABLISH A RECORD-KEEPING SYSTEM FOR STUDENTS

Andy Giesbrecht

Experienced adult readers sometimes keep lists of the books they read; students should have an opportunity to do the same thing. While this list becomes another way of documenting the accomplishments of a student in a SUCCESS class, it should not be considered an accurate way to award points or earn a certain report-card grade. Beginning readers and younger students will sometimes enjoy making long lists without spending much time "reading" any of the books on them. Students will tend to spend even more time writing down titles without doing much reading if they think there are prizes for reading the most books. One teacher delayed starting the student record-keeping until the right atmosphere of a community of readers had been established in her classroom. In such an atmosphere, keeping a list of books read does not require much time, nor does it become competitive, and it is a helpful record of what a reader has done in a year.

Figure 3-2 is an example of the kind of form that some teachers use for having students record the titles and authors of books they have read. When students begin to read longer, "chapter" books, it may be helpful

Figure 3-1

CLIPBOARD NOTES

Andy

Dominic — reading to Anthony; helping him

Jerome — daydreaming again

Jason — absent

Timothy

*Tawanna — 4th Grade Nothing — reading alone

Cedric

Tiffany — Say Cheese (was reading during math, too)

Thaddeus — talking to Shannon about illustrations

Shannon

Deadra

Hayley — is influencing other students to try Narnia

Sheena — got Girl Talk for Christmas

David — animal books — on his knees next to shelf of Nonfiction!

*Jamie — chose story to read to me from basal

Anthony — more attentive because of Dominic

Carla

*Scott — Mother Goose — trying to match illustrations to rhymes

Terrence — reading from basal with Jamie

*Al — Mother Goose with Scott

DeeDee — big stack of picture books

*Otis — comparing 2 books by Anthony Browne

*Sam — told me about ant queens — Ant Cities

* Conferences held today

Jan. 7
Rec. Rdng

for them to record what pages they read each day; Figure 3-3 is an example of the form needed for that kind of record-keeping. Most teachers keep all the reading lists for the entire class in one notebook or folder. They hand the forms out daily or make the notebook available to readers who need to use it. When a reader has filled in all the spaces on the form, he or she staples a blank form to the top, continuing to add blank forms throughout the year when they are needed. This way, each student's complete reading list is maintained all year.

ALLOW STUDENTS TIME TO CHECK OUT BOOKS TO READ AT HOME

As homework, students in a SUCCESS class read a book for at least thirty minutes every night. Some teachers take time at the end of each

Figure 3-2

READER FORM

Name _____ **List of the Books I've Read**

Title	Author	Date	Comments

Figure 3-3

DATED READER FORM

Name _____ **List of the Books I've Read**

Date	Title	Author	Page Started	Page Stopped	Comments

Recreational Reading module to ask students to decide which books to read that night. If the teacher jots down each student's choice, the list can serve as a record of checked-out books, as well as another documentation of the reading being done by each student throughout the year (see Figure 3-4). At the beginning of the next school day, the teacher or student librarian can mark off the books that are returned. The arrows on the form indicate that a student is keeping a book for more than one day.

▶ Reader Conferences

Teachers who are accustomed to having students complete worksheets and workbook pages in reading class, and who use sustained, silent reading as a supplementary activity rather than as the backbone of the reading program, ask how they can teach comprehension skills with SUCCESS and how they can find out if students are comprehending what they read. Teacher-student conferences and small-group discussions about books help teachers learn how well students are comprehending what they read and give them opportunities to teach skills. Perhaps more important, student readers appreciate the chance to share ideas about their reading with another interested reader. After all, adult readers who are enjoying a book usually find someone to talk to about it. "Have you read . . .?" the conversation begins.

MINI-CONFERENCES

The conversation that is easiest to start is the mini-conference, a one- or two-minute conversation with a reader, usually about what book he or she has chosen to read. The teacher approaches students with whom he or she wishes to speak and interrupts their reading for as brief a time as possible. Usually the teacher makes a note on the clipboard about each reader's plans.

"What are you reading today, Thaddeus?"

"*Ghost-Eye Tree,*" the student replies.

"I believe you've read that before. You must really like that book a lot."

"Yes, I do. It's my favorite book."

"Well, have a good time reading it again. Have you tried reading *White Dynamite and Curly Kidd*? It's another book by Bill Martin, Jr., and John Archambault. You might like it, too."

The teacher moves on to another student. "Scott, finish choosing your books and come back to your seat. It's time to start reading."

"Cedric has *Willy the Wimp,* and that's what I wanted."

"If he got it first, then you'll have to read something else first, and get that book later, when Cedric is finished with it. How about another Anthony Browne book, like *Gorilla*?"

Moving rather quickly from student to student, the teacher can help many readers settle down and get started, and then, later in the period, have some brief conversations, such as the following:

"Jamie, I see you've been reading some more of *New Kid on the Block* by Jack Prelutsky. What's your favorite poem today?"

"I think 'My Dog, He is an Ugly Dog' is so funny!"

"How about reading me the verse you like the best?"

EXTENDED CONVERSATIONS

At other times, the teacher will not interrupt so many students in one reading period; instead, he or she will have conversations with only three or four students. In an extended conference with each of these readers, the teacher can ask the child to read a longer portion of a book, perhaps a favorite part, or even the next part he or she is about to read. The teacher

Figure 3-4

CHECK-OUT LIST

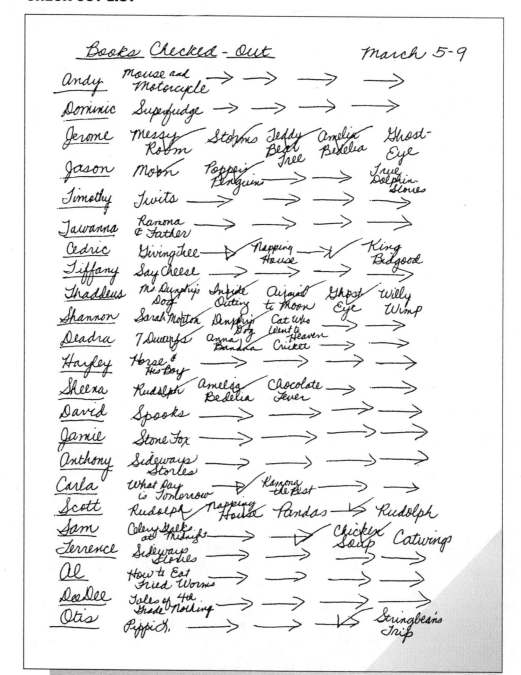

can ask prediction questions, such as, "What do you think is going to happen to a particular character?" Or, he or she can ask cause-and-effect questions, such as, "Why was the boy scared?" Or, the teacher can ask questions about the plans a reader is making, such as, "You've read two books by Beverly Cleary already. Are you planning to read another one? What do you like about her books?"

This kind of conversation is especially appropriate at progress-report and report-card times. The teacher and student can establish some goals for the student's reading in the coming grading period, and they can look back over the student's progress during the period that is coming to a close. The teacher might say, "In the past few weeks I've noticed that you have spent a lot of time looking at pictures in encyclopedias and books about weather. You haven't had time to read many stories. I think you might enjoy some books like *The Magic Schoolbus at the Waterworks* because you can learn a lot of information, but you can also get to know some funny characters and find out what happens to them. In the next three weeks I'd like you to concentrate on reading some stories, instead of books that are just for information. Can you find plenty of good stories on your own, or would you like me to help you make a list? Your friend Joe might be able to tell you about some of the stories he has especially liked, too."

A student might say, "Yes, I can tell that my reading is improving."

"What do you think has helped you improve?"

"*Willy the Wimp*. I really like that book, so I've learned all the words. I'm going to read *Willy the Champ* next. It's good, too."

GROUP DISCUSSIONS

The third approach to talking with students about their reading is to form some discussion groups. For example, the teacher may invite five people who have been reading poetry to discuss their reading. Someone who has concentrated on Shel Silverstein's books might read a favorite poem to the rest of the group. Someone else who likes Jack Prelutsky's books might point out that those poems are also very silly. Other children may show each other the poems about an approaching holiday that they found in their anthologies. In these discussions, students inevitably end up finding the same poem in more than one book, and they eagerly compare the different versions they have located.

Another group may be formed to discuss books by James Marshall, or those by Don and Audrey Wood. Fans of a particular author enjoy examining illustrations carefully and showing each other details they think no one else has noticed. The teacher could call together children who have read various folktales from different cultures such as *Mufaro's Beautiful Daughters* or *The Talking Eggs*.

Many third-graders are attempting to read "chapter" books for the first time. It could help some students to meet in a group with others who have been trying the same types of books. Some students may be trying to read a novel independently that the teacher has already read to the

*S*UCCESS stimulates optimum learning and effective time management. With SUCCESS, subject areas are easily integrated and students are able to experience realistic learning situations.

Donna F. Parker, teacher

class. It could help them to talk with other students who have also read parts of the novel on their own.

In these group discussions the teacher should not ask all the questions and wait for students to answer them. In fact, the teacher may choose to set up the group and then let it function without interfering.

SPONTANEOUS CONVERSATIONS

As helpful as conversations and group discussions can be, however, their importance should not be overestimated. Most of a reader's improvement in comprehension skills, as well as in word study skills, is due to the reading itself. Conference activities should interfere only minimally with the amount of time that students count on having to read every day. In a classroom community of readers, many spontaneous conversations take place daily, among students, as well as with the teacher, allowing frequent opportunities for readers to talk about their reading.

▶ Teacher Observations

Teachers do not have to rely only on conversations to learn about a student reader's comprehension skills. The following description of a student's activities during Recreational Reading is based entirely on a teacher's observation of him, not on any questions he was required to answer.

Notes about Sam represent a study of about a dozen possible ways to fool around when reading isn't yet a meaningful activity. The second day of school he spent a thirty-minute reading time looking around, looking at pictures in a book, then strolling around the room, asking if it was math time yet, and then drawing. The next day he started the period off better by reading with Quincy, but soon he was playing. The fourth day was devoted to a long search through all our books. He moved on to magazines the following day and finally found the book *Best Friends*. That book wasn't satisfying the following day, so he turned to a nonfiction book about bees. Before long, he was flexing his muscles on another student's desk and fiddling with his shoelaces. Then came three more days of drawing and collecting and hoarding books without reading any of them.

Case studies of four beginning readers in one third-grade class, based on the teacher's daily clipboard notes about those students, produced the following recommendations of how to best help those students:

Joe needs a partner who reads better than he does; he needs to be able to listen to others read.

On the other hand, Tim needs a partner who reads worse than he does, so he can show off.

Jim needs to be able to lie down, kneel, and lean on things while he reads.

In contrast, Scott is distracted if he is away from his usual seat.

Joe needs to experiment with books that are too hard.
But Scott gets frustrated with books that are too hard.

Tim needs stories and authors that he already knows; he needs to be able to figure out the story without reading every word just right. He likes to answer questions about the story.
But Jim needs to tell the teacher exactly what the words are, and he doesn't want to be asked questions about the story yet.

Following these recommendations helped four readers make tremendous progress. Meanwhile, twenty-two other third-graders in that class needed their own individual attention. Can a classroom teacher provide for such diverse needs? Yes, if he or she remembers to do three things:

- Learn as much as possible about each student by writing down observations and notes about conversations throughout the year;
- Periodically read his or her notes about a student, referring back to earlier notes that pertain to that student;
- Always schedule at least thirty minutes every day for students to read books they choose.

Instruction can be individualized in a SUCCESS classroom without much extra work and confusion because the students make so many choices on their own. And, instead of standing in front of the group talking, the teacher is able to work with individuals who need help of any kind. Because a SUCCESS teacher observes students carefully and documents what he or she observes, a study of the observations can reveal specific ways to help children who have great needs. Because the actual procedures of reading instruction during Recreational Reading are simple, the teacher has time to make observations and use the information to improve instruction.

Jessica Myers

▶ Changes Throughout the School Year

Besides the changes that one student goes through during the year in Recreational Reading, the teacher sees the class as a whole change. The following observations from one teacher's clipboard notes were made during the first half of a school year.

8-28   Today (the fourth day of school) they seem to realize that they need to be able to really read the books. More talking, less just looking at pictures.

9-7   Ugh! Fourteen students were all distracted at least part of the time. I don't remember so many people who played last year. Does this room arrangement hinder good reading?

9-12   Even though there was way too much commotion today, five beginning readers were much more excited about what they read.

9-19   More reading aloud than in past—more trading books than yesterday or Friday.

9-20   Now acquainted with more books, negotiating to get ones they want. Much, much more settled down than two weeks ago—orbiters are now working with partners.

10-15   Without asking, lots of moving to read with friends; lots of poetry—time to do some in writing.

10-23   When partners share, do they take turns? Read one book, then the other?

11-7   I am so excited to watch two of the beginning readers reading an Anthony Browne book together! It's amazing to see the changes since the beginning of the year!

11-21   Changed the rules today: only people who are reading difficult chapter books can move next to someone else.

11-22   It's hard to get back to habit of each person reading his own books at his own desk. The exception I'm making is if partners have multiple copies of same book—I hope this will be incentive to read harder books.

1-3   Taking a while to get back in pre-Christmas habit. Discouraging: one of the beginning readers has made great progress, but two others have not.

All year long, teachers who love books and who faithfully schedule Recreational Reading look forward to it every day. One teacher said that even when other times of the day were not going particularly well in her class, she could count on Recreational Reading to be a time when she could see that the class was truly a community of readers after all.

▶ Read-Aloud Time

Another favorite time of the day in many SUCCESS classes is read-aloud time. Most teachers are able to find fifteen to twenty minutes in the school day, in addition to the four SUCCESS modules, for reading to their classes. Plus, they read during every possible spare moment. Often, a teacher reads part of a book in the mini-lesson in the Writing module.

They read all kinds of books, picture books, and novels, and they see those books become favorites for students to try to read themselves later. Teachers choose the books they read aloud with different purposes in mind. Sometimes a book is related to a theme being studied by the class; most often the books are fun to read. Some books are suggested for read-aloud in the Lessons. These are only suggestions; a teacher's choice is encouraged!

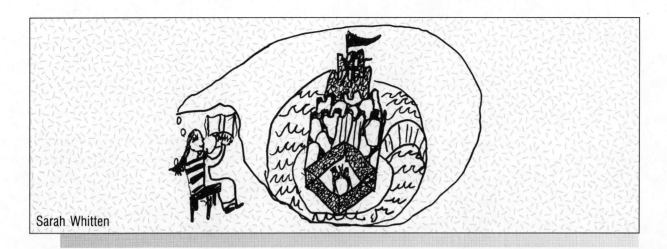

Sarah Whitten

Most teachers do stop and ask questions during the reading time, especially when they wonder if the students understand the significance of what has just been read. These questions and discussions could certainly be called effective comprehension instruction, but the teacher's main purpose during this time is to entertain the class with a great story.

▶ Some Suggested Books to Read Aloud to Third-Graders

Ackerman, Karen. *Song and Dance Man.* New York: Alfred A. Knopf, 1988.

Baker, Keith. *The Magic Fan.* San Diego: Harcourt Brace Jovanovich, 1989.

*Banks, Lynne Reid. *The Indian in the Cupboard.* New York: Avon Books, 1980.

Bayer, Jane. *A, My Name is Alice.* New York: Dial Books for Young Readers, 1984.

Baylor, Byrd. *The Way to Start a Day.* New York: Aladdin Books, 1977.

Berenzy, Alix. *A Frog Prince.* New York: Henry Holt and Co., 1989.

Birdseye, Tom. *Air Mail to the Moon.* New York: Holiday House, 1988.

Brown, Laurene Krasny, and Marc Brown. *Visiting the Art Museum.* New York: E. P. Dutton, 1986.

Browne, Anthony. *Piggybook.* New York: Alfred A. Knopf, 1986.

———. *Willy the Champ.* New York: Alfred A. Knopf, 1985.

———. *Willy the Wimp.* New York: Alfred A. Knopf, 1984.

Bunting, Eve. *The Wall.* New York: Clarion Books, 1990.

———. *The Wednesday Surprise.* New York: Clarion Books, 1989.

*Byars, Betsy. *The Not-Just-Anybody Family.* New York: Dell, 1986.

Charlip, Remy. *Fortunately.* New York: Four Winds Press, 1964.

Clements, Andrew. *Big Al.* Saxonville, MA: Picture Book Studio, 1988.

Cole, Joanna. *The Magic Schoolbus Inside the Earth.* New York: Scholastic, 1987.

*Dahl, Roald. *Danny the Champion of the World.* New York: Alfred A. Knopf, 1975.

**de Regniers, Beatrice. *Sing a Song of Popcorn.* New York: Scholastic, 1988.

Fox, Mem. *Shoes from Grandpa.* New York: Orchard Books, 1989.

———. *Wilfrid Gordon McDonald Partridge.* Brooklyn: Kane/Miller Book Publishers, 1985.

*Gardiner, John Reynolds. *Stone Fox.* New York: Thomas Y. Crowell, 1980.

Geraghty, Paul. *Over the Steamy Swamp.* London: Gulliver Books, 1988.

**Greenfield, Eloise. *Honey, I Love.* New York: Harper and Row, 1978.

* long books to be read chapter by chapter

** collections of poems, stories, and articles to be read throughout the year

**————. *Nathaniel Talking*. New York: Black Butterfly Children's Books, 1988.

**Hamilton, Virginia. *The People Could Fly: American Black Folk Tales*. New York: Alfred A. Knopf, 1985.

Houston, Gloria. *The Year of the Perfect Christmas Tree*. New York: Dial Books for Young Readers, 1988.

Howe, James. *Scared Silly*. New York: Morrow Junior Books, 1989.

Huck, Charlotte. *Princess Furball*. New York: Greenwillow Books, 1989.

Karlin, Barbara. *Cinderella*. Boston: Little, Brown and Co., 1989.

Kellogg, Steven. *The Island of the Skog*. New York: Dial Books for Young Readers, 1973.

**Lauber, Patricia. *The News about Dinosaurs*. New York: Bradbury Press, 1989.

Mahy, Margaret. *The Great White Man-Eating Shark*. New York: Dial Books for Young Readers, 1989.

Marshall, James. *Red Riding Hood*. New York: Dial Books for Young Readers, 1987.

————. *The Three Little Pigs*. New York: Dial Books for Young Readers, 1989.

————. *Wings, A Tale of Two Chickens*. New York: Viking Kestrel, 1986.

Martin, Bill, Jr., and John Archambault. *The Ghost-Eye Tree*. New York: Henry Holt and Co., 1985.

*Mathis, Sharon Bell. *The One Hundred Penny Box*. New York: Puffin Books, 1975.

*Mowat, Farley. *Owls in the Famlily*. New York: Bantam, 1961.

Munsch, Robert. *The Paperbag Princess*. Toronto: Annick Press, 1980.

Noble, Trinka Hakes. *Jimmy's Boa and Big Splash Birthday Bash*. New York: Dial Books for Young Readers, 1989.

**Prelutsky, Jack. *Something Big Has Been Here*. New York: Greenwillow Books, 1990.

*Rockwell, Thomas. *How to Eat Fried Worms*. New York: Dell Publishers, 1973.

*Sachar, Louis. *Sideways Stories from Wayside School*. New York: Avon Books, 1978.

San Souci, Robert. *The Talking Eggs*. New York: Dial Books for Young Readers, 1989.

————. *The Boy and the Ghost*. New York: Simon and Schuster, 1989.

Schroeder, Alan. *Ragtime Tumpie*. Boston: Little, Brown and Co., 1989.

**Schwartz, Alvin. *Scary Stories to Tell in the Dark*. New York: Harper and Row, 1981.

Schwartz, David. *If You Made a Million*. New York: Lothrop, Lee and Shepard, 1989.

Schieszka, Jon. *The True Story of the Three Little Pigs*. New York: Viking Penguin, 1989.

*Shreve, Susan. *The Flunking of Joshua T. Bates*. New York: Alfred A. Knopf, 1984.

**Silverstein, Shel. *Where the Sidewalk Ends*. New York: Harper and Row, 1974.

**Singer, Marilyn. *Turtle in July*. New York: Macmillan, 1989.

Steptoe, John. *Mufaro's Beautiful Daughters*. New York: Lothrop, Lee and Shepard, 1987.

Van Allsburg, Chris. *Jumanji*. Boston: Houghton Mifflin, 1981.

————. *The Polar Express*. Boston: Houghton Mifflin, 1985.

————. *Two Bad Ants*. Boston: Houghton Mifflin, 1988.

Viorst, Judith. *Alexander and the Terrible, Horrible, No Good, Very Bad Day*. New York: Atheneum, 1972.

————. *The Tenth Good Thing about Barney*. New York: Macmillan, 1971.

Waber, Bernard. *Ira Says Goodbye*. Boston: Houghton Mifflin, 1988.

*White, E. B. *Charlotte's Web*. New York: Harper and Row, 1952.

Williams, Vera B., and Jennifer Williams. *Stringbean's Trip to the Shining Sea*. New York: Greenwillow Books, 1988.

Wood, Don and Audrey. *Heckedy Peg*. San Diego: Harcourt Brace Jovanovich, 1987.

———. *King Bidgood's in the Bathtub*. San Diego: Harcourt Brace Jovanovich, 1985.

———. *The Napping House*. San Diego: Harcourt Brace Jovanovich, 1984.

Yolen, Jane. *Owl Moon*. New York: Philomel Books, 1987.

Yorinks, Arthur. *Hey, Al*. New York: Farrar, Straus and Giroux, 1986.

Young, Ed. *Lon Po Po, A Red Riding Hood Story from China*. New York: Philomel Books, 1989.

▶ Books, Books, Books

A description of procedures for Recreational Reading may be helpful, but until teachers and students get their hands on loads of wonderful books, it is only a hollow plan. SUCCESS classes have shelves of basals; anthologies of literature; stacks of paperbacks by authors such as Beverly Cleary, Betsy Byars, John Christopher, Patricia Reilly-Giff, Judy Blume, Robert Newton Peck, Laura Ingalls Wilder, Lynne Reid Banks, E. B. White, Roald Dahl, Peggy Parrish, James Howe, and many others; displays of picture books, including Caldecott winners and books by James Marshall, James Allard, Steven Kellogg, Anthony Browne, Chris Van Allsburg, Don and Audrey Wood, Eve Bunting, and many, many more. There are also poetry books and other nonfiction books.

The following list from a teacher's clipboard notes shows books being read in her class one day in October:

- *Ghost-Eye Tree* by Bill Martin, Jr., and John Archambault
- *The Polar Express* by Chris Van Allsburg
- *Miss Nelson is Missing* by James Allard
- *The Wednesday Surprise* by Eve Bunting
- *The Random House Book of Poetry*
- *Good Dog Carl* by Alexandra Day
- *Mother Goose*
- *Over the Steamy Swamp* by Paul Geraghty
- *If You Made a Million* by David Schwartz
- *The Island of the Skog* by Steven Kellogg
- *Willy the Wimp* by Anthony Browne
- *The Beast in Ms. Rooney's Room* by Patricia Reilly-Giff
- *Gorilla* by Anthony Browne
- *Heckedy Peg* by Don and Audrey Wood
- *Sing a Song of Popcorn* by Beatrice de Regniers
- *Scary Stories to Read in the Dark* by Allen Schwartz
- *How to Eat Fried Worms* by Thomas Rockwell
- *Farmer Boy* by Laura Ingalls Wilder

These books together replace a reading textbook to provide young readers with a richer and more personalized experience.

Chapter 4 The Writing Module

What is the purpose of the Writing module? It is to make it possible for a girl to write a funny poem about her big brother's new haircut, or for an animal-fanatic boy to compose a paragraph about how chihuahuas cannot possibly be as small as the encyclopedia says.

Letters, notes, advertisements, greeting cards, reports, stories, poems, lists, dialogues, jokes, and journals are all types of writing that are important for third-graders, not because they are included in the language arts curriculum, but because they are important means of communication in the lives of eight- and nine-year-old children. The Writing module sets aside the time for third-graders to work on various kinds of writing every day. This module also allows the teacher to introduce or review information that is helpful to writers through brief mini-lessons for the whole class and especially through numerous teacher-student conferences. The time set aside for the Writing module also includes opportunities for writers to share what they are writing with classmates and to seek suggestions from fellow writers.

The purpose of the Writing module is inextricably connected to those of the other modules in SUCCESS. Techniques and information from the Research module show up again as writers work on their compositions. Growing expertise with spelling, handwriting, and word knowledge introduced in the Word Study module enables a writer to work with more fluency. Reading quantities of wonderful literature in the Recreational Reading module feeds the love of stories and poems and provides an endless supply of ideas for plots, characters, styles of writing, and more. Teachers can easily capitalize on all of these connections by deliberately

Lesson 31

Writing

Theme: People or _____.

MINI-LESSON
Brainstorm list of people at school or _____.

COMPOSING
Write a list of people you can write about or _____.

SHARING Partners discuss their lists or _____.
Papers are dated and filed.

Ann-Sydney Harden

coordinating topics, materials, and skills among the modules; but even with no special attempts to develop thematic units, students who feel like members of a literary community make innumerable connections on their own.

Each day, the Lessons include an outline recommending how a teacher could plan to spend the Writing module time. As in the other modules, the blanks indicate where teachers are encouraged to add other emphases and substitute ideas that are more appropriate for their classes. The outlines for lessons in the Writing module include an emphasis on a broad theme for three weeks, which is coordinated with themes in the Word Study and/or Research modules. Throughout the three-week theme emphasis, some of the mini-lessons focus on developing ideas related to the theme itself; others pertain to writing mechanics; some are connected with what the teacher reads aloud or with reading the students have done on their own; some offer ideas for class publication projects; and others help writers help each other.

The example on page 48, Lesson 31, is the first in the sequence of lessons about people, so the mini-lesson is designed to generate lists of ideas for personal writing projects. By Lesson 40, the emphasis is on working toward the completion of pen pal letters that will be mailed (published) after Lesson 45. Some teachers will choose to substitute more mini-lessons about grammar and the mechanics of writing if those areas are stressed in the school; most teachers find that through editing for publication, these "skills" are appropriately emphasized on an individual basis.

The rest of this chapter explains what matters most in writing instruction in SUCCESS classes, along with choices teachers make to make the plans in the Lessons most effective.

▶ Principles of Effective Writing Instruction

To achieve the purpose of the Writing module, the following principles must be kept in mind:

1. Students need time for writing. Students must have at least thirty minutes for writing every day. If no more time is available, this half hour may include the five-minute mini-lesson and about five minutes for sharing, thus leaving twenty minutes for actual writing. More time can be added to this minimum amount, depending on some of the choices that teachers make about integrating other content-area subjects into the language arts program. For example, in a self-contained class, much science, health, and social studies information is included in the SUCCESS modules. For this reason some teachers can afford more than thirty minutes from their daily schedules for the Writing module. Children and teachers learn that writing takes time; without a dependable schedule of time set aside for writing, writers cannot truly "get into" their work. As they "get into" their writing, they deal with traditional comprehension skills, such as main idea, inference, sequence of events, and cause and effect. Comprehension cannot improve if writers and readers never have a chance to settle into an extended story.

2. Students must have daily opportunities to share their writing with classmates. Teachers will make many choices about how the sharing will take place. Sometimes there may be time for individuals to read their pieces to the entire class; at other times small groups may gather to hear each other's work. Often, students should be allowed to collaborate quietly during the writing time for the sake of seeking suggestions and help from other writers.

3. Students must have regular opportunities to "publish" pieces of their writing. As many of these publication opportunities as possible should be real, such as a writing contest sponsored by a local business, letters to pen pals, editorials about issues that affect the students, or guides to accompany content-area projects the students have prepared in the Research module.

Unless students believe they are writing for "real" reasons, no matter how many choices they are given about topics, they will tend to think that the only reason to write is because the teacher told them to. Writing instruction then becomes only another form of drilling the skills.

4. Editing must be emphasized appropriately. The main emphasis on writing mechanics and editing can be limited to the pieces that are to be published. Until the editing stage, students and teachers should be more interested in what the writer has to say than in the mechanics.

When teachers begin using the Writing module, one of their first concerns is how to handle children who ask the spelling of every word they write down. Correct spelling doesn't continue to be such a major issue for students once they learn that when they are writing a draft, it is all right to spell words incorrectly. Teachers may respond to spelling questions, "This is your draft, or sloppy copy, so spell the words the best you know how. You can find the correct spellings later if you choose to publish the piece."

Parents need to be aware of the distinction between sloppy copies and published pieces so that they can support their children's efforts as writers in the same way that the teacher does. Some teachers have rubber stamps that say "rough draft" or "sloppy copy."

5. The teacher leads brief mini-lessons, beginning each day's writing time with a short pre-writing activity that lasts no more than five minutes. The purposes of this lead-in time vary widely from reviewing writing mechanics, to using particular pieces of literature as models for student pieces, to discussing the management of writing materials in the classroom. Many mini-lessons may focus on topics and subject matter, thereby linking the writing time to other parts of the curriculum. No matter how critical the importance of the mini-lesson, however, it is most effective if kept very brief. In addition to losing some of its effectiveness by making it too long, a teacher who extends a mini-lesson beyond the recommended five minutes takes away some of the minimum amount of time needed by the writers for writing.

6. Skills are taught in context. The teacher must expect that most instruction will occur in individual or small-group discussions during the writing time, not during the mini-lesson. Otherwise, teachers would feel a greater need to give more examples, ask more questions, and explain more things in the mini-lesson. By giving students at least twenty minutes out of the Writing module to work on their own, the teacher has at least twenty minutes to help individuals with the skills they demonstrate the need to learn.

For example, in one class, Deadra shared her Christmas story with the teacher during the writing time. She had essentially written one sentence that had twelve independent clauses all connected with *and*. In the context of that story, which Deadra wanted to publish, the teacher showed her how to use fewer *and*s and more periods. That advice would have been wasted if it had been presented to the whole class at once.

The best instruction occurs in the context of the piece the child has chosen to write, not in impersonal examples. Teachers observe that the child who has demonstrated the need for instruction about a skill is not the only one who benefits from the teacher's individual attention. Those sitting around the student who is talking with the teacher cannot resist eavesdropping! Students tend to be more motivated to eavesdrop than to listen to the best mini-lesson in the world.

7. Students must consider their audience. The teacher must create the expectation that he or she is not the main audience for student's work. It is not the students' job to decide what the teacher wants to see in a composition; it is more important to decide what the intended audience wants, whether that audience is the judge of a contest, other students looking at a bulletin board, or mothers reading Mother's Day cards. Teachers help students develop an appropriate understanding of their audience by allowing them to share their writing with each other, by creating as many real-world publishing opportunities as possible, and by giving students helpful responses to their work without making judgments (see page 63).

8. Writing models help students. The teacher must make available a large variety of models of writing, including his or her own writing and that of well-known writers. Good models are readily available in the other modules of the SUCCESS program, and the brief mini-lessons in the Writing module create the possibility of including more models. Some teachers occasionally use part of the students' time for writing to sit down and work on their own pieces; they model the processes of drafting, conferring with someone else, revising, conferring some more, editing, and publishing. Students get to see the "sloppy copies" that adults produce! They get to hear the worries of a writer who is bogged down. As in Recreational Reading, the role of a model is important.

9. Students maintain manila writing folders where they keep all of their drafts, as well as copies of finished pieces. Folders are more appropriate than spiral-bound notebooks because writers often cut up drafts

and tape them together. Students are less comfortable with messy drafts if they use spirals.

Some teachers supply students with a second folder for writing. This folder is for copies of finished pieces. Students staple all of the sloppy copies and drafts that lead to the publication of the piece to the back of the copy. This second folder is documentation of the best writing a student can do, along with evidence of all the work that contributed to its completion.

Besides implementing the nine principles of effective writing instruction described so far to achieve the goals of the Writing module, the teacher must make two fundamental choices that affect the way the Writing module will work:

1. Will students be required to follow through on assignments that spring from the mini-lesson, or will they be allowed to plan their own writing projects, sometimes doing what the teacher has introduced?

2. Will the entire class edit and publish pieces of writing according to the same schedule, or will individual students be allowed to publish their own projects according to their own schedules?

Decisions about these issues make a difference in how students develop as writers. In a SUCCESS classroom or in any other language arts class, writing instruction that requires all students to follow the same schedule of drafting, editing, and publishing particular kinds of pieces can be excellent. Yet, many teachers who have used this format now believe that writing instruction is much better if students choose their own projects and work according to their own schedules. Outlines of lessons in the Writing module make it possible for a teacher to assign topics and schedules, or, instead, to allow students more flexibility to try various types of writing and working according to more individualized schedules.

▶ How to Lead the Writing Module

Considering the purpose of this module and the principles of effective writing instruction, certain things must happen every day in the Writing module in every SUCCESS class: a mini-lesson should last less than five minutes, students must have at least twenty minutes to write, and students should have about five minutes to share their work with other writers in some way. Throughout these three activities, teachers must make many decisions. The following describes the daily procedures in the Writing module and shows some of the decisions a teacher might make.

BRIEF MINI-LESSON (5 MINUTES)

The teacher starts off the Writing module with a brief mini-lesson. The Lessons give ideas for what to do, but a skillful teacher usually adapts the mini-lessons to suit something he or she has noticed about what the students have been doing in their writing. Sometimes the mini-lesson concerns class procedures, and sometimes it focuses on a mechanics-of-writing skill. One teacher favors mini-lessons designed to get the students to try a new kind of writing; some of these mini-lessons are simply

Figure 4-1

SUGGESTED TOPICS FOR WRITING MODULE

Lessons	Topics	Lessons	Topics
1–15	Animals	91–105	Friends
16–30	Places	106–120	Communication
31–45	People	121–135	Changes
46–60	Things to Do	136–150	Cities
61–75	Space/Holidays	151–165	Nutrition
76–90	Energy	166–180	Art

the reading of a poem or part of a picture book. Other mini-lessons are quick class discussions of a topic or the reading of a pen pal letter before students begin writing back to their pals. Still others are mainly for the purpose of announcing a contest or some other real reason for students to publish some writing.

For example, Mike, a third-grade teacher, said to his class, "Listen to this advertisement the witch received in *The Jolly Postman:* 'Boots come in five fashion colors: jet black, coal black' and so on. Do you need to advertise anything for sale?"

"Yeah, my little brother is for sale . . . cheap!"

"Our cat had kittens, and my mom says we have to sell all five of them."

The teacher continues. "What kind of information does an advertisement have to give?"

"The price."

"You have to make the thing sound good, or they won't buy it. I don't know how I could advertise my brother."

Mike concludes the mini-lesson. "You also have to tell who the seller is and how an interested buyer can get in touch. Now it's your turn to think of something to advertise and write an advertisement."

This lead-in could have been much, much longer. The teacher could have let everyone share an idea for something to sell; he could have heard lots of suggestions from lots of people. He could have shown examples of real advertisements and talked about all kinds of propaganda techniques. He could have talked about the need for capital letters in so many places in advertisements. Instead, his mini-lesson is less than five minutes long. It connects one of his students' favorite books with an idea for writing in the real world. It spurs students' thinking about what they have for sale, as well as gives a few reminders of the kind of facts they must include.

At another school, in a mini-lesson devoted to the correct use of commas in listing items in a series, Marilyn, the teacher, spoke to the class. "Jeremy, Jerome, and Jamie all have names that start with *J*. If I wrote that sentence in a story, what would I need to do to make it right?"

"Use capital *J*s."

"That's right. Anything special about the punctuation?"

"Period at the end."

"Good. I'm glad you know that. Anything else?"

The teacher could have expanded this mini-lesson to include many more examples. She could have asked students to write several sentences demonstrating commas separating items in a series. Instead, she talks with the class about one example, showing them the sentence on the board with its commas. Then, she asks everyone to watch out for places in their writing where they need to separate items in a series with commas.

Because she has spent less than five minutes presenting this lesson to the class, she has plenty of time to circulate among the writers, looking to see how they are using commas in sentences. If this skill is the proofreading emphasis for the day, the students will also get some feedback from others about their use of commas.

Effective mini-lessons can be content oriented, skill oriented, or process oriented. Every group of writers needs all three kinds of mini-lessons. Whatever the emphasis, the key for the teacher to remember is that the mini-lesson itself truly is mini. The maximum level of instruction occurs through individual and small-group interaction during writing and sharing times.

WRITING TIME (20 MINUTES MINIMUM)

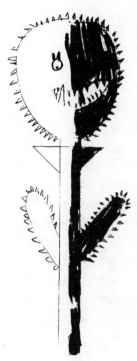

Jim Conant

Plan A Mike's students pick up their pencils and get to work. In his class, everyone is not required to respond immediately to the mini-lesson; many students go back to work on projects they began on other days. Hayley, on the other hand, has been scheming to raise money for ordering books from the book club, so she realizes she could advertise some of her old books for sale.

"These are too easy for me now, and some of the first- or second-graders might buy them." She wants to know if she can send her advertisements over to the classrooms of the younger children, and then she proceeds to write her first draft. It takes a few more days for her to complete the process of preparing her advertisements.

After assuring Hayley that she can put up her advertisements in the other classes, Mike moves on to other students. Two girls overheard Hayley's idea and decide they could advertise toys that they've outgrown to younger students. Four boys have been involved in writing a saga based on the Teenage Mutant Ninja Turtle characters. Mike talks briefly with them about introducing the characters well enough so that those who don't watch the TV show will understand what the story is about. Then he stops at another boy's desk to find out what his plan for the day is; it appears that he hasn't gotten started yet. Meanwhile, Mike has planned an editing conference with a couple of boys to help them determine where to put periods in their stories about a recent school assembly program.

When students are working on so many different projects at the same time, teachers keep careful records of each student's work. As students begin their writing, some teachers ask each student what he or she plans to do in writing that day. They record each student's plan on their clipboard sheet (see Figure 4-2). The process of determining and recording each student's plans is what Nancie Atwell calls "status of the class."* Atwell accomplishes this in much the same way a teacher calls the roll for attendance. She says status of the class can be completed in two minutes. Other teachers have discovered that they can do the job best by allowing students to get right to work following the mini-lesson and, without making everyone remain still and quiet, circulating to interview each student briefly. For these teachers, seeking the status of the class is actually another type of teacher-student conference. It takes from two minutes to five minutes to check in with everyone in the class.

One teacher says, emphatically, "Writing time is not quiet in my room." A quick survey of all the activity reveals the reason. During the writing time, students sometimes work together on collaborative projects; when working on individual projects, they sometimes seek help from each other. Still other students, who have reached the publishing stage of their work, are out of their seats to get crayons, glue, scissors, and other materials they need for putting together their completed work. Teachers may have to re-train themselves to listen to the content and quality of individual conversations rather than to react to the overall noise level in the classroom. Naturally, the teacher sets the limits for how much noise is acceptable. A lot of talking is a healthy characteristic of a writing class, but no one's talking should interfere with anyone else's work, in this classroom or any others.

In this not-so-quiet atmosphere teachers spend their time helping some students edit work for publication, asking other students how their work is progressing, urging others to try out their ideas on a friend, answering questions, and sometimes standing back to observe the whole scene. They use clipboards to keep notes about what they learn from their observations. Then, after observing students at work, teachers are able to question students more carefully about their plans and progress, especially those who seem to be having trouble.

More about writing conferences   As a general rule, teachers conducting conferences with writers should ask the writers questions instead of reading from their drafts. After a mini-lesson about poetry, using "Harriet Tubman" by Eloise Greenfield as a model, one teacher conducted conferences about various aspects of poetry writing.

The teacher asked Mary, "How's it going?"

---

*Nancie Atwell, *In the Middle: Writing, Reading, and Learning with Adolescents* (Portsmouth, NH: Boynton/Cook, 1987), p. 90.

Figure 4-2

CLIPBOARD NOTES

Andy - answering pen pal letter
Dominic poem about environment
Jerome continue draft of winter book
Jason - idea for refrain of poem
Timothy - animal poems
Tawanna - script for black history
Cedric - web, then poem draft
Tiffany - looked at Fortunately for more ideas
Thaddeus - about bubble gum in hair
Shannon script - b.h.
Deadra - poem
Hayley - her version of Girl Talk
Shelna - script - b.h.
David - 2nd draft. Tecnage M. N. Turtles
Jamie - idea from basal
Anthony - look at another poetry book
Carla script - b.h.
Scott - web, draft of poem
Sam - web, 1st verse of poem
Terrence - trouble getting idea
Al - web.
DeeDee script. b.h.
Otis - ideas from his new bike

Feb. 10
Writing.
mini-lesson-
Prelutsky,
"I Should Have
Stayed in Bed"
made webs
of bad things
that happen.
Connected to
Viorst,
Alex and the
Terrible, Horrible . . .

"I think I'm finished," she said. "Will you read it?"

"I'd love for you to read it to me." Mary read the poem, and the teacher observed that she had used the same line at the beginning and end of her poem. "I like the way you used the same line twice. Did you do that on purpose? Would you use that idea in other poems you write?"

The purpose of the conference was to give the writer some specific feedback on her poem, and perhaps to encourage her to experiment with a technique in another piece. The emphasis was on the content of the poem, not on the mechanics of writing. If the teacher had read the draft instead of asking Mary to read it, mechanics would have become the focus rather than content.

Deleshia Williams

In the same classroom, Quincy asked, "How do you write a poem?"

The teacher responded, "What have you thought of so far?"

"Well, I made this list of things, but how can I make a poem?"

"What are the things on the list? Is your poem going to tell about a person like the one about Harriet Tubman does?"

The purpose of this conference was to get Quincy to explain more about his own ideas for writing a piece, not to provide him with a set formula for poetry writing. Many teachers who confer with student writers describe a sensation of being able to see the wheels turning in the writers' minds while they ask and answer questions. Students who are telling the teacher what a piece of writing is about are often actually rehearsing and composing sentences that are yet to be written on the paper!

In still another conference that day, the teacher talked with Susan about some revisions for her poem. Susan said, "I've changed some things in my poem."

"Why do you like this new one better?"

Here, the purpose of the conference was to celebrate a revision! Writers—and students who overhear this conversation—benefit from comparing the latest version of a piece of writing to earlier versions to see what progress has been made. They are all encouraged to expect that early drafts can develop into better compositions.

After Marilyn gave her mini-lesson about commas separating items in a series, she held fifteen or sixteen short conferences about commas as she traveled around the room. She asked writers to show her where they had decided they needed commas. She complimented writers on their correct use of punctuation. She asked writers questions about their reasons for putting punctuation marks where they did. She showed writers what she was talking about in the example she had used in the mini-lesson. In short, she had a better chance to help the students who didn't already know about commas separating items in a series. Marilyn could even keep notes on her clipboard about various students and their success in using commas.

Plan B   For teachers who prefer more conformity to a schedule, the time for writing would be spent somewhat differently. In the case of our example, the students would all begin writing advertisements, following through with the suggestions introduced in the mini-lesson. The teacher decides whether or not to encourage collaboration and conferencing among students during the writing time, and the teacher still has the responsibility to circulate and confer with students. A student who completes the writing of an advertisement before writing time is over may choose to continue a previous assignment or construct a new project.

"I'm through! I've written an advertisement to sell my old bike," Justin says.

"You're happy with every bit of what you've written?" He nods. "Save your ad, then, because we will be sharing them in a few minutes. Did you need to go back to the poem you started the other day about your dog? You really had some good ideas going there, and I remember you were disappointed when writing time was over that day. Is there more you want to do with that piece?"

Happy with that suggestion, Justin looks through the papers in his folder until he finds the draft he had worked on earlier in the week. Another child may not eagerly shift his attention to something "old," and the teacher may suggest that he or she start a new project, perhaps something modeled after some recent reading.

Plan C Many teachers begin the year conducting the Writing module according to Plan B, and, after students have more experience trying out various types of writing and are working well with other writers in the room, these teachers shift to Plan A. One teacher gives students journals in which to write every day at the beginning of the year, in addition to the thirty minutes for a SUCCESS Writing module conducted with assigned topics and schedules. The journal-writing time easily introduces students to writing that isn't assigned. After a few weeks, Plan A replaces the assigned topics and schedules, and students begin to use their journal-writing time to do more work on their writing projects. Even teachers committed to allowing students the choices they are given in Plan A periodically operate their classes according to Plan B. For example, to celebrate a season of the year or to show off material the students have been learning in science, math, or social studies, the teacher may require everyone to contribute a piece of writing to a class exhibit. In this case, a topic is required of everyone, and a publication deadline governs the schedule for everyone.

SHARING TIME (5 MINUTES)

Ideally, writers share with each other constantly during the writing time, seeking advice and help, as well as trying out ideas on their friends. "D-O-G! That's how you spell dog!" "Have you seen Sam's new story about the Lamborghini?" In addition to this, teachers orchestrate some sharing at the end of each Writing lesson, choosing one of several approaches.

Figure 4-3

STUDENT WRITING

Greta Camp. 9/27/90

My name is
Johnny
I love apple trees.
So do the bees,
Thats why everyone
calls me Johnny
Apple Seed.
Over

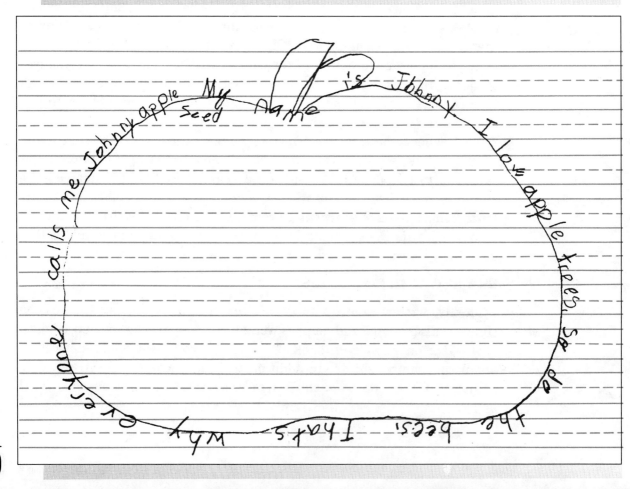

First, many third-grade teachers incorporate a proofreading activity in the sharing time. A particular writing skill is highlighted for attention during the mini-lesson or during writing time. The correct use of that skill is marked by the writer on his own paper. Then partners check each other's work. The partners also mark the part of the writing that they think is best and a part that needs help. The writing that is being proof-read is a draft, and the suggestions that the writer receives may be useful later if the piece is completely edited and "published." (See the section about proofreading, editing, and publishing for more information.) Meanwhile, the proofreading activity gives partners a specific reason to share their work and to pay attention to the details of each other's work.

In another approach, students form response, or sharing, groups. The most effective response groups have four or five members. During sharing time, each person reads to the group part of what he or she has written and asks for feedback from the other group members. This kind of sharing focuses only on the content of the writing since the writer does not show his or her paper to other students. The writer wants to know if friends like the story, not whether the spelling is good. The writer can seek editorial help from fellow students during the editing process if the piece is going to be published.

Teachers sometimes plan a whole-class gathering during which one or two writers share something they have been working on. In this kind of sharing, the writer can ask the rest of the group questions and the group can ask questions of the writer. As with the small groups, this kind of sharing emphasizes content. The teacher often invites a particular writer to share for a particular reason. For example, whole-class sharing works when a teacher has observed a student trying something new that would interest the rest of the class, or when a writer is trying to make a choice between two approaches to a problem, or when a student has revised a piece significantly and needs a chance to let other students hear the before and after versions. In another approach, a large number of writers share specific parts of their pieces.

Just as the "How do you spell. . . ?" syndrome can be cured when students become accustomed to the ideas of sloppy copies and editing times, students can learn that the teacher doesn't have to read everything they write. There are other valuable audiences available. If sharing time is not provided regularly, students remind the teacher of their need for it by demanding that he or she look at everything they write, leaving the teacher wondering, "Why are they sticking papers in my face all the time?"

Students need response to what they write, but it doesn't have to come from the teacher. The teacher's response isn't necessarily the best. Until they learn the delights of feedback from friends, third-graders' requests for attention from the teacher can be dramatic and annoying. Janet demanded attention from the teacher and threw a tantrum when that attention didn't come immediately. She wadded up the draft of her letter to Judy Blume, smoothed it out again, threw it on the floor, stomped on it, and then shook it in the air to see how much noise she could make.

Sometimes students are reluctant to share. One teacher read a student's "book" to the class during whole-class sharing time because he was too bashful to do it himself; the class spontaneously applauded! This spurred another reluctant writer to read his summary of *Danny the Champion of the World* to the class. It was well written, and he read it well. Whole-class sharing like this may not prompt a lot of specific tips to help writers, but the triumphant feeling that captures everyone in the room sparks immeasurable enthusiasm for writing.

Until students gain experience with various methods of sharing their writing, the mini-lessons at the beginning of the Writing module can focus on making the response writers get more helpful. In one mini-lesson, a teacher encouraged all the listeners to think of a question to ask a writer who was planning to share. "How did you write such a good story?" "What's it about?" To encourage students to listen better, volunteers were asked to tell what they remembered from the pieces that were read during that day's sharing.

Several writers shared with the whole class on a day that the mini-lesson had been about things that crawl. Three people wanted to share what they had written about babies that lived in their homes. Another student shared her piece about bears, which was complete with plenty of reasons why she included bears in the category of things that crawl.

Figure 4-4

STUDENT WRITING

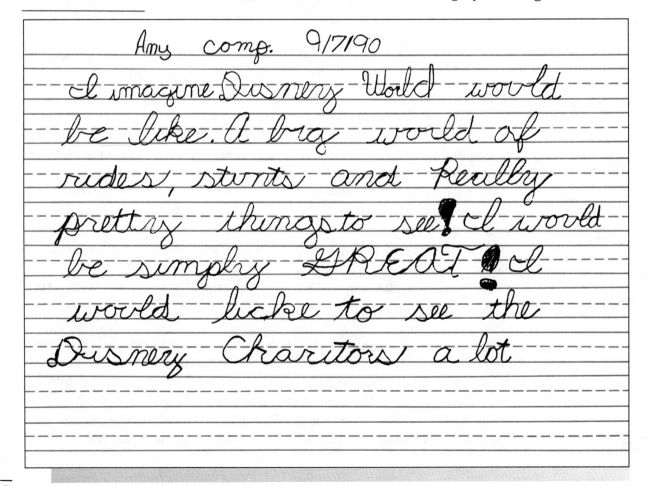

Amy comp. 9/7/90

I imagine Disney World would be like. A big world of rides, stunts and Really pretty things to see! I would be simply GREAT! I would licke to see the Disney Charitors a lot

Another student began to read her piece, then soon departed from the words on the page and told a revised version of what she had written. The final writer to share demonstrated how much he was influenced by a book he recently read about caterpillars.

No matter how impatient a teacher may feel to "get on with the lesson," students are eager to show off what they have accomplished and also to see what their classmates have written. Sharing time does not have to be a big production. Nothing can motivate learning more than simply reading one's ideas to a friend and finding out what that friend thinks.

Every day the Writing module ends with a time for everyone to file all the papers in their file folders for this module.

▶ The Proofreading, Editing, and Publishing Steps

Teachers and students in a SUCCESS class spend far more time focusing on the messages of their pieces of writing than on the mechanics of writing. In fact, early in the year teachers work to ease students' paralysis over not knowing how to spell a word. They encourage students to "guess and go." Teachers have seen students make far more progress in writing when the emphasis is first placed on finding something important to say. Then, after plenty of attention is given to figuring out what to say and how to say it, an appropriate amount of emphasis can be given to superficial issues of the mechanics of writing. Too often in the past, the priorities of emphasis have been reversed, leaving young writers so anxious about how to be correct in their writing that they have little time to concentrate on what they have to say.

In SUCCESS, students *do* progress in making their writing conform to the traditions of the English language, such as correct spelling, grammar, punctuation, and capitalization. Even though content of writing receives more emphasis, the Writing module helps students improve their use of the mechanics of writing as well. In traditional programs, teachers have to mark all the mechanical errors in every piece written by the students, making it impractical for students to write more than a paragraph or two each week. Because SUCCESS students write much more than do students in traditional programs, they apply the skills they are learning regularly.

Another reason SUCCESS students learn and improve their mechanics is that they find more motivation for correcting problems with mechanics because they write their pieces for other people to read, not just for the teacher to grade. They write stories for their friends to read. They write letters that pen pals will read. They write compositions that judges of contests will read. Knowing that real people will have to understand a message that the writer thinks is important causes him or her to pay more attention to the customs of the English language. The writer wouldn't want someone to misunderstand the message.

Children feel very good about themselves and their individual learning styles after experiencing a SUCCESS class!

Lisa Degnan, teacher

Teachers breaking away from traditional textbook and worksheet exercises in the language arts curriculum may wonder how they will teach the skills through this writers' workshop approach. After three days of circulating around the room during writing time, many teachers will recognize the multitude of teachable moments every day and realize how much more attentive the students are when they recognize the need for help in the context of their own stories. Teachers have always wondered how students could complete endless drill activities and still make errors in their own writing; often students don't appreciate the relevance of the mechanics of writing unless encountered in the context of their own work. In SUCCESS, much skill instruction takes place every day, and it is always in the context of pieces of writing done by each student.

In one classroom, a teacher taught a huge variety of skills all in one day through individual editing conferences. One child needed help seeing how much space to skip between words; several children were editing pieces with special attention to capital letters and periods; someone else needed to know about underlining book titles; two girls worked on distinguishing *to, too,* and *two* in their pieces; someone else was ready to talk about paragraphing and indenting; and others needed spelling help. This same list of skills, some of which cover broad areas such as all the possible reasons to use capital letters, could be developed into a year's lesson plans, if the skills were taught one at a time to the whole class. Instead, this teacher will work on the same variety of skills all year long, each child concentrating on the skills as they are needed as each piece is edited. One teacher asked, "Wouldn't it be more efficient to teach each skill to the class all at once?" Indeed it would, if only that approach were effective!

PARTNER PROOFREADING STRATEGY

The attention of all writers *can* be drawn to the same skill at the same time in the context of many different pieces through the partner proofreading strategy. Some plans in the Lessons suggest partner proofreading as part of sharing, along with a particular skill that will be the day's focus. The teacher can add proofreading emphases as often as they are needed.

Proofreading procedure

1. During mini-lesson time, or at the end of writing time, the teacher explains the proofreading thrust. If the thrust is a totally new concept, this explanation will be long enough to include one or two examples. Most of the thrusts are basic skills that have been discussed often in the contexts of pieces people have been writing all year. Even when the thrust is a relatively unfamiliar idea, however, the teacher knows that a long explanation will be futile.

The teacher introduces the thrust during the mini-lesson if it is something that wouldn't naturally be used in that day's writing. For example, if the thrust is the use of quotation marks around direct quotations, the writers need to know that at the beginning of their writing time; otherwise, they might not write any dialogue that day. On the other hand, if the thrust is capital letters at the beginning of sentences, there is no point in mentioning it during mini-lesson time.

2. At the end of writing time, writers are asked to put small checkmarks above some examples of the correct use of the day's proofreading thrust.

3. During sharing time, each writer gets a partner. The partners exchange papers. First, the proofreading partner writes his or her own name at the top of the writer's piece followed by "PR" to stand for "proofreader."

4. The proofreader reads the writer's paper to find out what it is about.

5. The proofreader checks the correctness of the proofreading thrust. If he or she agrees that the writer has used the thrust correctly, the proofreader places a second checkmark next to the one already made by the writer. If he or she thinks the thrust is not used correctly, the proofreader places an *X* next to the checkmark the writer made. If the proofreader can find another example of either the correct or incorrect use of the thrust, he or she points it out to the writer.

6. The proofreader chooses the part of the writer's piece that he or she thinks is the best and writes "good" in the margin near that part.

7. The proofreader chooses one part of the writer's piece that has a mistake or that he or she thinks could be improved in some way and writes "help!" in the margin near that underlined part.

8. The writers and proofreaders show each other the marks that they made and discuss the reasons for their decisions. Sometimes they get out grammar handbooks and dictionaries to prove who is correct!

Teachers use the partner proofreading strategy to draw writers' attention to editorial issues, but only in the context of *drafts* they are writing. The partner proofreading strategy is not designed to provide the thorough editing that must be done when a piece is going to be published. Some of the drafts that are proofread with partners may eventually be edited in a more complete way for publication. Meanwhile, the partner proofreading strategy helps students improve their proofreading skills so that they can proofread their own work more carefully. As the proofreaders help each other, everyone focuses on one mechanics-of-writing skill that the teacher designates.

EDITING FOR PUBLICATION

A writer needs help with thorough proofreading and editing when he or she has produced a final draft of a piece of writing and intends to publish it. Whether a pen pal letter ready to be mailed or an essay for a contest, the published pieces that come from a third-grade SUCCESS class need to be as correct as the writers can make them at that time. The goal is for all spelling, grammar, capitalization, and punctuation errors to be corrected. The published version of a writer's work always has more of those errors corrected than the final draft had, although, depending on the achievement level of that student, the writing may not be perfect.

Tiffany, a student in one third-grade class, wrote a letter to her new pen pal. Tiffany spends time every week with the school speech therapist, working on improving her pronunciation of consonant sounds. While helping her edit her letter, the classroom teacher helped her correct some spelling mistakes that probably resulted from some of her speech difficulties. Had those mistakes not been corrected, the pen pal would not have been able to understand what Tiffany had to say. In addition to the spelling mistakes, Tiffany also made errors with subject-verb agreement in many of her sentences. The teacher chose not to have Tiffany correct all those mistakes, deciding to save that "skill lesson" for another time. Compared to the last piece Tiffany had had edited for publication, her writing exhibited improvement in the use of capital letters and punctuation.

Teachers can help each student maintain an individual record and checklist of skills that need to be noticed during editing. After the teacher has worked on an editing project with a student, the teacher or the student can record two skills on the inside of that student's writing folder. The skills recorded should be ones that were emphasized during the editing conference. As the student edits his or her own work for a future publication, he or she will check the list inside the folder.

Teachers conduct editing conferences with students when the students decide they have done all they can to prepare their final drafts for publication. "Doing all they can" may mean working with a partner who can help edit; it may mean getting a dictionary to check the spelling of some words; and it may mean looking in one's writing folder for the kinds of mistakes the teacher has helped the writer correct in past papers. Teachers do the most effective editing with students when they can work with them during the writing time. Allowing students flexibility in scheduling their work on various writing projects means that while a student waits for an editing conference about a pen pal letter, he or she knows work can continue on the comic strip he or she is creating. SUCCESS students know that writers always have work to do.

Teachers often think of themselves as editors during the final two days before a publication is completed because they need to have so many editing conferences. The editing conferences are not, however, the most important conferences the teacher has with writers! The goals are for students to rely less and less on the teacher's editing service, and for all writers to think of the editing process as the final phase of the writing process. Deciding on one's message always takes precedence. The way the teacher chooses to use time and energy in the classroom conveys to the students what matters most about writing. If the teacher's conversations are more often about quotation marks than about the jokes a writer chooses to include in a story, the students unfortunately learn that punctuation matters more than the content of a story.

PUBLISHING

In order to reap the benefits of editing for publication, the class must be publishing fairly often. The plans in the Lessons suggest a class publication project every three weeks: class books, pen pal letters, museum exhibits, science fair projects, invitations, and so on. Teachers should design publication opportunities that are real and meaningful to the students in the class. Real publication opportunities will allow students to see that their writing can have an impact on the world.

If teachers allow students flexibility in following through on specific assignments, many students will choose to publish pieces of writing that are not assigned to the whole class. For example, Tiffany chose to write a card for her brother's birthday. That piece of writing needed to be edited for immediate publication!

This chapter ends the way it began. Students write things that are important to them. Through the teacher's decisions to provide time the students can count on for writing, freedom for the students to choose many of their own projects, and nonthreatening responses to their ideas, students come to think of themselves as authors.

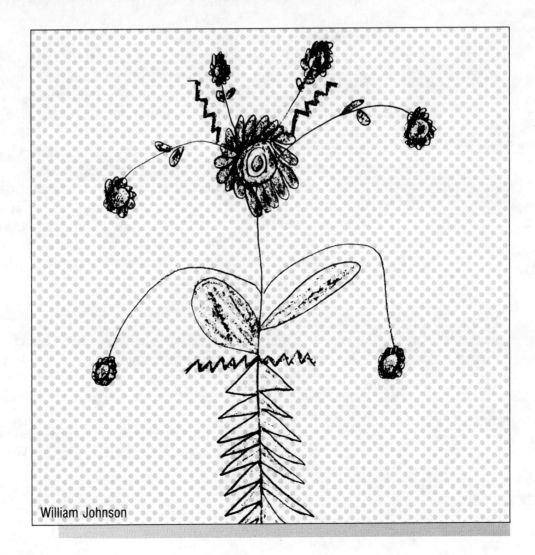

William Johnson

Chapter 5 The Word Study Module *Interactive Writing*

"Oh, yes, the SUCCESS program. That's the program with all the charts."

Many people think the Word Study module is the entire SUCCESS program. That may be because SUCCESS classrooms are covered with charts. Displaying a chart every day does give a classroom a distinctive look. People who take time to read the charts learn how personalized they are for the people in the class. Sometimes reading the charts is like reading a history of special events in the class.

Contrary to some people's impressions, however, the Word Study module is neither the entire SUCCESS program, nor the most important part of it. The Word Study module is a thirty-minute period reserved each day for focusing on a topic for the purposes of gaining information, examining spelling patterns in students' vocabulary, learning new vocabulary in context, practicing spelling of new words, and practicing written composition skills as well as handwriting. Throughout the thirty-minute module, students have opportunities to use all four language processes: speaking, listening, writing, and reading.

Many students think of this module as their time to spell; but others attribute their growth in reading to the attention they pay to words in this module. Still others, in schools where cursive handwriting is introduced in third grade, think the major purpose of this module is to work on handwriting. Every student thinks of the opportunity to get his or her idea written on the class chart. Every student is proud of the display of charts around the room and is eager to read them to any visitors.

Teachers recognize more direct teaching opportunities for the whole class in this module than in the other three. The emphasis on skills is very strong and is always in the context of language that comes from the students in the class. The results of good work in this module should be improved adherence to the customs of our language when students read and write in the other modules.

▶ How to Lead the Word Study Module

Three things happen in this module every day: a chart is made, students do some writing, and students participate in a spelling activity with a partner. For each of these three components, the teacher will make many decisions depending upon curriculum demands, student needs, and teachable moments that arise.

Teachers have been using this module in third-grade classes for many years. An example of a typical day's plan for the Word Study module appears on page 70.

THE LAST GREAT RACE

Josh Demske

Lesson **60**

Word Study

CHART DEVELOPMENT
Spelling Emphasis: *ou* or
  Other Emphasis:
- sentences or
- careers
  On the chart, the teacher writes
sentences volunteered by the students
using:
- *ou* words
- career vocabulary
- _____

WRITING
On their papers, students write: their
favorite words from the chart or other
words, phrases, or sentences that would
be appropriate for the chart.

SPELLING
Partners call out words for each other to
spell aloud.
  Papers are dated and filed.

HOMEWORK
Write a paragraph about careers you are
interested in. Use some *ou* words.

Using suggestions from the lesson outlines, teachers make many decisions about each of the three main activities in the Word Study module. Some typical decisions are described here, followed by a list of other decisions a teacher might make within the same framework of activities.

MAKE A CHART (10 TO 15 MINUTES)

The teacher tapes chart paper to the blackboard and writes on it the date, the lesson number, and the spelling emphasis. If choosing to incorporate cursive handwriting instruction in this module, he or she models the handwriting lesson for the day at the top of the chart. The letters emphasized in handwriting are the same as those in the spelling emphasis.

In some classrooms students practice handwriting before the chart is made. This is the procedure for handwriting practice: After the first few days of school, the teacher says almost nothing to the class at this point in the lesson. The students know to write the heading on their own papers and begin to practice writing the letters in cursive. The teacher immediately begins circulating among the students, helping individuals with handwriting. Many students need a model of the letters written on their own papers; some students trace over the teacher's model writing on their papers. (In other classrooms, handwriting practice is part of the "Students Write" step. See page 78.)

Next, if there is a topic emphasis in the lesson, the teacher leads a brief brainstorming discussion about the topic. Students volunteer words that include the spelling pattern or words that suit the topic, and the teacher writes these on the chart.

This part of the module changes over the course of the year (see Figure 5-1), depending on whether the class is in a phase of listing words, phrases, sentences, or paragraphs on the chart, and on whether the teacher chooses to give more emphasis to spelling, a grammar skill, or the topic. The Lessons include outlines of choices for what might be emphasized. What follows is the schedule of changes throughout the year, followed by a description of procedures for developing each kind of chart.

Lessons 1–21: Single Words   The teacher records words on the chart that students suggest. During Lesson 3, where the spelling emphasis is the lowercase *f*, students in one class gave this list of words: *flag, food, fat, fine, beef, finished, fork, Florida, California, floor, giraffe,* and *frog*. When a student said "Florida," the teacher wrote the word on the chart and pointed out, "That word does start with the letter *f*, but since it is the name of a particular place, it has to be capitalized." The next student thought of a state that had a lowercase *f* in its name.

Lessons 22–40: Phrases   The teacher asks volunteers to give phrases instead of individual words, or records words that volunteers give and then goes back and adds more words to make phrases.

In Lesson 38, the spelling emphasis is *L*, the topic emphasis is history, and the grammar emphasis is "proper noun." One teacher began with, "Who can think of a name or some other word that has to do with history? These will be words that we think we could find in the history books."

Students gave the following list of words they associated with history: *Martin Luther King, Clara Barton, lobster, Daniel Boone, King Solomon, Underground Railroad, Harriet Tubman, the Wright Brothers,* and *the Air Force*. Along the way, the teacher asked the volunteers questions such as, "Why is Clara Barton in the history books?"

"She started the Red Cross."

"What's the Underground Railroad?"

"It's the way slaves got to freedom before the Civil War."

"Was it a train?"

Once those were recorded on the chart paper, the teacher asked, "Which words on the chart are nouns?" and underlined all the words the students designated as nouns.

To emphasize adjectives, the teacher asked, "Can you think of any words to add to the chart that would tell more about the ideas? These words would have to make sense coming right in front of the nouns on the chart." Then students volunteered their adjective ideas, and the list

Figure 5-1

SCHEDULE OF CHANGES ON THE CHART

Lessons 1–21	Single Words	Lessons 80–90	One Paragraph
Lessons 22–40	Phrases	Lessons 91–180	Two or More
Lessons 41–79	Sentences		Paragraphs

changed to *red lobster, famous Daniel Boone, rich King Solomon, brave Harriet Tubman,* and *magnificent Air Force.* The teacher wrote the original list in one color ink and the adjectives in a new color.

Lessons 41–79: Sentences Volunteers give the teacher words that correspond to the spelling emphasis or to the topic, whichever he or she has chosen to emphasize. The teacher records these on the chalkboard next to the chart. After a good supply of words fills the chalkboard, the teacher calls on volunteers to compose sentences about the topic using some of the words on the chalkboard. He or she writes the sentence on the chart.

In Lesson 59 the spelling emphasis is *oi,* and the topic is "medicine." One teacher said to her class, "Today we're going to need some words that have *oi* for our chart. Who can think of some?"

The students suggested these words: *poinsettia* (because the teacher had brought one to school that day), *soil, boil, ointment, coins, spoil, foil, going, voice, oink.* The teacher recorded these suggestions on the chalkboard, not in a straight list, but grafitti-style. Then she said, "Our chart is mainly going to be about medicine today, so let's think of some sentences that have something to do with medicine. We want to use as many *oi* words as we can."

"*Poinsettias are poisonous if you eat them.*"

"What does that have to do with medicine?"

"If you ate a poinsettia, you'd have to take medicine to keep from dying."

Figure 5-2

PARTNER SPELLING TEST WITH WORD LIST

Rachel   Word Study   11/21/90

calendar   (ar)

cărnĭvăl

earn

Hallmark

Sears

Target

                    extraordinary
                    extraordinary
                    extraordinary

Figure 5-3

PARTNER SPELLING TEST WITH SENTENCES USING SPELLING WORDS

Forysia Word Study 12-17-80
gg ⑳

Ziggy went to the zoo with Maggie. They walked around the zoo. Ziggy saw a man juggling small appliances. Then Ziggy got hungry. While Ziggy was eating eggplant, he struggled with the trigger of the brake on the buggy. Then

they went home.
suggest it to Fraggle Rock
sugest it to Fraggle Rock

"Boil the water. That's what you have to do to keep from getting sick if the water is dirty."

"Put some ointment on your finger."

"What is ointment?"

"It's the medicine you put on cuts. It helps you get well."

These are three of the nine sentences that ended up on the chart that day. As the teacher recorded each sentence, she underlined the *oi* words that were included. On this particular day, every sentence did include at least one *oi* word. Sometimes every sentence won't have a word with the designated letters.

Lessons 80–90: One Paragraph   The procedure for developing these charts is the same as it is for sentences, except that in calling on volunteers to give sentences for the paragraph, the teacher asks questions about whether the sentence is a good one to begin the paragraph, to come next in the paragraph, to explain more about the previous sentence, or to conclude the paragraph. On these charts, students explain much more information than was necessary for the phrases or sentences on earlier charts.

In Lesson 81 the spelling emphasis is *re* and the topic is "literature." One teacher began this lesson by asking students to name words that had the letters *re*. The students volunteered several words, which the teacher recorded on the chalkboard. He then announced, "We're going to write a paragraph on our chart today, and it needs to be about literature. That means we can write about some of the books that you've been reading. Who wants to start off the paragraph? Remember that whatever the first sentence says will tell us what the whole page is going to be about."

He called on one student, whose hand was up, and he said, *"The Boy and the Ghost is a really scary story."*

The teacher said, "That's a good sentence. Do you think we can make up a whole paragraph about how scary that story is?"

The class nodded, since the teacher had just read that book by Robert San Souci to the class the day before.

As he wrote the sentence on the chart, the teacher said, "I have to do something special to some of the words in this sentence. Does anybody know what?"

"Underline *The Boy and the Ghost* because it's the title of a book," somebody said.

"Good. Now who has an idea for the next sentence? Maybe it could tell why this book is scary."

"The ghost's body comes apart." The teacher wrote that on the chart and called on someone else for another sentence.

"When the boy saw the ghost's legs, he said, 'Don't kick over my soup.'" The teacher recorded that sentence and asked the class about quotation marks and direct quotations. He called on someone else to tell another scary part of the book.

Figure 5-4

STUDENT SPELLING LIST AND STORY USING WORDS WITH SPELLING EMPHASIS

"ss"

Mike Word Study 12/11/90

It was not possible to do the homework that my professor gave me because the Sassers took it. They flussed it to. Then a massive earthquake came, It had a big mess

con it.
Mississippi
Mississippi
Sassy
Sassy
Pussycat
Pussycat

"The ghost's head flew in the house." The teacher wrote that sentence on the chart.

Then he said, "We're about to run out of room on the paper, so the next sentence needs to wrap up the paragraph. Who has an idea for a sentence that summarizes what we've been trying to say here?"

After some discussion, one student suggested, *"Some of our books are scary."*

Lessons 91–180: Two or More Paragraphs   The procedures for developing these charts are the same as they are for one paragraph, except for one additional step. The students name words that have the assigned spelling emphasis, and the teacher records those on the chalkboard. Then the teacher introduces the topic for the day and asks students to name the major ideas they wish to include on the chart. The teacher writes these in a separate corner of the chalkboard, and when the class is ready to compose the first paragraph, the first student to contribute to the chart decides which idea should come first.

Lesson 92 is about friends. This is the way a group of students who were seriously affected by Hurricane Hugo developed the chart. The spelling emphasis was *ox*, so the teacher recorded the *ox* words that the class volunteered on the chalkboard. Then she said, "Since our chart is going to be about friends today, let's see if we can think of some things to say about the way friends helped us after Hurricane Hugo."

"We could write about all the trucks."

"What do you mean?"

"Well, you know how they brought us things we needed."

"Good idea. I'll write *trucks* over here so we'll remember to write a paragraph about that. What else could we write about?"

"What about FEMA? They gave people some money to fix up their houses." (FEMA stands for Federal Emergency Management Agency.)

"And the Red Cross, too."

"Great. I'll write down *FEMA* and the *Red Cross*. Who wants to start off the first paragraph? Remember, that person gets to decide what idea we will write about first."

"Lots of trucks came to bring us stuff."

"Good beginning, but could you say what some of that stuff was, instead of saying *stuff*?"

"Lots of trucks came to bring us clothes, food, toys, and generators after Hugo."

"What else did the trucks bring?"

"Some trucks brought ice."

"What else do you know about the trucks?"

"They came from Georgia, Alabama, and other states."

"Let's start our second paragraph. You said it should be about the help we got from FEMA and the Red Cross. Who wants to start this part?"

"FEMA sent checks to people."

Shea Hutchings

"If it wasn't for Clara Barton, we wouldn't have a Red Cross to give us other things we need."

"Those are good sentences, but we have run out of room on our paper. What else could we say to finish this paragraph?"

No words with *ox* were used in the paragraphs on the chart.

After the words, phrases, sentences, or paragraphs are written on the chart paper, the teacher often goes back and asks the students to pick out all of a certain kind of word on the chart: all of the three-syllable words, all of the verbs, and so on. In going back over the chart, the teacher finds good opportunities for focusing on skills.

For example, in one class, after the chart for Lesson 59 was written, the teacher said, "We've been working on two-syllable words lately. Do we have any on our chart today?" After students volunteered to point them out, the teacher circled *ointment, finger, pocket,* and *lower,* the only two-syllable words on the chart that day. (Teachers are careful that they don't circle or underline so many things on the chart that it becomes illegible!)

It is a special privilege in some classes to be chosen to read the entire chart aloud. Another volunteer gives the chart a title. This decision usually requires the collaboration of several students, the consensus of the class, or a verdict by the teacher. The agreed-upon title for Lesson 81 was "A Scary Story" and the title for Lesson 92 was "Help after Hugo."

The teacher must remember to limit the "make a chart" part of the Word Study module to ten to fifteen minutes. Many teachable moments arise during this time, and the teacher has to decide when to pursue the teachable moment and when to pass it by. No matter how great the temptation, the teacher cannot digress from making the chart to teach all of the skills that pertain to the words and ideas offered by the students.

Knowing which teachable moments to pursue and which ones to skip is an art, a teaching skill that takes practice. This is one of the most difficult aspects of teaching this module. Most teachers are inclined to embellish too many of the teachable moments. Teachers need to remember that the very important ones will show up again and again on the chart throughout the school year, so they don't have to feel that the opportunity is gone forever. Rather than stressing skill instruction with every line of the chart, teachers accomplish more by waiting until the teachable moment comes up, and students are inquiring about something on the chart.

Sometimes teachers have commented that this module becomes boring. Making the chart is never boring if the emphasis is more on the topic and less on spelling. In the meaningful context of discussion about an important topic, children gain much experience with various spelling patterns, as well as with mechanics-of-writing skills.

STUDENTS WRITE (10 MINUTES)

"Now you may do your own writing on your paper."

After the chart is made, students begin to do their own writing for the day. The teacher did not tell the students exactly what to write or how much. The very least amount of writing required of every student is to make a list of the words he or she chooses to practice spelling. Words from which to choose are on the chart in Lessons 1 through 40, and from Lesson 41 onward, the chalkboard has lots of words that fit the day's spelling emphasis. Some students may have already started a list of words. Some may copy part or all of the chart the class made together.

By not giving explicit directions for writing, such as a minimum number of spelling words to write, the teacher creates an open-ended assignment for everyone. Each student is expected to do his or her best, and the teacher is able to question and encourage individuals while circulating among them.

As the year proceeds, more and more students are eager to write things on their papers that aren't on the chart. Some of them begin to do this without comment, but one student asked a teacher, "Can I copy the paragraph on the chart, but change it to make it better?" Wonderful! By not telling the students specifically what they are to write, the teacher is better able to encourage each student to do his or her best. The teacher can individually encourage students to try more challenging things.

When the class has reached the lessons for which it is to write three, four, and five paragraphs about a topic, the chart itself will probably have room for only two or three. Teachers may ask the students to write the remaining paragraphs on their own papers, composing those sentences themselves and perhaps using some of the ideas the class discussed.

Throughout the writing time, it is the teacher's job to circulate among the students, observing their progress and keeping notes on the

As a teacher, I am responsible for motivating, challenging, and enlightening my students. I [investigated this program] with the hope of expanding my teaching repertoire and providing my students with the best education possible.

Cynthia A. Nuckles, teacher

clipboard. The teacher makes suggestions, asks questions, and offers help when it is needed.

PARTNER SPELLING ACTIVITY (5 MINUTES)

At the end of this module, student partners work together to give each other a chance to practice spelling words aloud. The partners call out words from each other's spelling lists. (The spelling lists were written during the students' writing time.) Often it helps the caller and the speller if they have read over each other's lists together before the spelling activity begins. The first person calls out the words from the other person's paper and places a small checkmark over each letter that the speller says in the correct sequence. Then the second person calls out the words from the first person's list and makes checkmarks for each correct letter.

At the third-grade level, scoring for spelling is done by awarding one point for each letter in the proper sequence in each word on this list, even if the entire word is not spelled correctly. The speller may omit some letters, substitute incorrect letters, or reverse the order of letters and still get points for the correct letters that are included in the right order. The partner records the final score at the top of the page. Figure 5-2 shows a student's paper that has been marked by a partner.

What about reversed letters? Some teachers ask their students to give the speller one point for having two correct letters in the wrong order.

What about extra letters? No points are added on or taken off for extra letters.

What about omitted letters? Points are given for all the correct letters that are given, but are not subtracted for missing letters.

What's the advantage in spelling a word right if other people are getting points for words that are misspelled? The more letters a speller gets right, the more points he or she earns. Some teachers ask their students to give spellers a bonus point if the word is spelled exactly right.

Finally, students file their papers in their Word Study folders.

The teacher hangs the chart from each Word Study lesson on the wall. More and more charts should be added to the classroom display, pinned to bulletin boards, taped to walls, hung from clotheslines. The teacher should keep at least twenty to thirty charts on display at all times. The students read the charts, use them as spelling resources, and, best of all, are very proud of the charts they have created. Old charts are taken down to make room for new ones. The teacher can accumulate them and then give each student one to take home. Old charts are cherished prizes.

Teachers think of many ways to display and store charts. Some tie clotheslines from one end of the room to the other and use clothespins to attach the charts high over the heads of students. Others tape a row of charts across the windows of the classroom, nicely filtering the light in the room! SUCCESS teachers don't spend much time decorating bulletin boards, because all bulletin-board space is needed for displaying student

Best Friends

Sheena Manigault

work, including the charts. Some teachers store old charts by hanging two back to back on a coathanger and then hanging the coathanger on a chart rack.

▶ Teacher Decisions in the Word Study Module

Although the main routines of making charts, letting students write, and asking partners to call out words to each other happens in every SUCCESS classroom, teachers make many decisions about what to emphasize based upon their knowledge of the students in their classes and on the curriculum demands in their schools. All of the possibilities cannot be thoroughly covered in one thirty-minute session. The teacher must make some preliminary choices about what the emphases will be. Within the basic chart-writing-spelling format, more choices will be made based on the unexpected teachable moments that arise.

PRELIMINARY DECISIONS ABOUT MAKING THE CHART

Should the major emphasis of the chart be on a topic, a skill, or a spelling pattern? The example given from Lesson 3 showed the teacher's decision to emphasize the spelling pattern. In the example from Lesson 25, however, much more attention was given to the topic and the grammar emphasis. Teachers will look at the recommended emphases for a day's lesson and identify the major need of the class. They will also consider curriculum demands.

Should students search through printed materials for the designated spelling patterns? Or should the teacher lead a class discussion about an important topic the class has been studying? At the beginning of the year, it is usually best to let the words and information on the chart come from class discussion. Later in the year, some teachers notify students in advance of the letters in the spelling pattern by writing them at the top of the chart early in the school day. It is during this "advance notice" time that teachers see students scurrying around, grabbing dictionaries and checking glossaries, trying to find the best words, the most words, and so on. As a result, in these lessons, students have already listed some words on their papers before the class chart is made. Student enthusiasm for adding their own words to the class chart is even greater than before.

The disadvantage of students' locating words in print (instead of thinking of words they know that include the spelling emphasis) is that students will copy words that mean nothing to them. Teachers must ask more questions about the meanings of words that are volunteered if they are words students copied from print.

Class discussions about topics will still be the best way to begin when the topic is important to the curriculum. By beginning with topic discussions, teachers are able to link the language arts lesson to literature, math, social studies, and science topics.

Should the teacher stick to the topic in the lesson plan? The topics that are given in the Lessons relate to the whole range of typical curriculum topics, in addition to ones that are not usually found in third-grade materials. All of the topics are general enough so that the teacher can decide on a more specific aspect of the general topic, a specific topic that is helpful to a particular class at a particular time in the year. For example, the first time "music" is the topic, the students may think of their music class, and that is what the chart will be about that day. The next time, however, the teacher could suggest that, since they have already written about music class, maybe they would like to write about their favorite music on the radio. Still later in the year, when the class is preparing for the school's spring musical program, the chart could tell about that.

When the topic was "agriculture," one teacher led a discussion about the various farming techniques used by the Native Americans the students had been studying in social studies. When the topic was "math," the teacher led a discussion reviewing ideas about division, since the students were learning about it in math class. Another chart discussion allowed the students to review and explain the steps in a science experiment that had been done the day before.

Sometimes special events in the school and in the world affect the subject matter of the charts. On a day when a speaker from NASA visited a school, the scheduled topic was changed to "NASA." The day after Nelson Mandela was freed from prison in South Africa, a student brought in a news clipping with a picture. The scheduled topic for that day's chart was history, and it was easy to write a paragraph about very modern history.

Should the teacher stick to the sequence of spelling emphases in the Lessons?   The spelling emphases included in the lesson plans are to be used as a management system for insuring that students' attention is drawn to a variety of spelling combinations found in the language. The emphasis is not on letters that always come in a particular position in words, or ones that always make the same sound. Following the scheduled spelling emphases does not mean that the same words that are found in third-grade spelling books will be covered in the SUCCESS lessons, mainly because words in textbooks have been chosen to conform to a given pattern. In a SUCCESS class, students are always aware of exceptions and learn to use context in understanding words.

Teachers sometimes choose to draw students' attention to word families when they see that that is helpful. In Lesson 59, students had fun brainstorming words that ended with *oil*, once they recognized the pattern.

If a teacher chooses to substitute other spelling patterns for those given in the Lessons, he or she should do so, still thinking of these patterns only as a management system, not as a way to control the vocabulary used in the spelling activity.

Should the teacher have everyone spell words aloud as they are written on the chart?   At the beginning of the year when only words are being written on the chart, having students spell aloud as the words are written is a good way to encourage careful listening, as well as a helpful way for students to practice the correct spelling of some words. Later in the year, most teachers choose *some* words on the chart for the students to spell aloud. It would be monotonous to have students spelling all the words aloud. Having them spell some words still serves the original purpose of encouraging careful listening, since the students never know when they will need to be ready to spell aloud, and, also, giving extra practice in spelling some of the words.

Can the teacher choose some words to go on the chart?   Some teachers choose one or two words to go on the class chart. They may call these "teacher words," and they may require everyone to try to spell those words. Teachers usually do this if they are required to use a particular spelling textbook, or if they are responsible for a district or state word list for third grade. They find that most words on the mandated list are very ordinary and are used often on the charts, as well as in the other SUCCESS modules. Thus, they look for ways to incorporate the unusual words on charts in places where they would make sense.

Teachers can also choose words to put on the chart by revising sentences the students volunteer. If the sentence isn't in standard English, or if some words need to be changed to make it suit a paragraph better, the teacher may suggest a new version of the student's idea. That is what the teacher did in the example for Lesson 92, when she asked the student to replace *stuff* with a list of particular items.

Caution: A teacher who decides to put his or her own words and ideas on the chart needs to remember not to overdo it! Much of the students' motivation to spell and write things from the chart comes from their pride in having decided themselves what would be on it. If the teacher dictates more than just a small proportion of what is written, the students' sense of ownership will be taken away. Another risk in dictating things for the chart is that students will be required to write or spell something that they are not able to write or spell, thus the possibility of being successful will have been taken away.

What if the teacher isn't a good speller? Teachers who don't spell well can be excellent leaders of the Word Study module. They use the dictionary to check the spelling of words, and students learn that grown-ups really use the dictionary. They ask students to check words in the dictionary in order to "help the teacher." Finally it doesn't hurt for all SUCCESS teachers to have a colleague routinely proofread the charts that are displayed in the room.

DECISIONS ABOUT STUDENT WRITING

Will they do some writing before the chart is made or while the chart is being made? In the lessons that involve paragraph and sentence writing on the chart, the students brainstorm words that include the spelling emphasis before anything is written on the chart. Some teachers

SUCCESS gives me the freedom to do what is best for my children. It puts me in control of my classroom. It does this by simply treating me as a professional. The children see each other as equally worthwhile contributing members of the class. They are not grouped by arbitrary abilities. Every student has strengths and weaknesses. In SUCCESS, we build on the strengths instead of reinforcing the weaknesses.

Paul C. Moller, teacher

may decide to have the students write their spelling lists from the words that are written on the chalkboard. After the students have time to list their spelling words, the discussion leading to the development of the chart continues.

Some teachers ask students to sit close to the chart while all of the brainstorming and chart development takes place. The students then return to their seats to list their spelling words and write about the topic. In other classes, students stay at their seats throughout the chart development time. Teachers in those classes may permit students to write words on their papers during the class discussion time. The students have a better opportunity to listen and participate in the discussion if they are not writing on their papers, but some students need to do things on their own to be productive.

Can they copy the chart or should they write original words?   Especially at the beginning of the year, students may copy the class chart. Each student will choose parts of the class chart to write down, including the parts he or she has volunteered, as well as many parts contributed by other people. It is important that students understand everything that they copy. The class discussion that takes place while the words are being written on the chart gives everyone a chance to hear at least one interpretation of what the words are and what the sentences mean.

In addition, while circulating among the students during writing time, the teacher may question a student about something he or she is copying. "Now, what does this part say?"

Usually, as the year progresses, most third-graders are interested in writing original lists and information on their papers. The teacher is then challenged to help students spell their original ideas correctly! Again, the teacher needs to circulate during the student writing time.

DECISIONS ABOUT THE PARTNER SPELLING ACTIVITY

What if somebody "cheats"?   Some students work so hard to call out their partners' words that they don't realize the speller is looking right over their shoulder and *reading* the correct sequence of letters instead of spelling from memory. Other spellers are looking right at the chart or the chalkboard and calling out the letters they see, not the letters they know. Usually a student who resorts to "cheating" is someone who needs to take another look at a word, both for the sake of reading better as well as spelling better. That student may be gaining more from that extra look at a word than from spelling a word he or she already knows.

What happens to the spelling scores?   In most SUCCESS classes, nothing happens to the scores. The person calling out the words records the score at the top of the speller's paper, which is filed in his or her Word Study folder. The scores help the student to evaluate his or her own progress. The teacher is always asking, "Did you do better than

Desiree Jordan

yesterday? Better than you did last week?" Especially as they gain confidence and expertise, students challenge themselves to try harder words and earn more points.

Teachers may intervene in individual situations where "cheating" is occurring. But, sometimes they decide not to intervene, either because the student partner is handling the situation well, or because the "cheater" is learning more by cheating than if the teacher "caught" him or her.

Will students choose their own partners? Can they sit where they would like? Each teacher must decide on the best plan for this. At the beginning of the year, it is expeditious to assign partners according to who sits next to whom.

Later, allowing students to choose partners and workplaces is more fun and more motivating for the students, but spelling time is quieter and

I want to try the SUCCESS method because I feel it will help motivate the students in my class to read more, especially the students who may have trouble. It also gives me liberty, as a teacher, to make decisions on how and what needs to be taught to my children to help them improve in their reading and writing skills. I am excited about the possibility of using this type of teaching method!

Eleanor Sanda, teacher

more orderly if the teacher assigns partners and there is little student movement.

As usual, if students make poor choices of partners, the teacher can intervene in individual situations without interfering with the overall benefits of letting students choose their partners.

▶ Is **This** the Spelling Program?

This is *part* of the spelling program. In the Word Study module students focus on spelling patterns as they choose words that are appropriate for the class chart. They practice the spelling of those words as they write spelling lists, as they spell words aloud, and as they check their partner's oral spelling. Always, they consider the meaning and use of the words they spell when they explain their reasons for choosing a word and when they use the word in the context of the ideas for a chart.

Teachers help students correct their misspelled words as they circulate during the student writing part of this module. During all of the activities of this module students are motivated to spell correctly because they are working on words they have chosen for themselves and because they are spelling with and for their friends. The elements of competition and "showing off" cause students to spell more challenging words than the ones found on most published third-grade lists.

Now, for the rest of the spelling program. The true test of a spelling program comes when students write. It isn't the challenging words that they need to remember as much as it is the mundane words like *their, there*, and *they're*. Since SUCCESS students have frequent, extended, purposeful opportunities to write, they learn to spell the mundane words as well as the challenging ones. Students and teachers alike may think of

Word Study as the spelling time, but the Writing module is another time when good spelling is important. The Writing module is the other part of the spelling program.

Spelling instruction in SUCCESS may appear to rely on incidental opportunities to explore spelling patterns and words. However, making the chart, discussing words in the context of meaningful ideas, and giving students time to write and to take a partner spelling test every day create opportunities for deliberate attention to orthographic elements. Nevertheless, it may actually be the incidental spelling opportunities that arise for writers that cause SUCCESS students to improve their spelling. Because of the significance of a child's work in the Writing module in his or her growth as a speller, teachers determine spelling grades for the report card by evaluating work in the Word Study *and* the Writing modules.

▶ Homework

Still another decision every teacher must make is whether or not to give homework. The lessons in this module lend themselves to continued word study at home. Many students enjoy showing off at home the tough words they studied at school, and many more students enjoy exploring some words at home and sharing them the next day at school. For this reason, homework assignments are suggested in the Lessons. Some teachers give these assignments; other teachers modify the assignments to make them more relevant to the chart that was developed that day in class. Whatever way the teacher chooses for homework, it should be used consistently, and parents need to know what is expected.

▶ Decisions, Decisions, Decisions

Yes, the teacher is always thinking as he or she leads the Word Study module. He or she makes many decisions ahead of time and many more in deciding when to pursue teachable moments and when to pass them by. Even though there are plenty of useful options for teaching this module, SUCCESS teachers have discovered that certain things really matter most.

The main emphasis is on communication about a topic, not on fragmented skills. The teacher can direct attention to specific skills, and the students demonstrate increasing expertise in using them, but everyone's focus is on holistic use of all of the language processes.

Excellent opportunities for attention to structural analysis, syllabication, phonics instruction, grammar, and spelling exist in these lessons. Many more opportunities arise as students volunteer words and ideas for the chart. No matter how important a skill may be, or how new the skill may be for the class, the teacher must remember that the best instruction happens in the context of meaningful conversation. These meaningful conversations occur during the Word Study module in a SUCCESS classroom, allowing attention to be given to skills in an appropriate way.

Chapter 6 Evaluation, Communication, and Materials

SUCCESS teachers make many decisions in managing the materials they need, setting up their classrooms, keeping up with the information they gain about students, and communicating with parents, administrators, and others. The first five chapters of this book describe the major decisions, the characteristics of SUCCESS that account for its success with students. This chapter describes the logistical details.

▶

Information About Students: Evaluation and Assessment

In deciding to be less reliant on textbook materials for teaching, SUCCESS teachers decide to rely more on their own judgment in evaluating students' progress. Likewise, as teachers have learned that they can provide more appropriate instruction for their students through their own decisions rather than through a textbook, they have also learned that they can provide more helpful and appropriate information about their students at evaluation time than can published materials.

Helpful evaluation in SUCCESS is based on the teacher's knowledge of his or her students, knowledge that is readily available if the teacher is spending 75 percent of language arts instruction time circulating among students, observing and helping individuals and small groups. SUCCESS teachers document their knowledge by having the students maintain longitudinal records of their work in all the modules and through keeping notes about reading and writing conferences and observations.

STUDENTS RECORD MUCH INFORMATION THEMSELVES

In each module there is a system for students to use in keeping up with their own daily progress. They will need a form for Recreational Reading and a folder or a notebook for each of the other three modules.

Recreational Reading   Students use forms such as those on page 38 to record the names of books they read throughout the year. In addition to the students' lists, some teachers require every student to check out a book from the classroom collection to take home each night. The teacher's list of who checked out what book to read at home is another daily record of what students read.

Writing   Students have a file folder for filing everything they write during the Writing module. The contents of this folder will usually include a collection of drafts; some teachers keep a second folder for each student and file photocopies of "published" pieces of writing done by that student every month during the school year.

Chapter 6

Ann Schnell

Research Students have file folders for filing papers they write in this module throughout the year. Because much work in this module is done in groups, and because the emphasis is on searching for information more than on writing it down, students will not be able to file papers every day. The papers for the Research module are lists, notes, charts, and so on, not finished products. Nevertheless, reviewing a student's collection of papers in the Research folder shows his or her increasing skill at finding and noting more information as the year progresses.

Word Study Students produce a paper every day of the year to file in their Word Study folders. Because the same kinds of papers are produced daily, some teachers have students use spiral-bound notebooks for this module. Each day the student turns to the next clean page and begins to work.

In summary, each student needs forms for recording what books are read in Recreational Reading and three file folders for filing papers from the Writing, Research, and Word Study modules. Some teachers may choose to have an additional folder for each student for filing copies of "published" pieces of writing, and some teachers may prefer that students use spiral-bound notebooks instead of file folders for the Word Study module. (Notebooks are not as useful as folders in Research because students sometimes need to keep unusual papers, such as those with things pasted or drawn on them. Folders are also more useful than notebooks in the Writing module because students frequently pull out drafts written earlier in the year and work on revising pieces for publication.)

WHO KEEPS UP WITH THE FOLDERS, FORMS, AND NOTEBOOKS?

Teachers and students label, color code, or put stickers on the various folders and notebooks to differentiate them. Students are able to file the papers for each module in the correct folders each day. File folders are kept in boxes or stacked on shelves or tables in the classroom. Some teachers divide the students in the class into three or four groups, usually according to where the students sit in the classroom, or alphabetically. All of the folders for each member of each group are kept together in three or four different places in the room; that way only seven or eight students will file their work in the same place (see Figure 6-1).

Every student's work needs to be kept all year. Papers should not be sent home to parents for three reasons: keeping all papers creates a complete longitudinal record of the student's progress; even when parents have become acquainted with the SUCCESS philosophy, they sometimes don't understand why their child's work doesn't look like traditional "schoolwork"; and if papers aren't being sent home regularly, there is a greater chance parents will come in for conferences. Conferences with parents are most helpful when teacher and parents together examine a

Figure 6-1

CLASSROOM DIAGRAM

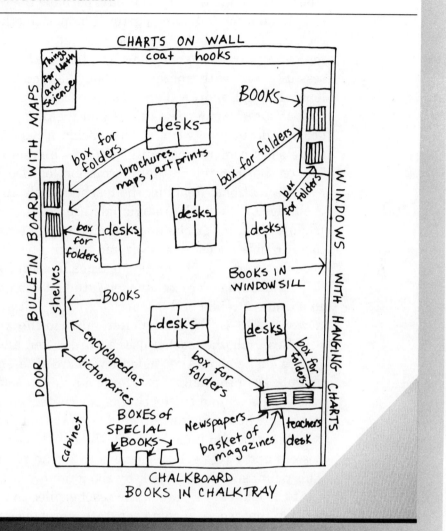

student's complete collection of papers for each module. In some schools where sending papers home is a tradition, teachers have students take home papers from other subject areas, as well as copies of "published" pieces of writing.

THE TEACHER KEEPS RECORDS

While the teacher is responsible for establishing the filing system for student work, the students maintain longitudinal records of their progress. In addition, teachers can keep three different kinds of records of their own: clipboard notes, conference notes, and periodic checklists.

Clipboard notes Teachers who use clipboard notes make many copies of a sheet with the class roster listed down the left side. They start out every day with a fresh stack of rosters on their clipboards, and they record interesting and helpful information throughout the day.

For example, at the beginning of Writing time, they label the top of their roster with the date and a specific objective they are stressing as the students do their writing that day, perhaps the correct use of capital letters. In addition to having partners help each other proofread for the correct use of capital letters, the teacher keeps notes on the clipboard, indicating with checkmarks which students are using capital letters successfully, and with another symbol, the students who are having problems. Through short conferences with students as they write, the teacher sees children trying new things and making progress toward achieving goals as developing writers. The teacher focuses primarily on *teaching* in these short conferences, but also learns a great deal about the students. The teacher can record the information learned in the clipboard notes.

In Recreational Reading, the teacher labels another roster and records the titles of the books individuals are reading at the beginning of the module time. He or she might decide to make notes about students who have trouble choosing a book and sticking with it. Clipboard notes are good for recording information learned in short conferences during Recreational Reading. For example, one student demonstrated a breakthrough in a conference: he had learned to employ initial consonants in decoding new words, even though he often misread the words.

In Research, the teacher uses a third roster, and during searching time, makes a note about the students who are differentiating names of people and places in the newspaper, for example. Sometimes observations of the whole class remind the teacher of the context in which an individual was working when a particular note was written. The teacher might write, "Students located information in the newspaper about safety. They made posters and wrote safety slogans. Students remembered rules from the safety film shown last week by the guidance counselor."

At the end of every week the teacher files the pages of clipboard notes written that week, keeping separate, chronological files of notes for each module. The teacher doesn't necessarily write a page of notes for every module every day, nor does he or she always write something next to every student's name. Looking back over several days of notes in a module is one way to check a student's progress, as well as a way to make certain no one is being overlooked.

Conference notes   Teachers make notebooks for recording notes about conferences with students, especially for keeping track of students' progress in the Recreational Reading module and the Writing module. Each sheet of notebook paper can have a student's name written at the top. The teacher writes the date of each extended conference with that student, and then records information to remember. This is the information that is needed for parent conferences.

For example, a teacher might write about Scott, "Sept. 10. Read *Owl Moon*. Good use of word attack skills to figure out new words. Difficulty with figurative language. Has had trouble settling down during RR time, doesn't have a plan for what to read next. I recommended *A Light in the Attic*."

The same kind of notetaking can be used in the Writing module, if only for notes about editing students' work at publication time. The teacher might write about Gerald, "Feb. 15. Essay about Black History Month. Good use of capital letters and punctuation. Has revised this piece two times, especially good job of rearranging sentences in logical order. Talked about paragraphing."

Over a period of time, each student's page in the conference notebook will have numerous entries describing changes and discussions, and perhaps goals that are set for improvement.

Periodic checklists   Some SUCCESS teachers design checklists, one page for each student, which list specific objectives that are being assessed in a three-week-long marking period, for example. Each week the teacher looks at each student's folders, assessing his or her accomplishments in regard to the specific objectives that were identified. The teacher rates each student's achievement on the checklist according to how that student is doing on the specific objectives. Most teachers who use the checklists also write narrative comments similar to those in clipboard notes and conference notebooks. The checklist gives a quick indication of skills that need to be reviewed in a new context; the narrative note describes a student's overall performance.

Kevin VanKleeck

Grading   Whether using clipboard notes, conference notebooks, checklists, or some combination of the three methods of documenting what he or she is learning about each student, the teacher still has to produce grades to go on report cards at some point. There are no test grades or scores on worksheets that can be averaged. SUCCESS teachers consider all the information that is recorded on notes and checklists, all the papers students have filed in their folders, and, especially, all the knowledge they have gained about students from working with them individually. The teacher then decides on the letter grades or numerical grades that best tell parents how each student is doing in language arts.

This method of deriving grades is subjective. SUCCESS teachers do not apologize for not being objective. They have made the criteria for success clear to parents and students: Anyone who does the best he or she can do in this class can succeed. Anyone who is having great difficulties is being *helped* to succeed—it's the teacher's job to help children who are having problems, not his or her job to label or judge them. Because of this attitude toward helping students, and because the SUCCESS routine allows teachers time to give extra help to students who need it, teachers typically give many good grades. If some students didn't deserve good grades, the teacher would have been working and working to find out why those students were doing badly, and then working and working to provide the help that was needed.

SUCCESS teachers have no trouble showing parents and students what they have learned about students' work and how a particular grade was determined. The teacher shows parents the collection of work in their child's folders. The papers of most students clearly show how they are progressing. The papers of a student who receives a poor grade will not show that kind of progress. In addition, in conferring with parents about grades and a child's progress, the teacher can refer to his or her clipboard, conference, or checklist notes to give specific examples of excellent or poor performance observed in class.

To some teachers, adding and averaging scores may be an easy approach to determining grades, but SUCCESS teachers find that deciding on a grade based on abundant information is a more meaningful one. Most parents are impressed by the way SUCCESS teachers can discuss what a particular student is actually able to do, not just what numerical score he or she received on last week's English test.

▶ Communication with Parents and Others

SUCCESS teachers are able to teach their students better when parents and administrators are enthusiastically supporting routines in the classrooms. To gain enthusiastic support, teachers confidently discuss what they do. The questions teachers are asked most often by administrators, other teachers, and parents are:

1. What is SUCCESS?

2. What materials do teachers need? How much do these things cost?

3. How is SUCCESS different from the traditional approaches—for students, teachers, and administrators?

4. Why does the teacher prefer to teach this way? What does he or she expect to accomplish?

5. What can administrators and parents do to help?

Teachers take initiative in acquainting parents with important information about SUCCESS by writing brief letters at the beginning of the year, making presentations at back-to-school-night programs, and perhaps by sending regular newsletters and holding special meetings.

HINTS ABOUT LETTERS TO PARENTS

1. Describe what SUCCESS is in a positive way, not by saying what students will not be doing. Remember that SUCCESS has been effective in many classrooms for more than ten years; no longer can it be called an innovative or experimental approach.

2. Ask parents to donate the magazines, catalogs, and so on that are needed.

3. A couple of weeks after the beginning of the year, invite parents to come and watch the class in action.

4. Let parents know that students' work is being filed for the whole year and that they are welcome to come in and see it and discuss their child with the teacher.

*S*UCCESS allows an excellent structure while, at the same time, a degree of flexibility. Also, I feel that through SUCCESS, my students are improving not only academics, but problem-solving and independent thinking skills. Using SUCCESS has helped me become self-challenging and helped my teaching of remedial children.

Barbara J. Silver, teacher

5. Encourage parents to support the nightly homework assignment: the child can read a book that he or she chooses or do a short written assignment.

HINTS ABOUT BACK-TO-SCHOOL-NIGHT PRESENTATIONS

1. Introduce the parents to SUCCESS procedures by involving them in some of the typical SUCCESS activities. Instead of telling them about Research or Word Study, let them participate in a shortened version of one of those activities.

2. Display edited pieces of students' writing and explain that many papers parents see will be drafts, not polished pieces of writing.

3. Display students' reading lists and make certain the classroom is full of books that parents can see.

4. Make certain the emphasis is on children, not programs!

VISITORS

Visitors to SUCCESS classes, administrators or parents, are welcome and are encouraged to talk with students, not simply to sit in a corner of the room. Many visitors learn how SUCCESS works by doing exactly what they see the teacher doing: circulating among students, inquiring about their reading, writing, and learning. They soon see how motivated students are and how personalized their projects are.

▶ Using SUCCESS with Special Schedules

Resource teachers and other teachers who don't have self-contained classes must make creative decisions about scheduling. SUCCESS is primarily considered a way of organizing language arts instruction in a regular classroom where two hours for the subject is standard, but resource teachers who teach smaller groups of students have adapted the activities to suit special needs. Also, classroom teachers who don't have a heterogeneous group of students for two hours have adapted the SUCCESS schedule to serve their purposes.

The biggest hurdle in adapting SUCCESS to resource classes of various kinds is scheduling enough time for all of the modules. Some teachers may only work with a group of students for thirty minutes a day. With less than two hours for language arts, the teachers decide how to divide up the time that is available to them. If the curriculum area for which the teacher is responsible is reading, then the Recreational Reading and Research modules may be more important than Writing and Word Study. In some cases, students who work on some SUCCESS modules in a resource class work on other modules in their homeroom class. In other cases, students who do all the modules in homeroom class can get extra help extending their projects in the resource room.

A classroom teacher who has a heterogeneous homeroom for language arts class but a so-called homogeneous group for reading class can also use SUCCESS. He or she might use the Writing and Word Study modules for language arts class in the homeroom, and then use Recreational Reading and Research with the reading class. The teacher will be able to draw interesting conclusions as it becomes clear how much more effectively he or she teaches the homeroom students who are also in the reading class; they may be the only students who do all four modules. The teacher will see how the modules complement each other and how difficult it is to teach some students with only two modules. Nevertheless, the teacher can include the objectives that are normally included in language arts and reading classes, even when the subjects are separated.

▶ The Materials

One of the attractive things about SUCCESS is its cost! Compared to the price of textbooks, workbooks, and kits, this is an inexpensive way to teach. The materials used in SUCCESS class are extremely important, however, and funds ought to be spent to purchase the most appropriate things. It is possible to teach well without spending much money at all; many teachers have begun teaching this way by making do with what they already have. Here is a list of the materials teachers and students need:

1. *Books.* An abundance of good books is needed. Some can be checked out from school and public libraries. Teachers check out fifty books at a time, keep them for a couple of weeks, and then get a new set. Teachers begin building a classroom library. They buy books, ask for donations, and check school closets for discarded books. Whenever money becomes available for materials, SUCCESS teachers spend it for books. Librarians have catalogs for ordering all kinds of children's books.

2. *Textbooks.* The textbooks that are typically assigned to students are suitable for most of the Research module activities. In addition, SUCCESS classes need an assortment of textbooks from other grade levels, not enough for the whole class, but one or two in a variety of different levels and subjects.

3. *Reference materials.* Third-graders use encyclopedias and dictionaries constantly. The encyclopedias do not have to be the most recent—incomplete, discarded sets are very useful. For many activities each student needs just one volume. The classroom supply of dictionaries should be a collection of several different kinds of dictionaries, not all of them elementary. Used paperback, college-level dictionaries are needed, too.

4. *Newspapers.* Old newspapers can be accumulated until there are enough for a class collection to be used in Research module activities. Ideally, one or two current papers should be delivered to each class every day. One copy of a major city's newspaper, such as the *Washington Post,* is enough. Some teachers pull out grocery ads, television schedules, and other special sections from old newspapers and keep stacks of those separate from the rest of the newspapers for special activities.

5. *Magazines.* Teachers keep a large basket filled with old magazines that can be cut apart for Research module activities. They have sepa-

Bethany Davidson

rate collections of magazines for reading: *National Geographic, Ranger Rick, Cobblestone,* and so on. Most teachers get all of their magazines through donations, although class subscriptions to a few would be helpful.

6. *Maps.* A United States map, a world map, and a state map should be displayed on the wall or bulletin board for reference at all times. A small box or basket full of miscellaneous maps is needed for Research module activities. These can be discarded road maps and maps that come out of *National Geographic.*

7. *Catalogs.* Teachers collect all kinds of catalogs and keep them in a separate box. Big department store catalogs are wonderful, but the little ones that come in the mail are adequate for the Research activities.

8. *Collections of nonfiction books about particular topics.* Depending on themes from content-area subjects that teachers decide to incorporate into the SUCCESS activities, collections of nonfiction books will be helpful for students seeking information. Often, teachers will check out a stack of appropriate books from the library and keep them on a special shelf. In particular, a collection of books, articles, and art prints is needed when the topic in Research is art. When music is the topic for Research module lessons, SUCCESS teachers borrow collections of appropriate books from the music teacher.

9. *Other assorted everyday reading materials.* Menus, telephone books, order forms, posters, junk mail, and so on are used in Research activities.

10. *Chart paper.* At least 180 sheets of approximately twenty-four-by-thirty-six-inch chart paper is needed for the Word Study module. Sometimes additional sheets are used in the Research module for group posters and class sharing.

11. *Markers and masking tape for writing and hanging the charts.*

12. *Plenty of paper for writing.*

13. *File folders and/or notebooks.* See the discussion about record-keeping and evaluation for more information about these folders and notebooks at the beginning of this chapter.

What do teachers do with all of this stuff? Are SUCCESS classrooms messy? SUCCESS teachers organize all of these materials so that they are accessible to the students. Books are in baskets, in boxes, and on shelves all over the room. Books for special topics are in a separate place. Textbooks are in stacks on shelves. One stack of newspapers, about thirty in all, is plenty; older issues are given away as newer ones come in. One large box or basket of magazines that can be cut up and stacks of magazines for reading are on shelves or tables. Encyclopedias and dictionaries are on shelves. Boxes of maps, catalogs, and miscellaneous reading materials are also on shelves or tables. The teacher arranges boxes for the storage of students' folders and notebooks for the four modules.

Having all of this material means that SUCCESS classrooms should be very neat and organized, not messy. The students use these things daily, so they learn to put things back where they belong. Or else they learn how frustrating it is when they cannot find material they need.

When school is out for the day and the students have gone home, two things about the SUCCESS classroom should catch the eye of a visitor: charts hang all over the place, and books fill the room. If the visitor looks closer, he or she will notice the stacks of other materials. A SUCCESS teacher needs to plan how to exhibit the charts easily and attractively and how to display plenty of books for students to see and use.

▶ A Community of Teachers

Being a decision-making, literate teacher who builds a community of readers and writers in the classroom is exciting. Perhaps the only way to add excitement to such a vocation is to bring like-minded teachers together. Teachers who work with other SUCCESS teachers share their successes, celebrate their discoveries, and puzzle over possible ways to help students who are having problems. SUCCESS teachers help each other make presentations to parents and administrators, just as they help each other regularly in planning SUCCESS lessons. They boost each other's confidence about being decision-making teachers.

This community of teachers makes an impression. Enthusiastic SUCCESS teachers who are focusing on children impress parents and administrators with their love of children and love of learning. SUCCESS is an organizational framework for language arts instruction that allows, and depends upon, each teacher's focus on his or her students.

Lessons

Walls, roof, and floor alone do not make a house a home, but the people inside certainly count on the building's firm framework. Similarly, these lessons do not constitute a rich language arts program in themselves, but the SUCCESS framework gives students and teachers freedom to form literary communities in schools.

The lesson plans are centered around themes that are highlighted in two or three of the modules. Blank lines indicate many opportunities for teachers to substitute different themes, either relating the activities in a day's lesson more closely, or making them more diverse in their themes.

Books are suggested in some lessons for the teacher to read aloud to the class. There is no prescribed list of books for SUCCESS. Teachers should read their own favorite books and investigate new books that become available to them. They should read some books over and over throughout the year, and they should consider scheduling books for reading aloud that enhance the class's study of a particular theme. Most important of all, the teacher should read aloud to the class every day. The titles marked with * will take several days to read, and titles marked with ** are collections of poetry and stories that should be regular resources for reading aloud.

Lesson 1

Research

LEAD-IN
Teacher introduces the Project Idea.
Topic: Animals or _Wash., DC_
Material: Magazines or _Newspapers_
Comprehension Skill: Main idea or
_____

SEARCH & RECORD
Group Size: 3 or _____
Project Idea: Cut out pictures of
animals from magazines. Glue on poster
and write labels or _____.

SHARING
Display posters or _sentence_ strips
    Papers are dated and filed.

Locate any info about DC.

Recreational Reading

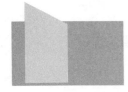

All students read books for approximately
30 minutes.

CONVERSATIONS
The teacher also reads silently. During
the last 10 minutes the teacher may
choose to talk with some individuals
about their reading.

CLIPBOARD NOTES
Teacher notes students' selections of
books.

READ-ALOUD BOOK
The Three Little Pigs by James Marshall
or _____

Writing

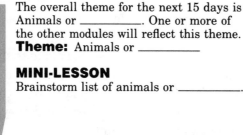

The overall theme for the next 15 days is
Animals or _____. One or more of
the other modules will reflect this theme.
Theme: Animals or _____

MINI-LESSON
Brainstorm list of animals or _____.

COMPOSING
Write list of animals or _____.

SHARING
Everyone tells the most interesting
animal listed or _____.
    Papers are dated and filed.

Word Study

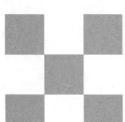

CHART DEVELOPMENT
Spelling Emphasis: *t* or _____
Other Emphasis: _____
    On the chart, the teacher lists *t* words
volunteered by students or _____.

WRITING
On their papers, students write their
favorite words from the chart and other
words, phrases, or sentences that would
be appropriate for the chart.

SPELLING
Partners call out words for each other to
spell aloud.
    Papers are dated and filed.

HOMEWORK
List names of things in your home that
have the letter *t* in them.

Lesson 2

Research

LEAD-IN
Teacher introduces the Project Idea.
Topic: Animals or _DC_
Material: Science textbooks or
Newspapers
Comprehension Skill: Details or
_____

Locate any info. about DC

SEARCH & RECORD
Group Size: Partners or _____
Project Idea: List names of animals found in textbook. Beside each name, write one fact or observation or _____.

SHARING
Everyone tells his or her best fact or observation or _____.
  Papers are dated and filed.

Recreational Reading

All students read books for approximately 30 minutes.

CONVERSATIONS
The teacher also reads silently. During the last 10 minutes the teacher may choose to talk with some individuals about their reading.

CLIPBOARD NOTES
Teacher notes students' selections of books.

READ-ALOUD BOOK
Danny the Champion of the World by Roald Dahl* or _____

Writing

Theme: Animals or _____

MINI-LESSON
Brainstorm list of 4-legged animals or _____.

COMPOSING
Write list of 4-legged animals or _____.

SHARING
Everyone tells the smallest 4-legged animal on his or her list or _____.
  Papers are dated and filed.

Word Study

CHART DEVELOPMENT
Spelling Emphasis: *c* or _____
Other Emphasis: _____
  On the chart, the teacher lists *c* words volunteered by students or _____.

WRITING
On their papers, students write their favorite words from the chart and other words, phrases, or sentences that would be appropriate for the chart.

SPELLING
Partners call out words for each other to spell aloud.
  Papers are dated and filed.

HOMEWORK
Make a list of words from the newspaper that have the letter *c*.

Lesson 3

Research

LEAD-IN
Teacher introduces the Project Idea.
Topic: Animals or ___DC___
Material: Magazines or _____
Comprehension Skill: Drawing
conclusions or _____

SEARCH & RECORD
Group Size: Partners or _____
Project Idea: Cut out a picture of an
animal. List details about things in the
picture with the animal or _____.

*Draw a picture about something
you learned.*

SHARING
Tell your partner what kind of home the
animal in the picture likes or _____.
　Papers are dated and filed.

Recreational Reading

All students read books for approximately
30 minutes.

CONVERSATIONS
The teacher also reads silently. During
the last 10 minutes the teacher may
choose to talk with some individuals
about their reading.

CLIPBOARD NOTES
Teacher notes students' selections of
books.

READ-ALOUD BOOK
_____

Writing

Theme: Animals or _____

MINI-LESSON
Students review lists written on previous
days and choose one animal to write more
about or _____.

COMPOSING
Write what you know about the chosen
animal or _____.

SHARING
Share with partner or _____.
　Papers are dated and filed.

Word Study

CHART DEVELOPMENT
Spelling Emphasis: *f* or _____
Other Emphasis: Names of animals
with *f* or _____
　On the chart, the teacher lists *f* words
volunteered by students, names of
animals with *f* volunteered by students,
or _____.

WRITING
On their papers, students write their
favorite words from the chart and other

words, phrases, or sentences that would
be appropriate for the chart.

SPELLING
Partners call out words for each other to
spell aloud.
　Papers are dated and filed.

HOMEWORK
Make a list of foods that have the letter *f*.

Lesson 4

Research

LEAD-IN
Teacher introduces the Project Idea.
Topic: Animals or ___DC___
Material: Magazines or _____
Comprehension Skill: Classification
or _____

SEARCH & RECORD
Group Size: 3 or 4 or _____
Project Idea: Cut out pictures of
animals from magazine. With group
members, group pictures that go together.
Glue on poster and label categories or
_____.

SHARING
Display posters or _____.
  Papers are dated and filed.

Recreational Reading

All students read books for approximately
30 minutes.

CONVERSATIONS
The teacher also reads silently. During
the last 10 minutes the teacher may
choose to talk with some individuals
about their reading.

CLIPBOARD NOTES
Teacher notes students' selections of
books.

READ-ALOUD BOOK
_____

Writing

Theme: Animals or _____

MINI-LESSON
Teacher reads a short selection from a
factual book about animals or
_____.

COMPOSING
Write facts or questions about animals or
_____.

SHARING
Everyone shares one sentence from his or
her writing or _____.
  Papers are dated and filed.

Word Study

CHART DEVELOPMENT
Spelling Emphasis: *l* or _____
Other Emphasis: products from
animals or _____
  On the chart, the teacher lists *l* words
volunteered by students, products from
animals volunteered by students, or
_____.

WRITING
On their papers, students write their
favorite words from the chart and other

words, phrases, or sentences that would
be appropriate for the chart.

SPELLING
Partners call out words for each other to
spell aloud.
  Papers are dated and filed.

HOMEWORK
Make a list of words that have *l* that you
saw on television.

Lesson **5**

Research

LEAD-IN
Teacher introduces the Project Idea.
Topic: Animals or _____
Material: Encyclopedias or _____
Comprehension Skill: Collecting data or _____

SEARCH & RECORD
Group Size: Partners or _____
Project Idea: Record names of animals found in a volume of an encyclopedia. Write one fact about each animal or _____.

SHARING
Show data to another team or _____.
   Papers are dated and filed.

Recreational Reading

All students read books for approximately 30 minutes.

CONVERSATIONS
The teacher also reads silently. During the last 10 minutes the teacher may choose to talk with some individuals about their reading.

CLIPBOARD NOTES
Teacher notes students' selections of books.

READ-ALOUD BOOK
Red Riding Hood by James Marshall or
_____

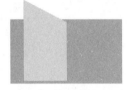

Writing

Theme: Animals or _____

MINI-LESSON
Teacher reads a poem about animals or _____.

COMPOSING
Write a poem about an animal or _____.

SHARING
Partners share or _____.
   Papers are dated and filed.

Word Study

CHART DEVELOPMENT
Spelling Emphasis: *b* or _____
Other Emphasis: nouns or
_____
   On the chart, the teacher lists *b* words volunteered by students, nouns with *b* volunteered by students, or _____.

WRITING
On their papers, students write their favorite words from the chart and other

words, phrases, or sentences that would be appropriate for the chart.

SPELLING
Partners call out words for each other to spell aloud.
   Papers are dated and filed.

HOMEWORK
Make a list of things used in a school that have the letter *b*.

Lesson 6

Research

LEAD-IN
Teacher introduces the Project Idea.
Topic: Animals or _____
Material: Textbooks or _____
Comprehension Skill: Cause and effect or _____

SEARCH & RECORD
Group Size: Partners or _____
Project Idea: Look for ways people use animals. Record information in a chart or _____.

SHARING
Teams volunteer information to go on class chart or _____.
   Papers are dated and filed.

Recreational Reading

All students read books for approximately 30 minutes.

CONVERSATIONS
The teacher also reads silently. During the last 10 minutes the teacher may choose to talk with some individuals about their reading.

CLIPBOARD NOTES
Teacher notes students' selections of books.

READ-ALOUD BOOK
_____

Writing

Theme: Animals or _____

MINI-LESSON
Teacher demonstrates correct use of capital letters in sentences about animals or _____.

COMPOSING
Continue an earlier draft. Check capital letters or _____.

SHARING
Proofread for correct use of capital letters or _____.
   Papers are dated and filed.

Word Study

CHART DEVELOPMENT
Spelling Emphasis: *j* or _____
Other Emphasis: nouns or

_____
   On the chart, the teacher lists *j* words volunteered by students, nouns with *j* volunteered by students, or _____.

WRITING
On their papers, students write their favorite words from the chart and other

words, phrases, or sentences that would be appropriate for the chart.

SPELLING
Partners call out words for each other to spell aloud.
   Papers are dated and filed.

HOMEWORK
Make a list of things for sale in a grocery store that have the letter *j*.

Lesson 7

Research

LEAD-IN
Teacher introduces the Project Idea.
Topic: Animals or _____
Material: Newspapers or _____
Comprehension Skill: Cause and effect or _____

SEARCH & RECORD
Group Size: 3 or 4 or _____
Project Idea: Cut out pictures of products that come from animals. Glue pictures on a poster and write labels or _____.

SHARING
Display posters or _____.
Papers are dated and filed.

Recreational Reading

All students read books for approximately 30 minutes.

CONVERSATIONS
The teacher also reads silently. During the last 10 minutes the teacher may choose to talk with some individuals about their reading.

CLIPBOARD NOTES
Teacher notes students' selections of books.

READ-ALOUD BOOK
_____

Writing

Theme: Animals or _____

MINI-LESSON
Teacher explains how to write a letter about a book you're reading or _____.

COMPOSING
Write a letter to a classmate or the teacher about a book you've read lately or _____.

SHARING
Deliver your letter or _____.
Papers are dated and filed.

Word Study

CHART DEVELOPMENT
Spelling Emphasis: *d* or _____
Other Emphasis: nouns or _____

On the chart, the teacher lists *d* words volunteered by students, nouns with *d* volunteered by students, or _____.

WRITING
On their papers, students write their favorite words from the chart and other words, phrases, or sentences that would be appropriate for the chart.

SPELLING
Partners call out words for each other to spell aloud.
Papers are dated and filed.

HOMEWORK
Make a list of things you would take with you on a trip that have the letter *d*.

Research

LEAD-IN
Teacher introduces the Project Idea.
Topic: Animals or _____
Material: Library books _____
Comprehension Skill: Comparison
or _____

SEARCH & RECORD
Group Size: Partners or _____
Project Idea: Locate pictures of baby animals. Write list of ways they are like their parents and ways they are different or _____.

SHARING
Show lists to other teams or _____.
Papers are dated and filed.

Recreational Reading

All students read books for approximately 30 minutes.

CONVERSATIONS
The teacher also reads silently. During the last 10 minutes the teacher may choose to talk with some individuals about their reading.

CLIPBOARD NOTES
Teacher notes students' selections of books.

READ-ALOUD BOOK
The Great White Man-Eating Shark by Margaret Mahy or _____

Writing

Theme: Animals or _____

MINI-LESSON
Teacher demonstrates how to begin writing a journal or _____.

COMPOSING
Write an entry in your journal or _____.

SHARING
Talk to a friend about your journal or _____.
Papers are dated and filed.

Word Study

CHART DEVELOPMENT
Spelling Emphasis: *h* or _____
Other Emphasis: nouns or _____

On the chart, the teacher lists *h* words volunteered by students, nouns with *h* volunteered by students, or _____.

WRITING
On their papers, students write their favorite words from the chart and other

words, phrases, or sentences that would be appropriate for the chart.

SPELLING
Partners call out words for each other to spell aloud.
Papers are dated and filed.

HOMEWORK
Make a list of words in the *Yellow Pages* that are nouns and have the letter *h*.

Lesson 9

Research

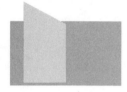

LEAD-IN
Teacher introduces the Project Idea.
Topic: Animals or _____
Material: Newspapers or _____
Comprehension Skill: Cause and effect or _____

SEARCH & RECORD
Group Size: Partners or _____
Project Idea: Locate animals in the news. Write reasons for the animals being in the news or _____.

SHARING
Volunteers tell the class the most interesting things they found or _____.
    Papers are dated and filed.

Recreational Reading

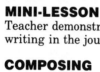

All students read books for approximately 30 minutes.

CONVERSATIONS
The teacher also reads silently. During the last 10 minutes the teacher may choose to talk with some individuals about their reading.

CLIPBOARD NOTES
Teacher notes students' selections of books.

READ-ALOUD BOOK
_____

Writing

Theme: Animals or _____

MINI-LESSON
Teacher demonstrates another idea for writing in the journal or _____.

COMPOSING
Write in your journal or _____.

SHARING
Share with partner or _____.
    Papers are dated and filed.

Word Study

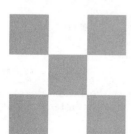

CHART DEVELOPMENT
Spelling Emphasis: *m* or _____
Other Emphasis: nouns or

    On the chart, the teacher lists *m* words volunteered by students, nouns with *m* volunteered by students, or _____.

WRITING
On their papers students write their favorite words from the chart and other words or phrases or sentences that would be appropriate for the chart.

SPELLING
Partners call out words for each other to spell aloud.
    Papers are dated and filed.

HOMEWORK
Write some rules that have words with the letter *m*. For example, "Clean up your mess."

Research

LEAD-IN
Teacher introduces the Project Idea.
Topic: Animals or _____
Material: Magazines or _____
Comprehension Skill: Drawing conclusions or _____

SEARCH & RECORD
Group Size: 3 or 4 or _____
Project Idea: Make a collage of pictures and words that shows how important animals are or _____.

SHARING
Display collages or _____.
 Papers are dated and filed.

Recreational Reading

All students read books for approximately 30 minutes.

CONVERSATIONS
The teacher also reads silently. During the last 10 minutes the teacher may choose to talk with some individuals about their reading.

CLIPBOARD NOTES
Teacher notes students' selections of books.

READ-ALOUD BOOK
_____

Writing

Theme: Animals or _____

MINI-LESSON
Teacher suggests how to choose a draft that can be revised and polished for publication. Class book about animals will be published as part of Lesson 15 or _____.

COMPOSING
Choose a piece to do more work on or _____.

SHARING
Everyone tells class what kind of piece he or she is planning to publish or

_____.
 Papers are dated and filed.

Word Study

CHART DEVELOPMENT
Spelling Emphasis: *r* or _____
Other Emphasis: nouns or

_____
 On the chart, the teacher lists *r* words volunteered by students, nouns with *r* volunteered by students, or _____.

WRITING
On their papers, students write their favorite words from the chart and other words, phrases, or sentences that would be appropriate for the chart.

SPELLING
Partners call out words for each other to spell aloud.
 Papers are dated and filed.

HOMEWORK
Write sentences containing color words that have the letter *r*. For example, "My favorite color is purple."

Lesson 11

Research

LEAD-IN
Teacher introduces the Project Idea.
Topic: School and home or _____
Material: Newspapers or _____
Comprehension Skill: Association of information or _____

SEARCH & RECORD
Group Size: Individuals or _____
Project Idea: Circle words in the newspaper that can be related to school or _____.

SHARING
Partners count each other's circled words or _____.
   Papers are dated and filed.

Recreational Reading

All students read books for approximately 30 minutes.

CONVERSATIONS
The teacher also reads silently. The teacher has some short conversations with readers. When appropriate, the main focus of these conversations is the way each student goes about choosing a book.

CLIPBOARD NOTES
Teacher notes students' selections of books and what they do as they examine books before selecting.

READ-ALOUD BOOK
The Napping House by Audrey Wood or _____

Writing

Theme: Animals or _____

MINI-LESSON
Class brainstorms examples of nouns or _____.

COMPOSING
Continue work on piece for publication. Mark nouns on draft or _____.

SHARING
Proofread partner's paper for identification of nouns or _____.
   Papers are dated and filed.

Word Study

CHART DEVELOPMENT
Spelling Emphasis: *g* or _____
Other Emphasis:
- verbs or _____
- animals or _____

   On the chart, the teacher lists words volunteered by students using:
- *g*
- verbs with *g*
- animal vocabulary
- _____

   On their papers, students write their favorite words from the chart or other words, phrases, or sentences that would be appropriate for the chart.

SPELLING
Partners call out words for each other to spell aloud.
   Papers are dated and filed.

HOMEWORK
Write words that have *g* having to do with animals.

S u c c e s **S** u c c e s **S** u c c e s **S** u c c e s **S** u c c e s **S** u c c e s **S** u c c e s **S** u c c e s **S**

Lesson **12**

Research

LEAD-IN
Teacher introduces the Project Idea.
Topic: School and home or _____
Material: Magazines or _____
Comprehension Skill: Association of information or _____

SEARCH & RECORD
Group Size: Partners or _____
Project Idea: Cut out pictures of items found in homes. Paste the 5 most important on your paper or _____.

SHARING
Compare your decisions about the most important items with the decisions made by others or _____.
    Papers are dated and filed.

Recreational Reading

All students read books for approximately 30 minutes.

CONVERSATIONS
The teacher also reads silently. The teacher has some short conversations with readers. When appropriate, the main focus of these conversations is the way each student goes about choosing a book.

CLIPBOARD NOTES
Teacher notes students' selections of books and what they do as they examine books before selecting.

READ-ALOUD BOOK
_____

Writing

Theme: Animals or _____

MINI-LESSON
Teacher discusses ways to help a fellow writer in a response group or _____.

COMPOSING
Continue with piece for publication or _____.

SHARING
Form response groups. Help each other with drafts or _____.
    Papers are dated and filed.

Word Study

CHART DEVELOPMENT
Spelling Emphasis: *v* or _____
Other Emphasis:
■ verbs or _____
■ animals or _____
    On the chart, the teacher lists words volunteered by students using:
■ *v*
■ verbs with *v*
■ animal vocabulary
■ _____

WRITING
On their papers, students write their favorite words from the chart or other words, phrases, or sentences that would be appropriate for the chart.

SPELLING
Partners call out words for each other to spell aloud.
    Papers are dated and filed.

HOMEWORK
Write and illustrate 3 verbs containing the letter *v*.

Lesson 13

Research

LEAD-IN
Teacher introduces the Project Idea.
Topic: School and home or _____
Material: Magazines or _____
Comprehension Skill: Classification
or _____

SEARCH & RECORD
Group Size: 3 or 4 or _____
Project Idea: Make a chart for
recording information about homes found
in a magazine. The chart will have two
columns: "Names of rooms in a house"
and "Contents of rooms," or _____.

SHARING
Partners or _____.
Papers are dated and filed.

Recreational Reading

All students read books for approximately
30 minutes.

CONVERSATIONS
The teacher also reads silently. The
teacher has some short conversations with
readers. When appropriate, the main
focus of these conversations is the way
each student goes about choosing a book.

CLIPBOARD NOTES
Teacher notes students' selections of
books and what they do as they examine
books before selecting.

READ-ALOUD BOOK
Mufaro's Beautiful Daughter by John
Steptoe or _____

Writing

Theme: Animals or _____

MINI-LESSON
Teacher discusses times and ways a
writer can ask for help or _____.

COMPOSING
Continue with piece for publication or
_____.

SHARING
Response groups or _____.
Papers are dated and filed.

Word Study

CHART DEVELOPMENT
Spelling Emphasis: _k_ or _____
Other Emphasis:
■ verbs or _____
■ animals or _____
On the chart, the teacher lists words
volunteered by students using:
■ _k_
■ verbs with _k_
■ animal vocabulary
■ _____

WRITING
On their papers, students write their
favorite words from the chart or other
words, phrases, or sentences that would
be appropriate for the chart.

SPELLING
Partners call out words for each other to
spell aloud.
Papers are dated and filed.

HOMEWORK
Write about the king of beasts. Circle the
verbs you use.

Research

LEAD-IN
Teacher introduces the Project Idea.
Topic: School and home or _____
Material: Health textbooks or _____

Comprehension Skill: Drawing conclusions or _____

SEARCH & RECORD
Group Size: Partners or _____
Project Idea: List places in homes and schools. Write safety rules for each place or _____.

SHARING
Teach another team your safety rules or _____.
Papers are dated and filed.

Recreational Reading

All students read books for approximately 30 minutes.

CONVERSATIONS
The teacher also reads silently. The teacher has some short conversations with readers. When appropriate, the main focus of these conversations is the way each student goes about choosing a book.

CLIPBOARD NOTES
Teacher notes students' selections of books and what they do as they examine books before selecting.

READ-ALOUD BOOK
_____

Writing

Theme: Animals or _____

MINI-LESSON
Teacher leads discussion of ideas for adding illustrations to pieces ready for publishing or _____.

COMPOSING
Continue with piece for publication. Add illustrations if desired or _____.

SHARING
Response groups or _____.
Papers are dated and filed.

Word Study

CHART DEVELOPMENT
Spelling Emphasis: *p* or _____
Other Emphasis:
- verbs or _____
- animals or _____
  On the chart, the teacher lists words volunteered by students using:
- *p*
- verbs with *p*
- animal vocabulary
- _____

WRITING
On their papers, students write their favorite words from the chart or other words, phrases, or sentences that would be appropriate for the chart.

SPELLING
Partners call out words for each other to spell aloud.
Papers are dated and filed.

HOMEWORK
Write verbs containing the letter *p* that tell about something you do.

Lesson 15

Research

LEAD-IN
Teacher introduces the Project Idea.
Topic: School and home or _____
Material: Social studies textbooks or _____

Comprehension Skill: Collecting data or _____

SEARCH & RECORD
Group Size: Partners or _____
Project Idea: List as many kinds of schools and homes as you can find in textbook. Write a question or statement to go with each or _____.

SHARING
Volunteers give examples for class list of kinds of schools and homes or _____.
Papers are dated and filed.

Recreational Reading

All students read books for approximately 30 minutes.

CONVERSATIONS
The teacher also reads silently. The teacher has some short conversations with readers. When appropriate, the main focus of these conversations is the way each student goes about choosing a book.

CLIPBOARD NOTES
Teacher notes students' selections of books and what they do as they examine books before selecting.

READ-ALOUD BOOK
Honey, I Love by Eloise Greenfield** or _____

Writing

Theme: Animals or _____

MINI-LESSON
Teacher presents plans for combining all published pieces in class book about animals or _____.

COMPOSING
Come to stopping point in writing. Participate in compiling book or _____.

SHARING
Teacher presents classbook to whole class or _____.
Papers are dated and filed.

Word Study

CHART DEVELOPMENT
Spelling Emphasis: *n* or _____
Other Emphasis:
- verbs or _____
- animals or _____
  On the chart, the teacher lists words volunteered by students using:
- *n*
- verbs with *n*
- animal vocabulary
- _____

WRITING
On their papers, students write their favorite words from the chart or other words, phrases, or sentences that would be appropriate for the chart.

SPELLING
Partners call out words for each other to spell aloud.
Papers are dated and filed.

HOMEWORK
Write a list of verbs you find in your math book.

Lesson **16**

Research

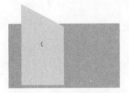

LEAD-IN
Teacher introduces the Project Idea.
Topic: School and home or _____
Material: Maps or _____
Comprehension Skill: Map reading
or _____

SEARCH & RECORD
Group Size: Partners or _____
Project Idea: Make lists of as many
places as possible that start with a
designated letter or _____.

SHARING
Make a class bar graph of the number of
places found starting with each letter or
_____.
   Papers are dated and filed.

Recreational Reading

All students read books for approximately
30 minutes.

CONVERSATIONS
The teacher also reads silently. The
teacher has some short conversations with
readers. When appropriate, the main
focus of these conversations is the way
each student goes about choosing a book.

CLIPBOARD NOTES
Teacher notes students' selections of
books and what they do as they examine
books before selecting.

READ-ALOUD BOOK
_____

Writing

The overall theme for the next 15 days is
Places or _____. One or more of the
other modules will reflect this theme.
Theme: Places or _____

MINI-LESSON
Brainstorm list of places students have
been or _____.

COMPOSING
Write list of places you have been or
_____.

SHARING
Share list with partner. Check places
where both have been or _____.
   Papers are dated and filed.

Word Study

CHART DEVELOPMENT
Spelling Emphasis: *qu* or
_____

Other Emphasis:
■ verbs or _____
■ world news or _____
   On the chart, the teacher lists words
volunteered by students using:
■ *qu*
■ verbs with *qu*
■ world news vocabulary
■ _____

WRITING
On their papers, students write their
favorite words from the chart or other
words, phrases, or sentences that would
be appropriate for the chart.

SPELLING
Partners call out words for each other to
spell aloud.
   Papers are dated and filed.

HOMEWORK
Write phrases and/or sentences about the
world. Use a *qu* word in some of your
phrases or sentences.

Lesson 17

Research

LEAD-IN
Teacher introduces the Project Idea.
Topic: School and home or _____
Material: Newspapers or _____
Comprehension Skill: Cause and effect or _____

SEARCH & RECORD
Group Size: Partners or _____
Project Idea: List places mentioned in captions. Write reason that each place is mentioned or _____.

SHARING
Tell another team what your team found or _____.
Papers are dated and filed.

Recreational Reading

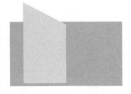

All students read books for approximately 30 minutes.

CONVERSATIONS
The teacher also reads silently. The teacher has some conversations with the readers. When appropriate, the main focus of these conversations is the way each student goes about choosing a book.

CLIPBOARD NOTES
Teacher notes students' selections of books and what they do as they examine books before selecting.

READ-ALOUD BOOK
_____

Writing

Theme: Places or _____

MINI-LESSON
Brainstorm list of places in stories the class has read or _____.

COMPOSING
Write list of places you have read about in books or _____.

SHARING
Whole-class sharing time. Students name the places on their lists where they would like to go or _____.
Papers are dated and filed.

Word Study

CHART DEVELOPMENT
Spelling Emphasis: *s* or _____
Other Emphasis:
- verbs or _____
- sports or _____
  On the chart, the teacher lists words volunteered by students using:
- *s*
- verbs with *s*
- sports vocabulary
- _____

WRITING
On their papers, students write their favorite words from the chart or other words, phrases, or sentences that would be appropriate for the chart.

SPELLING
Partners call out words for each other to spell aloud.
Papers are dated and filed.

HOMEWORK
Write sentences with verbs containing *s* that tell about sports you like.

116

Lesson 18

Research

LEAD-IN
Teacher introduces the Project Idea.
Topic: School and home or ——————
Material: Newspapers or ——————
Comprehension Skill: Facts or
——————

SEARCH & RECORD
Group Size: Partners or ——————
Project Idea: List places in the newspaper that you know something about. Write one fact about each or
——————.

SHARING
Teach another team some of your facts or
——————.
Papers are dated and filed.

Recreational Reading

All students read books for approximately 30 minutes.

CONVERSATIONS
The teacher also reads silently. The teacher has some short conversations with readers. When appropriate, the main focus of these conversations is the way each student goes about choosing a book.

CLIPBOARD NOTES
Teacher notes students' selections of books and what they do as they examine books before selecting.

READ-ALOUD BOOK
Miss Nelson is Missing by Harry Allard
or ——————

Writing

Theme: Places or ——————

MINI-LESSON
Teacher discusses how to choose a place from one of the writer's lists to write more about or ——————.

COMPOSING
Choose an idea for writing about a place or ——————.

SHARING
Discuss your plans for writing about a place with a partner or ——————.
Papers are dated and filed.

Word Study

CHART DEVELOPMENT
Spelling Emphasis: *w* or ——————
Other Emphasis:
■ verbs or ——————
■ our school or ——————
On the chart, the teacher lists words volunteered by students using:
■ *w*
■ verbs with *w*
■ our school
■ ——————

WRITING
On their papers, students write their favorite words from the chart or other words, phrases, or sentences that would be appropriate for the chart.

SPELLING
Partners call out words for each other to spell aloud.
Papers are dated and filed.

HOMEWORK
Write sentences with verbs containing *w* that tell about school.

Lesson **19**

Research

LEAD-IN
Teacher introduces the Project Idea.
Topic: School and home or _____
Material: Maps or _____
Comprehension Skill: Map reading
or _____

SEARCH & RECORD
Group Size: 3 or 4 or _____
Project Idea: List places on map
according to distance from our town
beginning with the closest or _____.

SHARING
Groups compare their lists or _____.
Papers are dated and filed.

Recreational Reading

All students read books for approximately
30 minutes.

CONVERSATIONS
The teacher also reads silently. The
teacher has some short conversations with
readers. When appropriate, the main
focus of these conversations is the way
each student goes about choosing a book.

CLIPBOARD NOTES
Teacher notes students' selections of
books and what they do as they examine
books before selecting.

READ-ALOUD BOOK
_____

Writing

Theme: Places or _____

MINI-LESSON
Teacher reads from a factual book about a
place and demonstrates how to write an
acrostic poem about the place or
_____.

COMPOSING
Write an acrostic poem about a place or
_____.

SHARING
Partners share their drafts of acrostic
poems or _____.
Papers are dated and filed.

Word Study

CHART DEVELOPMENT
Spelling Emphasis: x or _____
Other Emphasis:
- verbs or _____
- food or _____
  On the chart, the teacher lists words
volunterred by students using:
- x
- verbs with x
- food vocabulary
- _____

WRITING
On their papers, students write their
favorite words from the chart or other
words, phrases, or sentences that would
be appropriate for the chart.

SPELLING
Partners call out words for each other to
spell aloud.
Papers are dated and filed.

HOMEWORK
Write sentences with words containing
the letter x that tell about food.
Underline the verbs.

Lesson **20**

Research

LEAD-IN
Teacher introduces the Project Idea.
Topic: School and home or _____
Material: Newspapers or _____
Comprehension Skill: Classification
or _____

SEARCH & RECORD
Group Size: Partners or _____
Project Idea: List places found in
newspapers. Organize the list by cities,
states, countries, stores, etc., or
_____.

SHARING
Make class chart that classifies places
volunteered by students or _____.
    Papers are dated and filed.

Recreational Reading

All students read books for approximately
30 minutes.

CONVERSATIONS
The teacher also reads silently. The
teacher has some short conversations with
readers. When appropriate, the main
focus of these conversations is the way
each student goes about choosing a book.

CLIPBOARD NOTES
Teacher notes students' selections of
books and what they do as they examine
books before selecting.

READ-ALOUD BOOK
_____

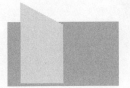

Writing

Theme: Places or _____

MINI-LESSON
Teacher reads a poem about a place or
_____.

COMPOSING
Write a draft of your own poem about a
place or _____.

SHARING
Share drafts of poems in response groups
or _____.
    Papers are dated and filed.

Word Study

CHART DEVELOPMENT
Spelling Emphasis: *y* or _____
Other Emphasis:
■ verbs or _____
■ science or _____
    On the chart, the teacher lists words
volunteered by students using:
■ *y*
■ verbs with *y*
■ science vocabulary
■ _____

WRITING
On their papers, students write their
favorite words from the chart or other
words, phrases, or sentences that would
be appropriate for the chart.

SPELLING
Partners call out words for each other to
spell aloud.
    Papers are dated and filed.

HOMEWORK
Write words from your science book that
have *y* or that are verbs.

119

Lesson 21

Research

LEAD-IN
Teacher introduces the Project Idea.
Topic: Land forms or _____
Material: Magazines or _____
Comprehension Skill: Comparison
or _____

SEARCH & RECORD
Group Size: 3 or 4 or _____
Project Idea: Cut out pictures of
various geographic features and organize
pictures into groups that go together or
_____.

SHARING
Display posters or _____.
  Papers are dated and filed.

Recreational Reading

All students read books for approximately
30 minutes.

CONVERSATIONS
The teacher also reads silently. The
teacher has some short conversations with
readers. When appropriate, the main
focus of these conversations is decoding
skills.

CLIPBOARD NOTES
Teacher notes students' selections of
books and their ability to decode well
enough to sustain attention to a story.

READ-ALOUD BOOK
Over the Steamy Swamp by Paul
Geraghty or _____

Writing

Theme: Places or _____

MINI-LESSON
Students volunteer sample sentences from
their drafts. Others add necessary
punctuation at ends of sentences or
_____.

COMPOSING
Continue draft or _____.

SHARING
Partners proofread for correct punctuation
at end of sentences or _____.
  Papers are dated and filed.

Word Study

CHART DEVELOPMENT
Spelling Emphasis: *z* or _____
Other Emphasis:
- verbs or _____
- land forms or _____
  On the chart, the teacher lists words
volunteered by students using:
- *z*
- verbs with *z*
- land form vocabulary
- _____

WRITING
On their papers, students write their
favorite words from the chart or other
words, phrases, or sentences that would
be appropriate for the chart.

SPELLING
Partners call out words for each other to
spell aloud.
  Papers are dated and filed.

HOMEWORK
Write sentences with verbs containing the
letter *z* that tell about sounds animals
make.

Research

LEAD-IN
Teacher introduces the Project Idea.
Topic: Land forms or _____
Material: Maps or _____
Comprehension Skill: Searching for details or _____

SEARCH & RECORD
Group Size: Partners or _____
Project Idea: List names of oceans, rivers, and mountains you find on the map. Make an observation about some of the things on your list. For instance, the Atlantic Ocean is between North America and Europe or _____.

SHARING
Volunteers show class what they located or _____.
   Papers are dated and filed.

Recreational Reading

All students read books for approximately 30 minutes.

CONVERSATIONS
The teacher also reads silently. The teacher has some short conversations with readers. When appropriate, the main focus of these conversations is decoding skills.

CLIPBOARD NOTES
Teacher notes students' selections of books and their ability to decode well enough to sustain attention to a story.

READ-ALOUD BOOK
_____

Writing

Theme: Places or _____

MINI-LESSON
Students look over lists of books they have read or _____.

COMPOSING
Write about one book on the list or _____.

SHARING
Students read what they have written to partners they think will enjoy the same book or _____.
   Papers are dated and filed.

Word Study

CHART DEVELOPMENT
Spelling Emphasis: *a* or _____
Other Emphasis:
■ adjective with noun or _____
■ land forms or _____
   On the chart, the teacher lists phrases volunteered by students using:
■ *a*
■ adjectives with nouns
■ land form vocabulary
■ _____

WRITING
On their papers, students write their favorite words from the chart or other words, phrases, or sentences that would be appropriate for the chart.

SPELLING
Partners call out words for each other to spell aloud.
   Papers are dated and filed.

HOMEWORK
Write sentences with adjectives and nouns containing the letter *a* that describe how the land looks around your home and school.

Lesson 23

Research

LEAD-IN
Teacher introduces the Project Idea.
Topic: Land forms or _____
Material: Social studies textbooks or
_____

Comprehension Skill: Classification
or _____

SEARCH & RECORD
Group Size: 4 or _____
Project Idea: Using ideas from the
textbook, draw pictures to show hot, cold,
dry, and wet places in the world or
_____.

SHARING
Display pictures or _____.
 Papers are dated and filed.

Recreational Reading

All students read books for approximately
30 minutes.

CONVERSATIONS
The teacher also reads silently. The
teacher has some short conversations with
readers. When appropriate, the main
focus of these conversations is decoding
skills.

CLIPBOARD NOTES
Teacher notes students' selections of
books and their ability to decode well
enough to sustain attention to a story.

READ-ALOUD BOOK
Stone Fox by John Gardiner* or
_____

Writing

Theme: Places or _____

MINI-LESSON
Teacher demonstrates ideas for writing
descriptions of places or _____.

COMPOSING
Write a description of a place or
_____.

SHARING
Volunteers read their descriptions to the
whole group or _____.
 Papers are dated and filed.

Word Study

CHART DEVELOPMENT
Spelling Emphasis: *e* or _____
Other Emphasis:
■ adjective with noun or _____
■ land forms or _____
 On the chart, the teacher lists phrases
volunteered by students using:
■ *e*
■ adjectives with nouns
■ land form vocabulary
■ _____

WRITING
On their papers, students write their
favorite words from the chart or other
words, phrases, or sentences that would
be appropriate for the chart.

SPELLING
Partners call out words for each other to
spell aloud.
 Papers are dated and filed.

HOMEWORK
Write sentences with adjectives and
nouns containing the letter *e* that
describe items in a department store.

Lesson 24

Research

LEAD-IN
Teacher introduces the Project Idea.
Topic: Land forms or _____
Material: Social studies textbooks or
_____

Comprehension Skill: Cause and
effect or _____

SEARCH & RECORD
Group Size: Partners or _____
Project Idea: Choose one region of the
world mentioned in the book. List some
resources there. Tell how abundance of a
resource affects that place. For example,
there are lots of trees where the Ojibwas
lived, therefore they made lots of things
out of wood or _____.

SHARING
Explain your conclusions to another team
or _____.
   Papers are dated and filed.

Recreational Reading

All students read books for approximately
30 minutes.

CONVERSATIONS
The teacher also reads silently. The
teacher has some short conversations with
readers. When appropriate, the main
focus of these conversations is decoding
skills.

CLIPBOARD NOTES
Teacher notes students' selections of
books and their ability to decode well
enough to sustain attention to a story.

READ-ALOUD BOOK
_____

Writing

Theme: Places or _____

MINI-LESSON
Teacher demonstrates how to decide what
information to include in a paragraph
that describes a place or _____.

COMPOSING
Continue work on description of a place.
Divide draft into paragraphs or
_____.

SHARING
Everyone reads topic sentences from their
drafts or _____.
   Papers are dated and filed.

Word Study

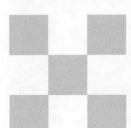

CHART DEVELOPMENT
Spelling Emphasis: *i* or _____
Other Emphasis:
■ adjectives with nouns or _____
■ land forms or _____
   On the chart, the teacher lists phrases
volunteered by students using:
■ *i*
■ adjectives with nouns
■ land form vocabulary
■ _____

WRITING
On their papers, students write their
favorite words from the chart or other
words, phrases, or sentences that would
be appropriate for the chart.

SPELLING
Partners call out words for each other to
spell aloud.
   Papers are dated and filed.

HOMEWORK
Write sentences with adjectives and
nouns containing the letter *i* that describe
your favorite school subject.

Lesson 25

Research

LEAD-IN
Teacher introduces the Project Idea.
Topic: Land forms or _____
Material: Social studies books or _____

Comprehension Skill: Cause and effect or _____

SEARCH & RECORD
Group Size: Partners or _____
Project Idea: List the resources of one region. Make a drawing that shows how people use their resources or _____.

SHARING
Display drawings or _____.
  Papers are dated and filed.

Recreational Reading

All students read books for approximately 30 minutes.

CONVERSATIONS
The teacher also reads silently. The teacher has some short conversations with readers. When appropriate, the main focus of these conversations is decoding skills.

CLIPBOARD NOTES
Teacher notes students' selections of books and their ability to decode well enough to sustain attention to a story.

READ-ALOUD BOOK
_____

Writing

Theme: Places or _____

MINI-LESSON
Teacher suggests that students might publish their writing about places as travel brochures. Teacher shows examples or _____.

COMPOSING
Work on revising draft of description of place to be used in travel brochure or _____.

SHARING
Read revision to partner or _____.
  Papers are dated and filed.

Word Study

CHART DEVELOPMENT
Spelling Emphasis: *o* or _____
Other Emphasis:
■ adjective with noun or _____
■ land forms or _____
  On the chart, the teacher lists phrases volunteered by students using:
■ *o*
■ adjectives with nouns
■ land form vocabulary
■ _____

WRITING
On their papers, students write their favorite words from the chart or other

words, phrases, or sentences that would be appropriate for the chart.

SPELLING
Partners call out words for each other to spell aloud.
  Papers are dated and filed.

HOMEWORK
Find and cut out sentences in the newspaper with adjectives and nouns containing the letter *o* that tell about events in your town.

Research

LEAD-IN
Teacher introduces the Project Idea.
Topic: Land forms or _____
Material: Newspapers or _____
Comprehension Skill: Association or _____

SEARCH & RECORD
Group Size: 3 or 4 or _____
Project Idea: Cut out articles, advertisements, and pictures associated with water. Glue on chart or _____.

SHARING
Display charts or _____.
Papers are dated and filed.

Recreational Reading

All students read books for approximately 30 minutes.

CONVERSATIONS
The teacher also reads silently. The teacher has some short conversations with readers. When appropriate, the main focus of these conversations is decoding skills.

CLIPBOARD NOTES
Teacher notes students' selections of books and their ability to decode well enough to sustain attention to a story.

READ-ALOUD BOOK
The Boy and the Ghost by Robert San Souci or _____

Writing

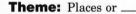

Theme: Places or _____

MINI-LESSON
Students volunteer sentences for travel brochures. Classmates check for subject-verb agreement or _____.

COMPOSING
Continue revising travel brochure or _____.

SHARING
Partners proofread for subject-verb agreement or _____.
Papers are dated and filed.

Word Study

CHART DEVELOPMENT
Spelling Emphasis: *u* or _____
Other Emphasis:
- adjective with noun or _____
- addition or _____
  On the chart, the teacher lists phrases volunteered by students using:
- *u*
- adjectives with nouns
- addition vocabulary
- _____

WRITING
On their papers, students write their favorite words from the chart or other words, phrases, or sentences that would be appropriate for the chart.

SPELLING
Partners call out words for each other to spell aloud.
Papers are dated and filed.

HOMEWORK
Write sentences explaining how you use addition to solve problems. Use *u* words.

Lesson **27**

Research

LEAD-IN
Teacher introduces the Project Idea.
Topic: Land forms or _____
Material: Newspapers or _____
Comprehension Skill: Comparisons
or _____

SEARCH & RECORD
Group Size: Partners or _____
Project Idea: Write comparisons of
places that seem to be opposites—trees/no
trees, rainfall/dry, cold/hot, or
_____.

SHARING
Show another team your conclusions or
_____.
Papers are dated and filed.

Recreational Reading

All students read books for approximately
30 minutes.

CONVERSATIONS
The teacher also reads silently. The
teacher has some short conversations with
readers. When appropriate, the main
focus of these conversations is decoding
skills.

CLIPBOARD NOTES
Teacher notes students' selections of
books and their ability to decode well
enough to sustain attention to a story.

READ-ALOUD BOOK
_____

Writing

Theme: Places or _____

MINI-LESSON
Demonstration of effective response
group. Emphasis on helping writers check
to see if all important information has
been included or _____.

COMPOSING
Continue work on brochure or
_____.

SHARING
Response groups or _____.
Papers are dated and filed.

Word Study

CHART DEVELOPMENT
Spelling Emphasis: *A* or _____
Other Emphasis:
- proper nouns or _____
- math or _____
  On the chart, the teacher lists phrases
and words volunteered by students using:
- *A*
- proper nouns
- math vocabulary
- _____

WRITING
On their papers, students write their
favorite words from the chart or other
words, phrases, or sentences that would
be appropriate for the chart.

SPELLING
Partners call out words for each other to
spell aloud.
Papers are dated and filed.

HOMEWORK
Look in a magazine and find names of
products containing the letter *A*. Write
them on a piece of paper.

Research

LEAD-IN
Teacher introduces the Project Idea.
Topic: Land forms or _____
Material: Social studies textbooks or _____

Comprehension Skill: Prediction or _____

SEARCH & RECORD
Group Size: Partners or _____
Project Idea: Choose a picture of a place in the book; list all the resources you see. Write a description of how the people's lives would change if you took away all of one resource. For example,

how would the Ojibwa have lived if they'd had no trees? or _____.

SHARING
Volunteers read predictions to class or _____.

Papers are dated and filed.

Recreational Reading

All students read books for approximately 30 minutes.

CONVERSATIONS
The teacher also reads silently. The teacher has some short conversations with readers. When appropriate, the main focus of these conversations is decoding skills.

CLIPBOARD NOTES
Teacher notes students' selections of books and their ability to decode well enough to sustain attention to a story.

READ-ALOUD BOOK
_____

Writing

Theme: Places or _____

MINI-LESSON
Discussion of ideas for illustrating travel brochures: maps, pictures, etc. or _____.

COMPOSING
Continue work on travel brochure. Begin illustrations or _____.

SHARING
Response groups or _____.
Papers are dated and filed.

Word Study

CHART DEVELOPMENT
Spelling Emphasis: *B* or _____
Other Emphasis:
- proper nouns or _____
- subtraction or _____
  On the chart, the teacher lists phrases and words volunteered by students using:
- *B*
- proper nouns
- subtraction vocabulary
- _____

WRITING
On their papers, students write their favorite words from the chart or other words, phrases, or sentences that would be appropriate for the chart.

SPELLING
Partners call out words for each other to spell aloud.
Papers are dated and filed.

HOMEWORK
Write sentences about how you know when to subtract when you are solving problems.

Lesson **29**

Research

LEAD-IN
Teacher introduces the Project Idea.
Topic: Land forms or _____
Material: Magazines or _____
Comprehension Skill: Comparison
or _____

SEARCH & RECORD
Group Size: 3 or 4 or _____
Project Idea: Cut out pictures of
places that have much in common with
the place where you live. For example, if
you live in Florida, don't cut out pictures
of snow, or _____.

SHARING
Everyone glues pictures onto class collage
or _____.
   Papers are dated and filed.

Recreational Reading

All students read books for approximately
30 minutes.

CONVERSATIONS
The teacher also reads silently. The
teacher has some short conversations with
readers. When appropriate, the main
focus of these conversations is decoding
skills.

CLIPBOARD NOTES
Teacher notes students' selections of
books and their ability to decode well
enough to sustain attention to a story.

READ-ALOUD BOOK
If You Made a Million by David Schwartz
or _____

Writing

Theme: Places or _____

MINI-LESSON
Editing information about checking
capital letters, especially in names of
places or _____.

COMPOSING
Complete revision of travel brochure. Edit
or _____.

SHARING
Partners help edit or _____.
   Papers are dated and filed.

Word Study

CHART DEVELOPMENT
Spelling Emphasis: *C* or _____
Other Emphasis:
- proper nouns or _____
- money or _____
   On the chart, the teacher lists phrases
and words volunteered by students using:
- *C*
- proper nouns
- money vocabulary
- _____

WRITING
On their papers, students write their
favorite words from the chart or other
words, phrases, or sentences that would
be appropriate for the chart.

SPELLING
Partners call out words for each other to
spell aloud.
   Papers are dated and filed.

HOMEWORK
Write sentences about how you use
money. Use proper nouns.

Lesson **30**

Research

LEAD-IN
Teacher introduces the Project Idea.
Topic: Land forms or _____
Material: Students select or _____
Comprehension Skill: Main idea or _____

SEARCH & RECORD
Group Size: Partners or _____
Project Idea: Write a summary of the most important information learned about land forms or _____.

SHARING
Volunteers read summaries to class or _____.
   Papers are dated and filed.

Recreational Reading

All students read books for approximately 30 minutes.

CONVERSATIONS
The teacher also reads silently. The teacher has some short conversations with readers. When appropriate, the main focus of these conversations is decoding skills.

CLIPBOARD NOTES
Teacher notes students' selections of books and their ability to decode well enough to sustain attention to a story.

READ-ALOUD BOOK
_____

Writing

Theme: Places or _____

MINI-LESSON
Teacher leads discussion of plans for assembling class collection of travel brochures or _____.

COMPOSING
Complete publication of travel brochure or _____.

SHARING
Whole-group sharing of completed collection of travel brochures or _____.
   Papers are dated and filed.

Word Study

CHART DEVELOPMENT
Spelling Emphasis: *D* or _____
Other Emphasis:
■ proper nouns or _____
■ measuring or _____
   On the chart, the teacher lists phrases volunteered by students using:
■ *D*
■ proper nouns
■ measuring vocabulary
■ _____

WRITING
On their papers, students write their favorite words from the chart or other words, phrases, or sentences that would be appropriate for the chart.

SPELLING
Partners call out words for each other to spell aloud.
   Papers are dated and filed.

HOMEWORK
Write sentences about things you have to measure when you cook.

Lesson **31**

Research

LEAD-IN
Teacher introduces the Project Idea.
Topic: People in the news or
_____

Material: Newspapers or _____
Comprehension Skill: Searching for information or _____

SEARCH & RECORD
Group Size: Partners or _____
Project Idea: List names of people found in the newspaper or _____.

SHARING
Tell another team 3 names you found or _____.
    Papers are dated and filed.

Recreational Reading

All students read books for approximately 30 minutes.

CONVERSATIONS
The teacher also reads silently. The teacher has some short conversations with readers. When appropriate, the main focus of these conversations is what each student is learning about authors.

CLIPBOARD NOTES
Teacher notes students' selections of books and whether they notice who the authors are.

READ-ALOUD BOOK
_____

Writing

The overall theme for the next 15 days is People or _____. One or more of the other modules will reflect this theme.
Theme: People or _____

MINI-LESSON
Brainstorm list of people at school or _____.

COMPOSING
Write list of people you can write about or _____.

SHARING
Partners discuss their lists or _____.
    Papers are dated and filed.

Word Study

CHART DEVELOPMENT
Spelling Emphasis: *E* or _____
Other Emphasis:
■ proper nouns or _____
■ art or _____
    On the chart, the teacher lists phrases and words volunteered by students using:
■ *E*
■ proper nouns
■ art vocabulary
■ _____

WRITING
On their papers, students write their favorite words from the chart or other words, phrases, or sentences that would be appropriate for the chart.

SPELLING
Partners call out words for each other to spell aloud.
    Papers are dated and filed.

HOMEWORK
Write a paragraph with words containing the letter *E* that describes your last art project.

Research

LEAD-IN
Teacher introduces the Project Idea.
Topic: People in the news or _____

Material: Newspapers or _____
Comprehension Skill: Cause and effect or _____

SEARCH & RECORD
Group Size: Partners or _____
Project Idea: Cut out a picture of people from the newspaper. Write reasons for the picture to be in the newspaper or _____.

SHARING
Volunteers share pictures and reasons with the whole group or _____.
Papers are dated and filed.

Recreational Reading

All students read books for approximately 30 minutes.

CONVERSATIONS
The teacher also reads silently. The teacher has some short conversations with readers. When appropriate, the main focus of these conversations is what each student is learning about authors.

CLIPBOARD NOTES
Teacher notes students' selections of books and whether they notice who the authors are.

READ-ALOUD BOOK
Two Bad Ants by Chris Van Allsburg or _____

Writing

Theme: People or _____

MINI-LESSON
Brainstorm list of people at home or _____.

COMPOSING
Write list of people at home you can write about or _____.

SHARING
Go over your list with another team or _____.
Papers are dated and filed.

Word Study

CHART DEVELOPMENT
Spelling Emphasis: _F_ or _____
Other Emphasis:
- proper nouns or _____
- literature or _____
  On the chart, the teacher lists phrases and words volunteered by students using:
- _F_
- proper nouns
- literature vocabulary
- _____

WRITING
On their papers, students write their favorite words from the chart or other words, phrases, or sentences that would be appropriate for the chart.

SPELLING
Partners call out words for each other to spell aloud.
Papers are dated and filed.

HOMEWORK
Write about your favorite book. Use some proper nouns.

Lesson **33**

Research

LEAD-IN
Teacher introduces the Project Idea.
Topic: People in the news or
_____

Material: Newspapers or _____
Comprehension Skill: Comparison
or _____

SEARCH & RECORD
Group Size: Individuals or _____
Project Idea: Cut out a picture of the
most important person you can find in the
newspaper. Write reasons you chose this
person or _____.

SHARING
Volunteers introduce their important
people to the class and explain why they
chose them or _____.
Papers are dated and filed.

Recreational Reading

All students read books for approximately
30 minutes.

CONVERSATIONS
The teacher also reads silently. The
teacher has some short conversations with
readers. When appropriate, the main
focus of these conversations is what each
student is learning about authors.

CLIPBOARD NOTES
Teacher notes students' selections of
books and whether they notice who the
authors are.

READ-ALOUD BOOK
_____

Writing

Theme: People or _____

MINI-LESSON
Read over lists of people and choose
someone to write more about or
_____.

COMPOSING
Begin writing about a person or
_____.

SHARING
Students read the first sentence of their
pieces about people or _____.
Papers are dated and filed.

Word Study

CHART DEVELOPMENT
Spelling Emphasis: *G* or _____
Other Emphasis:
■ proper nouns or _____
■ ecology or _____
On the chart, the teacher lists phrases
and words volunteered by students using:
■ *G*
■ proper nouns
■ ecology vocabulary
■ _____

WRITING
On their papers, students write their
favorite words from the chart or other
words, phrases, or sentences that would
be appropriate for the chart.

SPELLING
Partners call out words for each other to
spell aloud.
Papers are dated and filed.

HOMEWORK
Write a paragraph on energy conservation
using proper nouns that contain the letter
G.

Lesson 34

Research

LEAD-IN
Teacher introduces the Project Idea.
Topic: People in the news or _____

Material: Encyclopedias or books or _____

Comprehension Skill: Searching for facts or _____

SEARCH & RECORD
Group Size: 2 or 3 or _____
Project Idea: Find a person who is discussed in an encyclopedia or book. Make a list of facts about the person or _____.

SHARING
Everyone tells class the name of the person chosen and one fact or _____.
Papers are dated and filed.

Recreational Reading

All students read books for approximately 30 minutes.

CONVERSATIONS
The teacher also reads silently. The teacher has some short conversations with readers. When appropriate, the main focus of these conversations is what each student is learning about authors.

CLIPBOARD NOTES
Teacher notes students' selections of books and whether they notice who the authors are.

READ-ALOUD BOOK
_____

Writing

Theme: People or _____

MINI-LESSON
Teacher reads passage from a biography and discusses techniques the writer used or _____.

COMPOSING
Continue piece about person or begin a new piece about someone else or _____.

SHARING
Partners share or _____.
Papers are dated and filed.

Word Study

CHART DEVELOPMENT
Spelling Emphasis: *H* or _____
Other Emphasis:
■ proper nouns or _____
■ business or _____
   On the chart, the teacher lists phrases and words volunteered by students using:
■ *H*
■ proper nouns
■ business vocabulary
■ _____

WRITING
On their papers, students write their favorite words from the chart or other words, phrases, or sentences that would be appropriate for the chart.

SPELLING
Partners call out words for each other to spell aloud.
   Papers are dated and filed.

HOMEWORK
Find proper nouns containing the letter *H* in a newspaper advertisement. Write these on a piece of paper.

Lesson 35

Research

LEAD-IN
Teacher introduces the Project Idea.
Topic: People in the news or
_____

Material: Newspapers or _____
Comprehension Skill: Searching for
facts or _____

SEARCH & RECORD
Group Size: Individuals or _____
Project Idea: List people in the news.
Record facts about each one or
_____.

SHARING
Partners share or _____.
    Papers are dated and filed.

Recreational Reading

All students read books for approximately
30 minutes.

CONVERSATIONS
The teacher also reads silently. The
teacher has some short conversations with
readers. When appropriate, the main
focus of these conversations is what each
student is learning about authors.

CLIPBOARD NOTES
Teacher notes students' selections of
books and whether they notice who the
authors are.

READ-ALOUD BOOK
Fortunately by Remy Charlip or
_____

Writing

Theme: People or _____

MINI-LESSON
Teacher reads a poem about a person,
such as "Harriet Tubman" by Eloise
Greenfield or _____.

COMPOSING
Write about someone you've already
written on, this time in a poem or
_____.

SHARING
Volunteers share poems with class or
_____.
    Papers are dated and filed.

Word Study

CHART DEVELOPMENT
Spelling Emphasis: *I* or _____
Other Emphasis:
- proper nouns or _____
- science or _____
    On the chart, the teacher lists phrases
and words volunteered by students using:
- *I*
- proper nouns
- science vocabulary
- _____

WRITING
On their papers, students write their
favorite words from the chart or other
words, phrases, or sentences that would
be appropriate for the chart.

SPELLING
Partners call out words for each other to
spell aloud.
    Papers are dated and filed.

HOMEWORK
Write sentences about what you learned
in science today. Use some proper nouns.

Research

LEAD-IN
Teacher introduces the Project Idea.
Topic: People in the news or

_____

Material: Encyclopedias or _____
Comprehension Skill: Drawing
conclusions or _____

SEARCH & RECORD
Group Size: Partners or _____
Project Idea: List people you find in
the encyclopedia who helped other people.
Make a chart that shows how they helped
others or _____ .

SHARING
Explain how people helped others or

_____ .

Papers are dated and filed.

Recreational Reading

All students read books for approximately
30 minutes.

CONVERSATIONS
The teacher also reads silently. The
teacher has some short conversations with
readers. When appropriate, the main
focus of these conversations is what each
student is learning about authors.

CLIPBOARD NOTES
Teacher notes students' selections of
books and whether they notice who the
authors are.

READ-ALOUD BOOK
_____

Writing

Theme: People or _____

MINI-LESSON
Volunteers name words from their drafts
that need to be capitalized. Discussion of
reasons for capitalization or _____ .

COMPOSING
Continue work on previous draft or
_____ .

SHARING
Partners proofread drafts for correct use
of capital letters or _____ .
Papers are dated and filed.

Word Study

CHART DEVELOPMENT
Spelling Emphasis: *J* or _____
Other Emphasis:
- proper nouns or _____
- geography or _____
  On the chart, the teacher lists phrases
and words volunteered by students using:
- *J*
- proper nouns
- geography vocabulary
- _____

WRITING
On their papers, students write their
favorite words from the chart or other
words, phrases, or sentences that would
be appropriate for the chart.

SPELLING
Partners call out words for each other to
spell aloud.
Papers are dated and filed.

HOMEWORK
Write the names of important places that
contain the letter *J*.

Lesson **37**

Research

LEAD-IN
Teacher introduces the Project Idea.
Topic: People in the news or

_____

Material: Magazines or _____
Comprehension Skill: Classification
or _____

SEARCH & RECORD
Group Size: 3 or 4 or _____
Project Idea: Cut out pictures of
people. Paste them on poster in groups
according to where they live: in cities, in
cold places, etc., or _____.

SHARING
Display posters or _____.
    Papers are dated and filed.

Recreational Reading

All students read books for approximately
30 minutes.

CONVERSATIONS
The teacher also reads silently. The
teacher has some short conversations with
readers. When appropriate, the main
focus of these conversations is what each
student is learning about authors.

CLIPBOARD NOTES
Teacher notes students' selections of
books and whether they notice who the
authors are.

READ-ALOUD BOOK

_____

Writing

Theme: People or _____

MINI-LESSON
Go over list of books read recently or
_____.

COMPOSING
Write about a book you've read recently
or _____.

SHARING
Partners share or _____.
    Papers are dated and filed.

Word Study

CHART DEVELOPMENT
Spelling Emphasis: *K* or _____
Other Emphasis:
■ proper nouns or _____
■ health or _____
    On the chart, the teacher lists phrases
and words volunteered by students using:
■ *K*
■ proper nouns
■ health vocabulary
■ _____

WRITING
On their papers, students write their
favorite words from the chart or other
words, phrases, or sentences that would
be appropriate for the chart.

SPELLING
Partners call out words for each other to
spell aloud.
    Papers are dated and filed.

HOMEWORK
Make a list of foods that are good for you.
Make another list of foods that are not
good for you.

Lesson **38**

Research

LEAD-IN
Teacher introduces the Project Idea.
Topic: People in the news or
_____

Material: Magazines or _____
Comprehension Skill: Comparison
or _____

SEARCH & RECORD
Group Size: 3 or 4 or _____
Project Idea: Cut out pictures of
people. Paste them on a poster in the
order of their ages or _____.

SHARING
Display posters or _____.
 Papers are dated and filed.

Recreational Reading

All students read books for approximately
30 minutes.

CONVERSATIONS
The teacher also reads silently. The
teacher has some short conversations with
readers. When appropriate, the main
focus of these conversations is what each
student is learning about authors.

CLIPBOARD NOTES
Teacher notes students' selections of
books and whether they notice who the
authors are.

READ-ALOUD BOOK
Air Mail to the Moon by Tom Birdseye or
_____

Writing

Theme: People or _____

MINI-LESSON
Teacher introduces pen pal letter project
or _____.

COMPOSING
Write introductory letter to pen pal.
Write imaginary letter to famous person
or _____.

SHARING
Partners share or _____.
 Papers are dated and filed.

Word Study

CHART DEVELOPMENT
Spelling Emphasis: *L* or _____
Other Emphasis:
■ proper nouns or _____
■ history or _____
 On the chart, the teacher lists phrases
and words volunteered by students using:
■ *L*
■ proper nouns
■ history vocabulary
■ _____

WRITING
On their papers, students write their
favorite words from the chart or other
words, phrases, or sentences that would
be appropriate for the chart.

SPELLING
Partners call out words for each other to
spell aloud.
 Papers are dated and filed.

HOMEWORK
Make a list of famous people in American
history. How many of them have the
letter *L* in their names?

137

Lesson 39

Research

LEAD-IN
Teacher introduces the Project Idea.
Topic: People in the news or
_____

Material: Newspapers or _____
Comprehension Skill:
Characterization or _____

SEARCH & RECORD
Group Size: Partners or _____
Project Idea: List names of people in
the news. Beside each, write one
accomplishment of that person or
_____.

SHARING
Volunteers tell class about a person on
their lists or _____.
  Papers are dated and filed.

Recreational Reading

All students read books for approximately
30 minutes.

CONVERSATIONS
The teacher also reads silently. The
teacher has some short conversations with
readers. When appropriate, the main
focus of these conversations is what each
student is learning about authors.

CLIPBOARD NOTES
Teacher notes students' selections of
books and whether they notice who the
authors are.

READ-ALOUD BOOK
_____

Writing

Theme: People or _____

MINI-LESSON
Demonstration of format of friendly letter
or _____.

COMPOSING
Continue work on letter or _____.

SHARING
Read letter to partner or _____.
  Papers are dated and filed.

Word Study

CHART DEVELOPMENT
Spelling Emphasis: _M_ or _____
Other Emphasis:
■ proper nouns or _____
■ education or _____
  On the chart, the teacher lists phrases
and words volunteered by students using:
■ _M_
■ proper nouns
■ education vocabulary
■ _____

WRITING
On their papers, students write their
favorite words from the chart or other
words, phrases, or sentences that would
be appropriate for the chart.

SPELLING
Partners call out words for each other to
spell aloud.
  Papers are dated and filed.

HOMEWORK
Write a story about one of your teachers.
See how many words containing the letter
_M_ you can use.

138

Lesson **40**

Research

LEAD-IN
Teacher introduces the Project Idea.
Topic: People in the news or _____

Material: Students choose or _____

Comprehension Skill: Main idea or _____

SEARCH & RECORD
Group Size: Individuals or partners or _____

Project Idea: Search for the most important information about people in the news. Write a summary of what you find or _____.

SHARING
Volunteers tell class what they found or _____.
Papers are dated and filed.

Recreational Reading

All students read books for approximately 30 minutes.

CONVERSATIONS
The teacher also reads silently. The teacher has some short conversations with readers. When appropriate, the main focus of these conversations is what each student is learning about authors.

CLIPBOARD NOTES
Teacher notes students' selections of books and whether they notice who the authors are.

READ-ALOUD BOOK
_____

Writing

Theme: People or _____

MINI-LESSON
Announcement of deadline for mailing pen pal letters or for publishing imaginary correspondence or _____.

COMPOSING
Continue drafts or _____.

SHARING
Share with partner or _____.
Papers are dated and filed.

Word Study

CHART DEVELOPMENT
Spelling Emphasis: *N* or _____
Other Emphasis:
■ proper nouns or _____
■ agriculture or _____
On the chart, the teacher lists phrases and words volunteered by students using:
■ *N*
■ proper nouns
■ agriculture vocabulary
■ _____

WRITING
On their papers, students write their favorite words from the chart or other words, phrases, or sentences that would be appropriate for the chart.

SPELLING
Partners call out words for each other to spell aloud.
Papers are dated and filed.

HOMEWORK
Write some sentences about agriculture near your home. Use some proper nouns.

Lesson 41

Research

LEAD-IN
Teacher introduces the Project Idea.
Topic: Government or _____
Material: Newspapers or _____
Comprehension Skill: Association of information or _____

SEARCH & RECORD
Group Size: 3 or 4 or _____
Project Idea: Circle items in the newspaper associated with government or _____.

SHARING
Group representatives tell the class the ideas they found most often in their search or _____.
Papers are dated and filed.

Recreational Reading

All students read books for approximately 30 minutes.

CONVERSATIONS
The teacher also reads silently. The teacher has some short conversations with readers. When appropriate, the main focus of these conversations is each student's ability to tell what a book is mainly about.

CLIPBOARD NOTES
Teacher notes students' selections of books and whether they are developing preferences for particular types of books.

READ-ALOUD BOOK
The Flunking of Joshua T. Bates by Susan Shreve* or _____

Writing

Theme: People or _____

MINI-LESSON
Teacher asks volunteers to read sentences from their drafts that have present-tense verbs and sentences that have past-tense verbs or _____.

COMPOSING
Continue work on draft or _____.

SHARING
Proofread with partner. Check for correct use of verbs or _____.
Papers are dated and filed.

Word Study

CHART DEVELOPMENT
Spelling Emphasis: *O* or _____
Other Emphasis:
■ sentences or _____
■ government or _____
On the chart, the teacher lists sentences volunteered by students using:
■ *O*
■ government vocabulary
■ _____

WRITING
On their papers, students write their favorite words from the chart or other

words, phrases, or sentences that would be appropriate for the chart.

SPELLING
Partners call out words for each other to spell aloud.
Papers are dated and filed.

HOMEWORK
Write sentences about government. Use some words with the letter *O*.

Research

LEAD-IN
Teacher introduces the Project Idea.
Topic: Government or _____
Material: Newspapers or _____
Comprehension Skill: Details or
_____

SEARCH & RECORD
Group Size: Partners or _____
Project Idea: List names of people
who work for the government. Beside
each, write what that person does or
_____.

SHARING
Show your list to another team or
_____.
  Papers are dated and filed.

Recreational Reading

All students read books for approximately
30 minutes.

CONVERSATIONS
The teacher also reads silently. The
teacher has some short conversations with
readers. When appropriate, the main
focus of these conversations is each
student's ability to tell what a book is
mainly about.

CLIPBOARD NOTES
Teacher notes students' selections of
books and whether they are developing
preferences for particular types of books.

READ-ALOUD BOOK
_____

Writing

Theme: People or _____

MINI-LESSON
Teacher leads discussion of ideas for
helping writers with their letters in
response groups or _____.

COMPOSING
Continue draft or _____.

SHARING
Response group members share drafts of
letters or _____.
  Papers are dated and filed.

Word Study

CHART DEVELOPMENT
Spelling Emphasis: P or _____
Other Emphasis:
■ sentences or _____
■ government or _____
  On the chart, the teacher lists
sentences volunteered by students using:
■ P
■ government vocabulary
■ _____

WRITING
On their papers, students write their
favorite words from the chart or other

words, phrases, or sentences that would
be appropriate for the chart.

SPELLING
Partners call out words for each other to
spell aloud.
  Papers are dated and filed.

HOMEWORK
Write some sentences about the president
of the United States.

Lesson **43**

Research

LEAD-IN
Teacher introduces the Project Idea.
Topic: Government or _____
Material: Newspapers or _____
Comprehension Skill: Cause and effect or _____

SEARCH & RECORD
Group Size: Partners or _____
Project Idea: List things that the government does. Beside each, tell why or _____.

SHARING
Partners ask each other "why" questions: Why does the government do these things? or _____.
Papers are dated and filed.

Recreational Reading

All students read books for approximately 30 minutes.

CONVERSATIONS
The teacher also reads silently. The teacher has some short conversations with readers. When appropriate, the main focus of these conversations is each student's ability to tell what a book is mainly about.

CLIPBOARD NOTES
Teacher notes students' selections of books and whether they are developing preferences for particular types of books.

READ-ALOUD BOOK
_____

Writing

Theme: People or _____

MINI-LESSON
Teacher leads discussion of ideas about things to include with pen pal letters such as photographs or _____.

COMPOSING
Continue draft or _____

SHARING
Partners discuss extra materials to enclose in letters or _____.
Papers are dated and filed.

Word Study

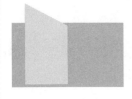

CHART DEVELOPMENT
Spelling Emphasis: *Qu* or
_____

Other Emphasis:
■ sentences or _____
■ government or _____
On the chart, the teacher lists sentences volunteered by students using:
■ *Qu*
■ government vocabulary
■ _____

WRITING
On their papers, students write their favorite words from the chart or other words, phrases, or sentences that would be appropriate for the chart.

SPELLING
Partners call out words for each other to spell aloud.
Papers are dated and filed.

HOMEWORK
Write some sentences about a queen.

Lesson **44**

Research

LEAD-IN
Teacher introduces the Project Idea.
Topic: Government or _____
Material: Social studies textbooks or
_____

Comprehension Skill: Questions or
_____

SEARCH & RECORD
Group Size: Partners or_____
Project Idea: List places associated
with government. Write questions about
each place or _____ .

SHARING
Partners share what they learned or
_____ .

Papers are dated and filed.

Recreational Reading

All students read books for approximately
30 minutes.

CONVERSATIONS
The teacher also reads silently. The
teacher has some short conversations with
readers. When appropriate, the main
focus of these conversations is each
student's ability to tell what a book is
mainly about.

CLIPBOARD NOTES
Teacher notes students' selections of
books and whether they are developing
preferences for particular types of books.

READ-ALOUD BOOK
Scared Silly by James Howe or
_____

Writing

Theme: People or _____

MINI-LESSON
Teacher leads discussion of what should
be carefully edited in letters or
_____

COMPOSING
Edit final draft of letter or _____ .

SHARING
Partners help each other edit or
_____ .

Papers are dated and filed.

Word Study

CHART DEVELOPMENT
Spelling Emphasis: *R* or _____
Other Emphasis:
- sentences or _____
- government or _____
  On the chart, the teacher lists
sentences volunteered by students using:
- *R*
- government vocabulary
- _____

WRITING
On their papers, students write their
favorite words from the chart or other

words, phrases, or sentences that would
be appropriate for the chart.

SPELLING
Partners call out words for each other to
spell aloud.
  Papers are dated and filed.

HOMEWORK
Write about some places that have the
letter *R*.

Lesson 45

Research

LEAD-IN
Teacher introduces the Project Idea.
Topic: Government or _____.
Material: Newspapers or _____.
Comprehension Skill: Classification or _____

SEARCH & RECORD
Group Size: 3 or 4 or _____.
Project Idea: Cut out articles and pictures associated with government. Group according to local, state, or federal government and glue on poster or
_____.

SHARING
Display posters or _____.
 Papers are dated and filed.

Recreational Reading

All students read books for approximately 30 minutes.

CONVERSATIONS
The teacher also reads silently. The teacher has some short conversations with readers. When appropriate, the main focus of these conversations is each student's ability to tell what a book is mainly about.

CLIPBOARD NOTES
Teacher notes students' selections of books and whether they are developing preferences for particular types of books.

READ-ALOUD BOOK
_____

Writing

Theme: People or _____.

MINI-LESSON
Instructions for preparing letters for mailing or _____.

COMPOSING
Prepare final copy of letter or _____.

SHARING
Share completed letters or _____.
 Papers are dated and filed.

Word Study

CHART DEVELOPMENT
Spelling Emphasis: _S_ or _____
Other Emphasis:
- sentences or _____
- government or _____
 On the chart, the teacher lists sentences volunteered by students using:
- _S_
- government vocabulary
- _____

WRITING
On their papers, students write their favorite words from the chart or other

words, phrases, or sentences that would be appropriate for the chart.

SPELLING
Partners call out words for each other to spell aloud.
 Papers are dated and filed.

HOMEWORK
Would Snoopy make a good president? Write sentences telling why or why not.

144

Lesson **46**

Research

LEAD-IN
Teacher introduces the Project Idea.
Topic: Government or _____
Material: Social studies books or _____

Comprehension Skill: Cause and effect or _____

SEARCH & RECORD
Group Size: Partners or _____
Project Idea: Make a chart that lists ways people influence government and ways government influences people or _____.

SHARING
Volunteers share conclusions with class or _____.

Papers are dated and filed.

Recreational Reading

All students read books for approximately 30 minutes.

CONVERSATIONS
The teacher also reads silently. The teacher has some short conversations with readers. When appropriate, the main focus of these conversations is each student's ability to tell what a book is mainly about.

CLIPBOARD NOTES
Teacher notes students' selections of books and whether they are developing preferences for particular types of books.

READ-ALOUD BOOK
_____

Writing

The overall theme for the next 15 days is Things to do or _____. One or more of the other modules will reflect this theme.
Theme: Things to do or _____

MINI-LESSON
Brainstorm list of things people do or _____.

COMPOSING
Write list of things to do or _____.

SHARING
Everyone shares an idea from list of things to do or _____.
Papers are dated and filed.

Word Study

CHART DEVELOPMENT
Spelling Emphasis: *T* or _____
Other Emphasis:
■ sentences or _____
■ medicine or _____
On the chart, the teacher lists sentences volunteered by students using:
■ *T*
■ medicine vocabulary
■ _____

WRITING
On their papers, students write their favorite words from the chart or other

words, phrases, or sentences that would be appropriate for the chart.

SPELLING
Partners call out words for each other to spell aloud.
Papers are dated and filed.

HOMEWORK
Make a list of things you usually do on Tuesdays and Thursdays.

Lesson **47**

Research

LEAD-IN
Teacher introduces the Project Idea.
Topic: Government or _____
Material: Magazines or _____
Comprehension Skill: Cause and effect or _____

SEARCH & RECORD
Group Size: Partners or _____
Project Idea: Cut out pictures that show the influence of government. Glue on posters and write captions or _____ .

SHARING
Display posters or _____ .
   Papers are dated and filed.

Recreational Reading

All students read books for approximately 30 minutes.

CONVERSATIONS
The teacher also reads silently. The teacher has some short conversations with readers. When appropriate, the main focus of these conversations is each student's ability to tell what a book is mainly about.

CLIPBOARD NOTES
Teacher notes students' selections of books and whether they are developing preferences for particular types of books.

READ-ALOUD BOOK
Willy the Wimp by Anthony Browne or
_____

Writing

Theme: Things to do or _____

MINI-LESSON
Brainstorm things you'd like to learn how to do or _____ .

COMPOSING
Write about one thing you'd like to learn how to do or _____ .

SHARING
Volunteers read their lists or _____ .
   Papers are dated and filed.

Word Study

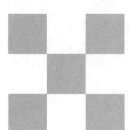

CHART DEVELOPMENT
Spelling Emphasis: *U* or _____
Other Emphasis:
- sentences or _____
- music or _____
   On the chart, the teacher lists sentences volunteered by students using:
- *U*
- music vocabulary
- _____

WRITING
On their papers, students write their favorite words from the chart or other

words, phrases, or sentences that would be appropriate for the chart.

SPELLING
Partners call out words for each other to spell aloud.
   Papers are dated and filed.

HOMEWORK
Write a song using as many words containing *U* as you can.

146

Lesson 48

Research

LEAD-IN
Teacher introduces the Project Idea.
Topic: Government or _____
Material: Magazines or _____
Comprehension Skill: Prediction or
_____

SEARCH & RECORD
Group Size: 3 or 4 or _____
Project Idea: Cut out pictures of
problems you think government might
help solve. Write predictions of ways
government might help or _____.

SHARING
Share with class or _____.
  Papers are dated and filed.

Recreational Reading

All students read books for approximately
30 minutes.

CONVERSATIONS
The teacher also reads silently. The
teacher has some short conversations with
readers. When appropriate, the main
focus of these conversations is each
student's ability to tell what a book is
mainly about.

CLIPBOARD NOTES
Teacher notes students' selections of
books and whether they are developing
preferences for particular types of books.

READ-ALOUD BOOK
_____

Writing

Theme: Things to do or _____

MINI-LESSON
Discussion of lists made in previous
lessons and how to decide whether to
continue a piece already begun, or write
a new draft on another topic, or
_____.

COMPOSING
Continue piece from lesson 47 or write a
new draft about things to do or
_____.

SHARING
Share with a partner or _____.
  Papers are dated and filed.

Word Study

CHART DEVELOPMENT
Spelling Emphasis: *V* or _____
Other Emphasis:
- sentences or _____
- literature or _____
  On the chart, the teacher lists
sentences volunteered by students using:
- *V*
- literature vocabulary
- _____

WRITING
On their papers students write their
favorite words from the chart or other

words, phrases, or sentences that would
be appropriate for the chart.

SPELLING
Partners call out words for each other to
spell aloud.
  Papers are dated and filed.

HOMEWORK
Write a poem containing as many words
containing *V* as you can.

Lesson 49

Research

LEAD-IN
Teacher introduces the Project Idea.
Topic: Government or _____
Material: Telephone books or _____

Comprehension Skill: Cause and effect or _____

SEARCH & RECORD
Group Size: Partners or _____
Project Idea: List government offices and phone numbers. Next to each, write a reason for calling or _____.

SHARING
Volunteers share one office they put on the calling list or _____.
  Papers are dated and filed.

Recreational Reading

All students read books for approximately 30 minutes.

CONVERSATIONS
The teacher also reads silently. The teacher has some short conversations with readers. When appropriate, the main focus of these conversations is each student's ability to tell what a book is mainly about.

CLIPBOARD NOTES
Teacher notes students' selections of books and whether they are developing preferences for particular types of books.

READ-ALOUD BOOK
_____

Writing

Theme: Things to do or _____

MINI-LESSON
Teacher reads from factual book about something to do, such as a career, a hobby, an experiment, a trick, etc. or _____.

COMPOSING
Write about a new topic explained in the reading or continue previous draft or _____.

SHARING
Everyone shares his or her topic or _____.
  Papers are dated and filed.

Word Study

CHART DEVELOPMENT
Spelling Emphasis: *W* or _____
Other Emphasis:
■ sentences or _____
■ math or _____
  On the chart, the teacher lists sentences volunteered by students using:
■ *W*
■ math vocabulary
■ _____

WRITING
On their papers, students write their favorite words from the chart or other

words, phrases, or sentences that would be appropriate for the chart.

SPELLING
Partners call out words for each other to spell aloud.
  Papers are dated and filed.

HOMEWORK
Write some story problems. Use words with the letter *W*.

Lesson 50

Research

LEAD-IN
Teacher introduces the Project Idea.
Topic: Government or _____
Material: Students choose or
_____

Comprehension Skill: Main idea or
_____

SEARCH & RECORD
Group Size: Partners or _____
Project Idea: Search for most important information about government. Write summary of information learned or
_____

SHARING
Volunteers share conclusions with class or _____.
   Papers are dated and filed.

Recreational Reading

All students read books for approximately 30 minutes.

CONVERSATIONS
The teacher also reads silently. The teacher has some short conversations with readers. When appropriate, the main focus of these conversations is each student's ability to tell what a book is mainly about.

CLIPBOARD NOTES
Teacher notes students' selections of books and whether they are developing preferences for particular types of books.

READ-ALOUD BOOK
Willy the Champ by Anthony Browne or _____

Writing

Theme: Things to do or _____

MINI-LESSON
Teacher reads poem about something to do or _____.

COMPOSING
Write poem about something to do. The topic might be the same as in the piece you've already written or _____.

SHARING
Response groups compare prose and poetry pieces about things to do or _____.
   Papers are dated and filed.

Word Study

CHART DEVELOPMENT
Spelling Emphasis: X or _____
Other Emphasis:
■ sentences or _____
■ art or _____
   On the chart, the teacher lists sentences volunteered by students using:
■ X
■ art vocabulary
■ _____

WRITING
On their papers, students write their favorite words from the chart or other

words, phrases, or sentences that would be appropriate for the chart.

SPELLING
Partners call out words for each other to spell aloud.
   Papers are dated and filed.

HOMEWORK
Write about things you can draw that have X shapes in them.

Lesson **51**

Research

LEAD-IN
Teacher introduces the Project Idea.
Topic: Public health or _____
Material: Health textbooks or _____

Comprehension Skbll: Details or _____

SEARCH & RECORD
Group Size: Partners or _____
Project Idea: List people in the textbook who work to keep us healthy. Next to each one, write what they do or _____.

SHARING
Volunteers read to whole class or _____.
   Papers are dated and filed.

Recreational Reading

All students read books for approximately 30 minutes.

CONVERSATIONS
The teacher also reads silently. The teacher has some short conversations with readers. When appropriate, the main focus of these conversations is each student's ability to discuss the characters in the book he or she is reading.

CLIPBOARD NOTES
Teacher notes students' selections of books and whether they talk with friends about the behavior of characters.

READ-ALOUD BOOK
_____

Writing

Theme: Things to do or _____

MINI-LESSON
Students review their lists of books read or _____.

COMPOSING
Write about one of your favorite books or _____.

SHARING
Response groups share write-ups about books or _____.
   Papers are dated and filed.

Word Study

CHART DEVELOPMENT
Spelling Emphasis: *Y* or _____
Other Emphasis:
■ sentences or _____
■ public health or _____
   On the chart, the teacher lists sentences volunteered by students using:
■ *Y* words
■ public health vocabulary
■ _____

WRITING
On their papers, students write their favorite words from the chart or other

words, phrases, or sentences that would be appropriate for the chart.

SPELLING
Partners call out words for each other to spell aloud.
   Papers are dated and filed.

HOMEWORK
Write what you learned about public health today. Use some words that have the letter *Y*.

Research

LEAD-IN
Teacher introduces the Project Idea.
Topic: Public health or _____
Material: Magazines or _____
Comprehension Skill: Association
or _____

SEARCH & RECORD
Group Size: Partners or _____
Project Idea: Cut out advertisements
related to health. Explain to your partner
how each ad is health-related or
_____.

SHARING
Volunteers display their best
advertisements or _____.
  Papers are dated and filed.

Recreational Reading

All students read books for approximately
30 minutes.

CONVERSATIONS
The teacher also reads silently. The
teacher has some short conversations with
readers. When appropriate, the main
focus of these conversations is each
student's ability to discuss the characters
in the book he or she is reading.

CLIPBOARD NOTES
Teacher notes students' selections of
books and whether they talk with friends
about the behavior of characters.

READ-ALOUD BOOK
_____

Writing

Theme: Things to do or _____

MINI-LESSON
Demonstration of eliminating run-on
sentences or _____.

COMPOSING
Continue previous piece or _____.

SHARING
Partners check each other's work for run-
on sentences or _____.
  Papers are dated and filed.

Word Study

CHART DEVELOPMENT
Spelling Emphasis: Z or _____
Other Emphasis:
■ sentences or _____
■ public health or _____
  On the chart, the teacher lists
sentences volunteered by students using:
■ Z
■ public health vocabulary
■ _____

WRITING
On their papers, students write their
favorite words from the chart or other

words, phrases, or sentences that would
be appropriate for the chart.

SPELLING
Partners call out words for each other to
spell aloud.
  Papers are dated and filed.

HOMEWORK
Write sentences with 2-syllable words
containing the letter Z.

Lesson **53**

Research

LEAD-IN
Teacher introduces the Project Idea.
Topic: Public health or _____
Material: Telephone books or
_____

Comprehension Skill: Cause and
effect or _____

SEARCH & RECORD
Group Size: 3 or 4 or _____
Project Idea: List names and
telephone numbers to call for help in
health emergencies or for routine
questions or _____.

SHARING
Tell the names you wrote on your list and
why you would need to call each one or
_____.
 Papers are dated and filed.

Recreational Reading

All students read books for approximately
30 minutes.

CONVERSATIONS
The teacher also reads silently. The
teacher has some short conversations with
readers. When appropriate, the main
focus of these conversations is each
student's ability to discuss the characters
in the book he or she is reading.

CLIPBOARD NOTES
Teacher notes students' selections of
books and whether they talk with friends
about the behavior of characters.

READ-ALOUD BOOK
Nathaniel Talking by Eloise Greenfield**
or _____

Writing

Theme: Things to do or _____

MINI-LESSON
Demonstration of invitation writing.
(Consider inviting guests to make
presentations about what they do for a
living or to view some class projects, such
as exhibits about health) or _____.

COMPOSING
If appropriate, write an invitation or
_____.

SHARING
Partners check each other's invitations for
necessary information or _____.
 Papers are dated and filed.

Word Study

CHART DEVELOPMENT
Spelling Emphasis: *ai* or _____
Other Emphasis:
■ sentences or _____
■ public health or _____
 On the chart, the teacher lists
sentences volunteered by students using:
■ *ai*
■ public health vocabulary
■ _____

WRITING
On their papers, students write their
favorite words from the chart or other

words, phrases, or sentences that would
be appropriate for the chart.

SPELLING
Partners call out words for each other to
spell aloud.
 Papers are dated and filed.

HOMEWORK
Write some sentences about public health
services that help you.

Lesson **54**

Research

LEAD-IN
Teacher introduces the Project Idea.
Topic: Public health or _____
Material: Health books or _____
Comprehension Skill: Details or
_____

SEARCH & RECORD
Group Size: Partners or _____
Project Idea: Choose a health professional. Draw pictures to show what that person does to help us be healthy. Write questions you would like to ask him or her or _____ .

SHARING
Display pictures or _____
Papers are dated and filed.

Recreational Reading

All students read books for approximately 30 minutes.

CONVERSATIONS
The teacher also reads silently. The teacher has some short conversations with readers. When appropriate, the main focus of these conversations is each student's ability to discuss the characters in the book he or she is reading.

CLIPBOARD NOTES
Teacher notes students' selections of books and whether they talk with friends about the behavior of characters.

READ-ALOUD BOOK
_____

Writing

Theme: Things to do or _____

MINI-LESSON
Demonstration of helpful editing of an invitation or _____ .

COMPOSING
Complete invitation or _____ .

SHARING
Partners edit each other's invitations or _____ .
Papers are dated and filed.

Word Study

CHART DEVELOPMENT
Spelling Emphasis: _au_ or
_____
Other Emphasis:
- sentences or _____
- public health or _____
  On the chart, the teacher lists phrases and words volunteered by students using:
- _au_
- public health vocabulary
- _____

WRITING
On their papers, students write their favorite words from the chart or other words, phrases, or sentences that would be appropriate for the chart.

SPELLING
Partners call out words for each other to spell aloud.
Papers are dated and filed.

HOMEWORK
Find words in the newspaper containing the letter cluster _au_. Write them on a piece of paper. Do any relate to public health?

Lesson **55**

Research

LEAD-IN
Teacher introduces the Project Idea.
Topic: Public health or _____
Material: Magazines or _____
Comprehension Skill: Main idea or
_____

SEARCH & RECORD
Group Size: 3 or 4 or _____
Project Idea: Cut out pictures to illustrate safety rules. Paste them on a chart and write the rules underneath or
_____.

SHARING
Display charts or _____.
   Papers are dated and filed.

Recreational Reading

All students read books for approximately 30 minutes.

CONVERSATIONS
The teacher also reads silently. The teacher has some short conversations with readers. When appropriate, the main focus of these conversations is each student's ability to discuss the characters in the book he or she is reading.

CLIPBOARD NOTES
Teacher notes students' selections of books and whether they talk with friends about the behavior of characters.

READ-ALOUD BOOK
_____

Writing

Theme: Things to do or _____

MINI-LESSON
Tips on necessary information to include in advertisements. (Consider making advertisements for health exhibit or guest speaker) or _____.

COMPOSING
Write advertisements or _____.

SHARING
Volunteers share drafts of advertisements. Identify main ideas that are most obvious or _____.
   Papers are dated and filed.

Word Study

CHART DEVELOPMENT
Spelling Emphasis: *ee* or _____
Other Emphasis:
■ sentences or _____
■ public health or _____
   On the chart, the teacher lists sentences volunteered by students using:
■ *ee*
■ public health vocabulary
■ _____

WRITING
On their papers, students write their favorite words from the chart or other

words, phrases, or sentences that would be appropriate for the chart.

SPELLING
Partners call out words for each other to spell aloud.
   Papers are dated and filed.

HOMEWORK
Write about ways public health agencies help meet people's needs. Use some *ee* words.

Lesson 56

Research

LEAD-IN
Teacher introduces the Project Idea.
Topic: Public health or _____
Material: Health books or _____
Comprehension Skill: Classification or _____

SEARCH & RECORD
Group Size: Partners or _____
Project Idea: On index cards, write statements that give health advice. Organize the cards into groups that go together or _____.

SHARING
Volunteers tell the names of the categories into which they sorted their cards or _____.
Papers are dated and filed.

Recreational Reading

All students read books for approximately 30 minutes.

CONVERSATIONS
The teacher also reads silently. The teacher has some short conversations with readers. When appropriate, the main focus of these conversations is each student's ability to discuss the characters in the book he or she is reading.

CLIPBOARD NOTES
Teacher notes students' selections of books and whether they talk with friends about the behavior of characters.

READ-ALOUD BOOK
Piggybook by Anthony Browne or _____

Writing

Theme: Things to do or _____

MINI-LESSON
Demonstration of variety of sentence patterns or _____.

COMPOSING
Continue previous pieces or _____.

SHARING
Partners check each other's work to make sure sentence patterns are varied, especially to eliminate "and then . . . and then . . . and then" or _____.
Papers are dated and filed.

Word Study

CHART DEVELOPMENT
Spelling Emphasis: *ea* or _____

Other Emphasis:
- sentences or _____
- history or _____
  On the chart, the teacher lists sentences volunteered by students using:
- *ea*
- history vocabulary
- _____

WRITING
On their papers, students write their favorite words from the chart or other words, phrases, or sentences that would be appropriate for the chart.

SPELLING
Partners call out words for each other to spell aloud.
Papers are dated and filed.

HOMEWORK
Write sentences using the following words: breathe, defeat, deaf, and leaf.

155

Lesson 57

Research

LEAD-IN
Teacher introduces the Project Idea.
Topic: Public health or _____
Material: Encyclopedias and library books or _____
Comprehension Skill: Details or _____

SEARCH & RECORD
Group Size: 3 or 4 or _____
Project Idea: Find information about the career of a particular type of health professional and list facts about it or _____.

SHARING
Each group tells the three most interesting facts it found or _____.
    Papers are dated and filed.

Recreational Reading

All students read books for approximately 30 minutes.

CONVERSATIONS
The teacher also reads silently. The teacher has some short conversations with readers. When appropriate, the main focus of these conversations is each student's ability to discuss the characters in the book he or she is reading.

CLIPBOARD NOTES
Teacher notes students' selections of books and whether they talk with friends about the behavior of characters.

READ-ALOUD BOOK
_____

Writing

Theme: Things to do or _____

MINI-LESSON
Response group demonstrates asking writers good questions or _____.

COMPOSING
Continue previous drafts or _____.

SHARING
Response group members ask writers about their pieces or _____.
    Papers are dated and filed.

Word Study

CHART DEVELOPMENT
Spelling Emphasis: *oo* or _____

Other Emphasis:
■ sentences or _____
■ business or _____
    On the chart, the teacher lists sentences volunteered by students using:
■ *oo*
■ business vocabulary
■ _____

WRITING
On their papers, students write their favorite words from the chart or other words, phrases, or sentences that would be appropriate for the chart.

SPELLING
Partners call out words for each other to spell aloud.
    Papers are dated and filed.

HOMEWORK
Write sentences about your favorite businesses.

Lesson **58**

Research

LEAD-IN
Teacher introduces the Project Idea.
Topic: Public health or _____
Material: Newspapers or _____
Comprehension Skill: Sequence of events or _____

SEARCH & RECORD
Group Size: Partners or _____
Project Idea: Locate health-related story. List events in the story in sequence or _____.

SHARING
Show another team the events you chose or _____.
   Papers are dated and filed.

Recreational Reading

All students read books for approximately 30 minutes.

CONVERSATIONS
The teacher also reads silently. The teacher has some short conversations with readers. When appropriate, the main focus of these conversations is each student's ability to discuss the characters in the book he or she is reading.

CLIPBOARD NOTES
Teacher notes students' selections of books and whether they talk with friends about the behavior of characters.

READ-ALOUD BOOK
_____

Writing

Theme: Things to do or _____

MINI-LESSON
Tips for editing posters: focus on main idea, necessary details are included or _____.

COMPOSING
Complete and edit posters or _____.

SHARING
Partners help each other edit or _____.
   Papers are dated and filed.

Word Study

CHART DEVELOPMENT
Spelling Emphasis: *oa* or _____

Other Emphasis:
- sentences or _____
- education or _____
   On the chart, the teacher lists sentences volunteered by students using:
- *oa*
- education vocabulary
- _____

WRITING
On their papers, students write their favorite words from the chart or other words, phrases, or sentences that would be appropriate for the chart.

SPELLING
Partners call out words for each other to spell aloud.
   Papers are dated and filed.

HOMEWORK
Write sentences about your favorite things at school.

Lesson **59**

Research

LEAD-IN
Teacher introduces the Project Idea.
Topic: Public health or _____
Material: Health books or _____
Comprehension Skill: Comparison or _____

SEARCH & RECORD
Group Size: Partners or _____
Project Idea: Find two different health professionals in books. List ways they are alike and ways they are different or _____.

SHARING
Volunteers share comparisons with class or _____.
Papers are dated and filed.

Recreational Reading

All students read books for approximately 30 minutes.

CONVERSATIONS
The teacher also reads silently. The teacher has some short conversations with readers. When appropriate, the main focus of these conversations is each student's ability to discuss the characters in the book he or she is reading.

CLIPBOARD NOTES
Teacher notes students' selections of books and whether they talk with friends about the behavior of characters.

READ-ALOUD BOOK
The Ghost-Eye Tree by Bill Martin, Jr., and John Archambault or _____

Writing

Theme: Things to do or _____

MINI-LESSON
Ideas for appropriate lettering and colors for posters or _____.

COMPOSING
Make final poster or _____.

SHARING
Ask partner for help or _____.
Papers are dated and filed.

Word Study

CHART DEVELOPMENT
Spelling Emphasis: *oi* or _____
Other Emphasis:
- sentences or _____
- medicine or _____
On the chart, the teacher lists sentences volunteered by students using:
- *oi*
- medicine vocabulary
- _____

WRITING
On their papers, students write their favorite words from the chart or other

words, phrases, or sentences that would be appropriate for the chart.

SPELLING
Partners call out words for each other to spell aloud.
Papers are dated and filed.

HOMEWORK
Write a paragraph about good ideas for staying healthy.

Lesson **60**

Research

LEAD-IN
Teacher introduces the Project Idea.
Topic: Public health or _____
Material: Students choose or _____

Comprehension Skill: Main idea or _____

SEARCH & RECORD
Group Size: Individuals or partners or _____

Project Idea: Choose most important thing about public health to study. Write summary of new information found or _____.

SHARING
Volunteers share with class or _____.
   Papers are dated and filed.

Recreational Reading

All students read books for approximately 30 minutes.

CONVERSATIONS
The teacher also reads silently. The teacher has some short conversations with readers. When appropriate, the main focus of these conversations is each student's ability to discuss the characters in the book he or she is reading.

CLIPBOARD NOTES
Teacher notes students' selections of books and whether they talk with friends about the behavior of characters.

READ-ALOUD BOOK
Turtle in July by Marilyn Singer** or _____

Writing

Theme: Things to do or _____

MINI-LESSON
Instructions about displaying posters or _____.

COMPOSING
Complete poster or _____.

SHARING
Display posters or _____.
   Papers are dated and filed.

Word Study

CHART DEVELOPMENT
Spelling Emphasis: *ou* or _____

Other Emphasis:
- sentences or _____
- careers or _____
  On the chart, the teacher lists sentences volunteered by students using:
- *ou*
- career vocabulary
- _____

WRITING
On their papers, students write their favorite words from the chart or other words, phrases, or sentences that would be appropriate for the chart.

SPELLING
Partners call out words for each other to spell aloud.
   Papers are dated and filed.

HOMEWORK
Write a paragraph about careers that interest you. Use some *ou* words.

Lesson 61

Research

LEAD-IN
Teacher introduces the Project Idea.
Topic: Space or _____
Material: Textbooks or _____
Comprehension Skill: Details or
_____

SEARCH & RECORD
Group Size: Partners or _____
Project Idea: Partners look for names
of planets and list them, writing a fact
next to each or _____.

SHARING
Share with another team or _____.
   Papers are dated and filed.

Recreational Reading

All students read books for approximately
30 minutes.

CONVERSATIONS
The teacher also reads silently. The
teacher has some short conversations with
readers. When appropriate, the main
focus of these conversations is on each
student's assessment of his or her own
improvement as a reader.

CLIPBOARD NOTES
Teacher notes students' selections of
books and whether their reading interests
seem to be changing.

READ-ALOUD BOOK
Charlotte's Web by E. B. White* or
_____

Writing

The overall theme for the next 15 days is
Space, Holidays, or _____. One or
more of the other modules will reflect
these themes.
Theme: Space, Holidays, or _____

MINI-LESSON
Brainstorm list of ideas about space
(holidays) or _____.

COMPOSING
Write list of ideas about space (holidays)
or _____.

SHARING
Everyone shares best idea on list or
_____.
   Papers are dated and filed.

Word Study

CHART DEVELOPMENT
Spelling Emphasis: *ay* or
_____

Other Emphasis:
■ sentences or _____
■ holidays or _____
   On the chart, the teacher lists
sentences volunteered by students using:
■ *ay* words
■ holiday vocabulary
■ _____

WRITING
On their papers, students write their
favorite words from the chart or other
words, phrases, or sentences that would
be appropriate for the chart.

SPELLING
Partners call out words for each other to
spell aloud.
   Papers are dated and filed.

HOMEWORK
Write about games you hope you will play
during the holidays.

Research

LEAD-IN
Teacher introduces the Project Idea.
Topic: Space or _____
Material: Textbooks and encyclopedias
or _____
Comprehension Skill: Comparison
or _____

SEARCH & RECORD
Group Size: Partners or _____
Project Idea: Partners list ways
Earth and the rest of space are the same
and ways they are different from each
other or _____.

SHARING
Compare lists with another team or
_____.
    Papers are dated and filed.

Recreational Reading

All students read books for approximately
30 minutes.

CONVERSATIONS
The teacher also reads silently. The
teacher has some short conversations with
readers. When appropriate, the main
focus of these conversations is on each
student's assessment of his or her own
improvement as a reader.

CLIPBOARD NOTES
Teacher notes students' selections of
books and whether their reading interests
seem to be changing.

READ-ALOUD BOOK
_____

Writing

Theme: Space, Holidays, or _____

MINI-LESSON
Brainstorm list of ideas about traveling in
space (preparing for the holidays) or
_____

COMPOSING
Write list of ideas or _____.

SHARING
Talk about lists with partner or
_____.
    Papers are dated and filed.

Word Study

CHART DEVELOPMENT
Spelling Emphasis: *ey* or _____
Other Emphasis:
■ sentences or _____
▲ holidays or _____
    On the chart, the teacher lists
sentences volunteered by students using:
■ *ey* words
■ holiday vocabulary
■ _____

WRITING
On their papers, students write their
favorite words from the chart or other

words, phrases, or sentences that would
be appropriate for the chart.

SPELLING
Partners call out words for each other to
spell aloud.
    Papers are dated and filed.

HOMEWORK
Look in the *Yellow Pages* of the telephone
book and find names of restaurants that
contain the letter cluster *ey*.

161

Lesson **63**

Research

LEAD-IN
Teacher introduces the Project Idea.
Topic: Space or _____
Material: Catalogs or _____
Comprehension Skill: Cause and effect or _____

SEARCH & RECORD
Group Size: 3 or 4 or _____
Project Idea: Write a shopping list of things you would want if you were going to live in space or _____.

SHARING
Show another group your list. Tell why you chose each thing on the list or _____.

Papers are dated and filed.

Recreational Reading

All students read books for approximately 30 minutes.

CONVERSATIONS
The teacher also reads silently. The teacher has some short conversations with readers. When appropriate, the main focus of these conversations is on each student's assessment of his or her own improvement as a reader.

CLIPBOARD NOTES
Teacher notes students' selections of books and whether their reading interests seem to be changing.

READ-ALOUD BOOK
_____

Writing

Theme: Space, Holidays, or _____

MINI-LESSON
Choose an idea from a previous list to write more about or _____.

COMPOSING
Write first draft of piece about an idea on the list or _____.

SHARING
Volunteers share leads with class or _____.

Papers are dated and filed.

Word Study

CHART DEVELOPMENT
Spelling Emphasis: *aw* or _____

Other Emphasis:
■ sentences or _____
■ holidays or _____
 On the chart, the teacher lists sentences volunteered by students using:
■ *aw* words
■ holiday vocabulary
■ _____

WRITING
On their papers, students write their favorite words from the chart or other words, phrases, or sentences that would be appropriate for the chart.

SPELLING
Partners call out words for each other to spell aloud.
 Papers are dated and filed.

HOMEWORK
Write about holiday surprises in your family. Use some *aw* words.

162

Research

LEAD-IN
Teacher introduces the Project Idea.
Topic: Space or _____
Material: Textbooks or _____
Comprehension Skill: Study questions or _____

SEARCH & RECORD
Group Size: Individuals or partners or _____

Project Idea: Without looking in the textbook, list all the facts you know about space. Then write some questions about space. Use your text to find the answers and other information or _____.

SHARING
Show someone else what you found out or _____.
Papers are dated and filed.

Recreational Reading

All students read books for approximately 30 minutes.

CONVERSATIONS
The teacher also reads silently. The teacher has some short conversations with readers. When appropriate, the main focus of these conversations is on each student's assessment of his or her own improvement as a reader.

CLIPBOARD NOTES
Teacher notes students' selections of books and whether their reading interests seem to be changing.

READ-ALOUD BOOK
Heckedy Peg by Audrey Wood or _____

Writing

Theme: Space, Holidays, or _____

MINI-LESSON
Teacher shares factual information about space (holidays) or _____.

COMPOSING
Write response to factual information or _____.

SHARING
Volunteers share important ideas from their pieces or _____.
Papers are dated and filed.

Word Study

CHART DEVELOPMENT
Spelling Emphasis: *ar* or _____

Other Emphasis:
■ sentences or _____
■ holidays or _____
On the chart, the teacher lists sentences volunteered by students using:
■ *ar* words
■ holiday vocabulary
■ _____

WRITING
On their papers, students write their favorite words from the chart or other words, phrases, or sentences that would be appropriate for the chart.

SPELLING
Partners call out words for each other to spell aloud.
Papers are dated and filed.

HOMEWORK
Look in the telephone book and find 3-syllable words containing *ar*. Write them on a piece of paper.

Lesson 65

Research

LEAD-IN
Teacher introduces the Project Idea.
Topic: Space or _____
Material: Science and library books or _____

Comprehension Skill: Comparison or _____

SEARCH & RECORD
Group Size: 3 or 4 or _____
Project Idea: Find pictures of the planets and information about their sizes. Draw pictures of them and arrange them according to their sizes or _____.

SHARING
Each group reports to the class or _____.
  Papers are dated and filed.

Recreational Reading

All students read books for approximately 30 minutes.

CONVERSATIONS
The teacher also reads silently. The teacher has some short conversations with readers. When appropriate, the main focus of these conversations is on each student's assessment of his or her own improvement as a reader.

CLIPBOARD NOTES
Teacher notes students' selections of books and whether their reading interests seem to be changing.

READ-ALOUD BOOK
_____

Writing

Theme: Space, Holidays, or _____

MINI-LESSON
Teacher shares poem about space (holidays). Students discuss techniques that writers can learn from the poem, such as repetition, rhyme, etc. or _____

COMPOSING
Write draft of poem or _____.

SHARING
Partners share poems or _____.
  Papers are dated and filed.

Word Study

CHART DEVELOPMENT
Spelling Emphasis: _er_ or _____
Other Emphasis:
■ sentences or _____
■ holidays or _____
  On the chart, the teacher lists sentences volunteered by students using:
■ _er_ words
■ holiday vocabulary
■ _____

WRITING
On their papers, students write their favorite words from the chart or other

words, phrases, or sentences that would be appropriate for the chart.

SPELLING
Partners call out words for each other to spell aloud.
  Papers are dated and filed.

HOMEWORK
Write about holiday art. Use words with _er_.

Lesson 66

Research

LEAD-IN
Teacher introduces the Project Idea.
Topic: Space or _____
Material: Science and library books or _____

Comprehension Skill: Comparison or _____

SEARCH & RECORD
Group Size: Partners or _____
Project Idea: Choose 2 planets. Write a list of ways the planets are alike and a list of ways they are different or _____.

SHARING
Show another team your comparison or _____.

Papers are dated and filed.

Recreational Reading

All students read books for approximately 30 minutes.

CONVERSATIONS
The teacher also reads silently. The teacher has some short conversations with readers. When appropriate, the main focus of these conversations is on each student's assessment of his or her own improvement as a reader.

CLIPBOARD NOTES
Teacher notes students' selections of books and whether their reading interests seem to be changing.

READ-ALOUD BOOK
_____

Writing

Theme: Space, Holidays, or _____

MINI-LESSON
Demonstration of correct capitalization in writing about space (holidays) or _____.

COMPOSING
Continue earlier prose or _____.

SHARING
Partners proofread for correct capitalization or _____.
Papers are dated and filed.

Word Study

CHART DEVELOPMENT
Spelling Emphasis: *ir* or _____
Other Emphasis:
■ sentences or _____
■ holiday music or _____
   On the chart, the teacher lists sentences volunteered by students using:
■ *ir* words
■ holiday music vocabulary
■ _____

WRITING
On their papers, students write their favorite words from the chart or other

words, phrases, or sentences that would be appropriate for the chart.

SPELLING
Partners call out words for each other to spell aloud.
Papers are dated and filed.

HOMEWORK
Write about your favorite holiday song.

165

Lesson 67

Research

LEAD-IN
Teacher introduces the Project Idea.
Topic: Space or _____
Material: Library books or _____
Comprehension Skill: Cause and effect or _____

SEARCH & RECORD
Group Size: Partners or _____
Project Idea: Find pictures of astronauts. Write a list of ways their suits differ from your clothes or _____.

SHARING
Each team tells the class one of its observations or _____.
   Papers are dated and filed.

Recreational Reading

All students read books for approximately 30 minutes.

CONVERSATIONS
The teacher also reads silently. The teacher has some short conversations with readers. When appropriate, the main focus of these conversations is on each student's assessment of his or her own improvement as a reader.

CLIPBOARD NOTES
Teacher notes students' selections of books and whether their reading interests seem to be changing.

READ-ALOUD BOOK
King Bidgood's in the Bathtub by Audrey Wood or _____

Writing

Theme: Space, Holidays, or _____

MINI-LESSON
Students review lists of books they have read or _____.

COMPOSING
Write about a book you have read lately or _____.

SHARING
Response groups share write-ups about books or _____.
   Papers are dated and filed.

Word Study

CHART DEVELOPMENT
Spelling Emphasis: *ur* or _____

Other Emphasis:
■ sentences or _____
■ holiday business or _____
   On the chart, the teacher lists sentences volunteered by students using:
■ *ur* words
■ holiday business vocabulary
■ _____

WRITING
On their papers, students write their favorite words from the chart or other words, phrases, or sentences that would be appropriate for the chart.

SPELLING
Partners call out words for each other to spell aloud.
   Papers are dated and filed.

HOMEWORK
Write about a holiday shopping trip.

Lesson **68**

Research

LEAD-IN
Teacher introduces the Project Idea.
Topic: Space or _____.
Material: Magazines or _____.
Comprehension Skill: Comparison
or _____.

SEARCH & RECORD
Group Size: 3 or 4 or _____.
Project Idea: Cut out pictures of
items that could not be used in space the
way you use them at home. Organize
them in groups and glue on a poster or
_____.

SHARING
Display posters or _____.
 Papers are dated and filed.

Recreational Reading

All students read books for approximately
30 minutes.

CONVERSATIONS
The teacher also reads silently. The
teacher has some short conversations with
readers. When appropriate, the main
focus of these conversations is on each
student's assessment of his or her own
improvement as a reader.

CLIPBOARD NOTES
Teacher notes students' selections of
books and whether their reading interests
seem to be changing.

READ-ALOUD BOOK
_____

Writing

Theme: Holidays or _____.

MINI-LESSON
Brainstorm ideas for writings that could
be used as gifts for special people during
the holidays, for example, anthologies of
student writing, gift certificates for chores
to be done throughout the year, etc., or
_____.

COMPOSING
Begin draft of gift project or _____.

SHARING
Everyone tells partner what the person
who will receive the gift especially likes
or _____.
 Papers are dated and filed.

Word Study

CHART DEVELOPMENT
Spelling Emphasis: *ew* or
_____

Other Emphasis:
■ sentences or _____
■ holiday messages or _____
 On the chart, the teacher lists
sentences volunteered by students using:
■ *ew* words
■ holiday message vocabulary
■ _____

WRITING
On their papers, students write their
favorite words from the chart or other
words, phrases, or sentences that would
be appropriate for the chart.

SPELLING
Partners call out words for each other to
spell aloud.
 Papers are dated and filed.

HOMEWORK
Write some holiday messages.

Lesson **69**

Research

LEAD-IN
Teacher introduces the Project Idea.
Topic: Space or _____
Material: Magazines or _____
Comprehension Skill: Cause and effect or _____

SEARCH & RECORD
Group Size: Partners or _____
Project Idea: Cut out pictures that show gravity at work. Write sentences to explain how you can tell gravity is working or _____.

SHARING
Show another team your pictures and explain what you know about gravity or _____.

Papers are dated and filed.

Recreational Reading

All students read books for approximately 30 minutes.

CONVERSATIONS
The teacher also reads silently. The teacher has some short conversations with readers. When appropriate, the main focus of these conversations is on each student's assessment of his or her own improvement as a reader.

CLIPBOARD NOTES
Teacher notes students' selections of books and whether their reading interests seem to be changing.

READ-ALOUD BOOK
_____

Writing

Theme: Holidays or _____

MINI-LESSON
Teacher leads discussion about audience. Will the person who receives the gift like it? or _____.

COMPOSING
Continue project or _____.

SHARING
Tell partner why you think the person who receives your writing will like it or _____.

Papers are dated and filed.

Word Study

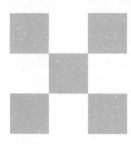

CHART DEVELOPMENT
Spelling Emphasis: *ow* or _____

Other Emphasis:
- sentences or _____
- holiday food or _____
  On the chart, the teacher lists sentences volunteered by students using:
- *ow* words
- holiday food vocabulary
- _____

WRITING
On their papers, students write their favorite words from the chart or other words, phrases, or sentences that would be appropriate for the chart.

SPELLING
Partners call out words for each other to spell aloud.
Papers are dated and filed.

HOMEWORK
Write a list of your favorite holiday foods. Write directions for making your most favorite.

Research

LEAD-IN
Teacher introduces the Project Idea.
Topic: Space or _____
Material: Science and library books or

_____

Comprehension Skill: Main idea or

_____

SEARCH & RECORD
Group Size: Individuals or _____
Project Idea: Study information that
is new to you. Draw a picture and write
notes to tell the most important thing you
found out or _____.

SHARING
Show a friend what you found out or

_____.

Papers are dated and filed.

Recreational Reading

All students read books for approximately
30 minutes.

CONVERSATIONS
The teacher also reads silently. The
teacher has some short conversations with
readers. When appropriate, the main
focus of these conversations is on each
student's assessment of his or her own
improvement as a reader.

CLIPBOARD NOTES
Teacher notes students' selections of
books and whether their reading interests
seem to be changing.

READ-ALOUD BOOK
Ira Says Goodbye by Bernard Waber or

_____

Writing

Theme: Holidays or _____

MINI-LESSON
Review suggestions for neat handwriting
or _____.

COMPOSING
Continue preparation of gift or

_____.

SHARING
Partners show each other how they are
improving their handwriting or

_____.

Papers are dated and filed.

Word Study

CHART DEVELOPMENT
Spelling Emphasis: *igh* or _____

_____

Other Emphasis:
- sentences or _____
- holiday memories or _____
  On the chart, the teacher lists
sentences volunteered by students using:
- *igh* words
- holiday memory vocabulary
- _____

WRITING
On their papers, students write their
favorite words from the chart or other
words, phrases, or sentences that would
be appropriate for the chart.

SPELLING
Partners call out words for each other to
spell aloud.
  Papers are dated and filed.

HOMEWORK
Write a story about something you
remember from last year's holidays.

Lesson 71

Research

LEAD-IN
Teacher introduces the Project Idea.
Topic: Holidays or _____
Material: Catalogs or _____
Comprehension Skill: Comparison
or _____

SEARCH & RECORD
Group Size: Partners or _____
Project Idea: Cut out pictures of five
items you would like to receive for the
holidays. Glue the pictures on a poster.
Write a description and the price next to
each or _____.

SHARING
Display posters or _____.
    Papers are dated and filed.

Recreational Reading

All students read books for approximately
30 minutes.

CONVERSATIONS
The teacher also reads silently. The
teacher has some short conversations with
readers. When appropriate, the main
focus of these conversations is on each
student's criteria for choosing a book.

CLIPBOARD NOTES
Teacher notes students' selections of
books.

READ-ALOUD BOOK
_____

Writing

Theme: Holidays or _____

MINI-LESSON
Teacher reviews strategies for checking
spelling while editing or _____.

COMPOSING
Edit piece. Pay special attention to
spelling or _____.

SHARING
Partners proofread each other's drafts for
spelling or _____.
    Papers are dated and filed.

Word Study

CHART DEVELOPMENT
Spelling Emphasis: *cc* or _____
Other Emphasis:
■ sentences or _____
■ health or _____
    On the chart, the teacher lists
sentences volunteered by students using:
■ *cc* words
■ health vocabulary
■ _____

WRITING
On their papers, students write their
favorite words from the chart or other

words, phrases, or sentences that would
be appropriate for the chart.

SPELLING
Partners call out words for each other to
spell aloud.
    Papers are dated and filed.

HOMEWORK
Write sentences giving your opinion about
using tobacco.

Research

LEAD-IN
Teacher introduces the Project Idea.
Topic: Holidays or _____
Material: Newspapers or _____
Comprehension Skill: Classifying or
_____

SEARCH & RECORD
Group Size: Partners or _____
Project Idea: Cut out pictures of
holiday symbols. Organize them into
groups and glue them on a poster. Write
a label for each group or _____.

SHARING
Display posters or _____.
　Papers are dated and filed.

Recreational Reading

All students read books for approximately
30 minutes.

CONVERSATIONS
The teacher also reads silently. The
teacher has some short conversations with
readers. When appropriate, the main
focus of these conversations is on each
student's criteria for choosing a book.

CLIPBOARD NOTES
Teacher notes students' selections of
books.

READ-ALOUD BOOK
_____

Writing

Theme: Holidays or _____

MINI-LESSON
Suggestions about gift wrapping or
_____.

COMPOSING
Recopy final draft. Prepare piece for
wrapping or _____.

SHARING
Share completed gifts before wrapping or
_____.
　Papers are dated and filed.

Word Study

CHART DEVELOPMENT
Spelling Emphasis: *ff* or _____
Other Emphasis:
■ sentences or _____
■ history or _____
　On the chart, the teacher lists
sentences volunteered by students using:
■ *ff* words
■ history vocabulary
■ _____

WRITING
On their papers, students write their
favorite words from the chart or other

words, phrases, or sentences that would
be appropriate for the chart.

SPELLING
Partners call out words for each other to
spell aloud.
　Papers are dated and filed.

HOMEWORK
Look in the newspaper for 3-syllable
words containing the letters *ff*. Write
them on a piece of paper.

Lesson 73

Research

LEAD-IN
Teacher introduces the Project Idea.
Topic: Holidays or _____
Material: Magazines or _____
Comprehension Skill: Main idea or _____

SEARCH & RECORD
Group Size: Partners or _____
Project Idea: Choose one picture that shows a holiday event. Write sentences to tell the main idea of the picture or _____.

SHARING
Tell another team about your picture or _____.
    Papers are dated and filed.

Recreational Reading

All students read books for approximately 30 minutes.

CONVERSATIONS
The teacher also reads silently. The teacher has some short conversations with readers. When appropriate, the main focus of these conversations is on each student's criteria for choosing a book.

CLIPBOARD NOTES
Teacher notes students' selections of books.

READ-ALOUD BOOK
The Polar Express by Chris Van Allsburg or _____

Writing

Theme: Holidays or _____

MINI-LESSON
Teacher demonstrates letter format or _____.

COMPOSING
Write a letter to someone important whom you will not see during the holidays or _____.

SHARING
Edit, publish, and mail the letter or _____.
    Papers are dated and filed.

Word Study

CHART DEVELOPMENT
Spelling Emphasis: *mm* or _____

Other Emphasis:
- sentences or _____
- education or _____
  On the chart, the teacher lists sentences volunteered by students using:
- *mm* words
- education vocabulary
- _____

WRITING
On their papers, students write their favorite words from the chart or other words, phrases, or sentences that would be appropriate for the chart.

SPELLING
Partners call out words for each other to spell aloud.
    Papers are dated and filed.

HOMEWORK
Write a summary of a television program you have seen.

Research

LEAD-IN
Teacher introduces the Project Idea.
Topic: Holidays or _____
Material: Old holiday greeting cards or _____

Comprehension Skill: Cause and effect or _____

SEARCH & RECORD
Group Size: Partners or _____
Project Idea: Study old cards and take notes. Decide who would like each card and write your reasons down or _____.

SHARING
Show partner your cards and your decisions or _____.
    Papers are dated and filed.

Recreational Reading

All students read books for approximately 30 minutes.

CONVERSATIONS
The teacher also reads silently. The teacher has some short conversations with readers. When appropriate, the main focus of these conversations is on each student's criteria for choosing a book.

CLIPBOARD NOTES
Teacher notes students' selections of books.

READ-ALOUD BOOK

_____

Writing

Theme: Holidays or _____

MINI-LESSON
Teacher demonstrates use of rhymes or _____.

COMPOSING
Write songs or poems for holidays or _____.

SHARING
Response groups share poems or _____.
    Papers are dated and filed.

Word Study

CHART DEVELOPMENT
Spelling Emphasis: *ll* or _____
Other Emphasis:
- sentences or _____
- agriculture or _____
    On the chart, the teacher lists sentences volunteered by students using:
- *ll* words
- agriculture vocabulary
- _____

WRITING
On their papers, students write their favorite words from the chart or other

words, phrases, or sentences that would be appropriate for the chart.

SPELLING
Partners call out words for each other to spell aloud.
    Papers are dated and filed.

HOMEWORK
Draw a picture of a lollipop. If lollipops could be grown, how would you grow them? Write a story about what you would do.

Lesson 75

Research

LEAD-IN
Teacher introduces the Project Idea.
Topic: Holidays or _____
Material: Newspapers or _____
Comprehension Skill: Sequence of events or _____

SEARCH & RECORD
Group Size: Partners or _____
Project Idea: Find information in the newspaper about events that happen before the holiday. Then find information about the holiday. Last, find information about something that happens after the holiday. Write notes or _____.

SHARING
Tell another team what you found out or _____.
   Papers are dated and filed.

Recreational Reading

All students read books for approximately 30 minutes.

CONVERSATIONS
The teacher also reads silently. The teacher has some short conversations with readers. When appropriate, the main focus of these conversations is on each student's criteria for choosing a book.

CLIPBOARD NOTES
Teacher notes students' selections of books.

READ-ALOUD BOOK
The Year of the Perfect Christmas Tree by Gloria Houston or _____

Writing

Theme: Holidays or _____

MINI-LESSON
Teacher leads discussion of ideas for holiday greetings or _____.

COMPOSING
Write holiday cards or _____.

SHARING
Edit, publish, and deliver cards or _____.
   Papers are dated and filed.

Word Study

CHART DEVELOPMENT
Spelling Emphasis: *ss* or _____
Other Emphasis:
- sentences or _____
- world news or _____
On the chart, the teacher lists sentences volunteered by students using:
- *ss* words
- world news vocabulary
- _____

WRITING
On their papers, students write their favorite words from the chart or other words, phrases, or sentences that would be appropriate for the chart.

SPELLING
Partners call out words for each other to spell aloud.
   Papers are dated and filed.

HOMEWORK
Write about the news story you think is most interesting.

Research

LEAD-IN
Teacher introduces the Project Idea.
Topic: Energy or _____
Material: Magazines or _____
Comprehension Skill: Main idea or
_____

SEARCH & RECORD
Group Size: 3 or 4 or _____
Project Idea: Cut out pictures related
to energy. Paste pictures on poster and
write captions for them or _____.

SHARING
Display posters or _____.
  Papers are dated and filed.

Recreational Reading

All students read books for approximately
30 minutes.

CONVERSATIONS
The teacher also reads silently. The
teacher has some short conversations with
readers. When appropriate, the main
focus of these conversations is on each
student's criteria for choosing a book.

CLIPBOARD NOTES
Teacher notes students' selections of
books.

READ-ALOUD BOOK
_____

Writing

The overall theme for the next 15 days is
Energy or _____. One or more of the
other modules will reflect this theme.
Theme: Energy or _____

MINI-LESSON
Brainstorm list of ideas about energy,
especially about where it comes from or
_____.

COMPOSING
Write list of ideas about energy or
_____.

SHARING
Everyone shares best idea on his or her
list or _____.
  Papers are dated and filed.

Word Study

CHART DEVELOPMENT
Spelling Emphasis: *bb* or _____

Other Emphasis:
■ sentences or _____
■ business or _____
  On the chart, the teacher lists
sentences volunteered by students using:
■ *bb* words
■ business vocabulary
■ _____

WRITING
On their papers, students write their
favorite words from the chart or other
words, phrases, or sentences that would
be appropriate for the chart.

SPELLING
Partners call out words for each other to
spell aloud.
  Papers are dated and filed.

HOMEWORK
Write a list of words that have double
consonants.

Lesson 77

Research

LEAD-IN
Teacher introduces the Project Idea.
Topic: Energy or _____
Material: Science books or _____
Comprehension Skill: Cause and
effect or _____

SEARCH & RECORD
Group Size: Partners or _____
Project Idea: Look for information
about energy. Write list of ways it is used
or _____.

SHARING
Tell another team about the things on
your list or _____.
   Papers are dated and filed.

Recreational Reading

All students read books for approximately
30 minutes.

CONVERSATIONS
The teacher also reads silently. The
teacher has some short conversations with
readers. When appropriate, the main
focus of these conversations is on each
student's criteria for choosing a book.

CLIPBOARD NOTES
Teacher notes students' selections of
books.

READ-ALOUD BOOK
_____

Writing

Theme: Energy or _____

MINI-LESSON
Brainstorm list of ways energy is used or
_____.

COMPOSING
Write list of ways energy is used or
_____.

SHARING
Everyone shares most important ways
energy is used or _____.
   Papers are dated and filed.

Word Study

CHART DEVELOPMENT
Spelling Emphasis: *dd* or
_____

Other Emphasis:
- sentences or _____
- communication or _____
   On the chart, the teacher lists
sentences volunteered by students using:
- *dd* words
- communication vocabulary
- _____

WRITING
On their papers, students write their
favorite words from the chart or other
words, phrases, or sentences that would
be appropriate for the chart.

SPELLING
Partners call out words for each other to
spell aloud.
   Papers are dated and filed.

HOMEWORK
Look at a television schedule for words
that contain *dd*. Write them on a piece of
paper.

S u c c e s **S** u c c e s **S** u c c e s **S** u c c e s **S** u c c e s **S** u c c e s **S** u c c e s **S** u c c e **S**

Lesson **78**

Research

LEAD-IN
Teacher introduces the Project Idea.
Topic: Energy or _____
Material: Science books or _____
Comprehension Skill: Cause and effect or _____

SEARCH & RECORD
Group Size: Partners or _____
Project Idea: Look for information about energy. Write a list of ways energy is produced or _____ .

SHARING
Tell another team what you found or _____ .

   Papers are dated and filed.

Recreational Reading

All students read books for approximately 30 minutes.

CONVERSATIONS
The teacher also reads silently. The teacher has some short conversations with readers. When appropriate, the main focus of these conversations is on each student's criteria for choosing a book.

CLIPBOARD NOTES
Teacher notes students' selections of books.

READ-ALOUD BOOK
The Paperbag Princess by Robert Munsch or _____

Writing

Theme: Energy or _____

MINI-LESSON
Students review lists from previous days to choose an idea about which to write more or _____ .

COMPOSING
Begin draft based on an idea from list or _____ .

SHARING
Everyone shares his or her topic or _____ .

   Papers are dated and filed.

Word Study

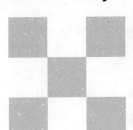

CHART DEVELOPMENT
Spelling Emphasis: *gg* or

_____
Other Emphasis:
■ sentences or _____
■ medicine or _____
   On the chart, the teacher lists sentences volunteered by students using:
■ *gg* words
■ medicine vocabulary
■ _____

WRITING
On their papers, students write their favorite words from the chart or other words, phrases, or sentences that would be appropriate for the chart.

SPELLING
Partners call out words for each other to spell aloud.
   Papers are dated and filed.

HOMEWORK
Look for words in the newspaper that have double consonants. Write them on a piece of paper.

Lesson 79

Research

LEAD-IN
Teacher introduces the Project Idea.
Topic: Energy or _____
Material: Newspapers or _____
Comprehension Skill: Details or _____

SEARCH & RECORD
Group Size: Partners or _____
Project Idea: Find an article related to energy. Write questions that can be answered by reading the article or _____.

SHARING
Trade articles and questions with your partner. Find the answers to your partner's questions or _____.
  Papers are dated and filed.

Recreational Reading

All students read books for approximately 30 minutes.

CONVERSATIONS
The teacher also reads silently. The teacher has some short conversations with readers. When appropriate, the main focus of these conversations is on each student's criteria for choosing a book.

CLIPBOARD NOTES
Teacher notes students' selections of books.

READ-ALOUD BOOK
_____

Writing

Theme: Energy or _____

MINI-LESSON
Teacher shares factual information about energy or _____.

COMPOSING
Students write journal entry about facts presented by teacher or _____.

SHARING
Volunteers review important information or _____.
  Papers are dated and filed.

Word Study

CHART DEVELOPMENT
Spelling Emphasis: *tt* or _____
Other Emphasis:
▪ sentences or _____
▪ local news or _____
  On the chart, the teacher lists sentences volunteered by students using:
▪ *tt* words
▪ local news vocabulary
▪ _____

WRITING
On their papers, students write their favorite words from the chart or other

words, phrases, or sentences that would be appropriate for the chart.

SPELLING
Partners call out words for each other to spell aloud.
  Papers are dated and filed.

HOMEWORK
Write about the news you learned today.

Research

LEAD-IN
Teacher introduces the Project Idea.
Topic: Energy or _____
Material: Magazines or _____
Comprehension Skill: Classification
or _____

SEARCH & RECORD
Group Size: 3 or 4 or _____
Project Idea: Find pictures of energy
being used. Classify according to where
energy is being used: at home, at work, at
play, for travel, etc. Glue to poster or
_____.

SHARING
Display posters or _____.
Papers are dated and filed.

Recreational Reading

All students read books for approximately
30 minutes.

CONVERSATIONS
The teacher also reads silently. The
teacher has some short conversations with
readers. When appropriate, the main
focus of these conversations is on each
student's criteria for choosing a book.

CLIPBOARD NOTES
Teacher notes students' selections of
books.

READ-ALOUD BOOK
_____

Writing

Theme: Energy or _____

MINI-LESSON
Teacher demonstrates model for writing a
poem, such as an acrostic or _____.

COMPOSING
Students include some of the facts they
know about energy in drafts of poems or
_____.

SHARING
Partners share drafts or _____.
Papers are dated and filed.

Word Study

CHART DEVELOPMENT
Spelling Emphasis: *si* or _____
Other Emphasis:
■ paragraphs or _____
■ literature or _____
   On the chart, the teacher writes a
paragraph of sentences volunteered by
students using:
■ *si* words
■ literature vocabulary
■ _____

WRITING
On their papers, students write their
favorite words from the chart and other
words, phrases, or sentences that would
be appropriate for the chart.

SPELLING
Partners call out words for each other to
spell aloud.
   Papers are dated and filed.

HOMEWORK
Write a paragraph about your favorite
book.

Lesson 81

Research

LEAD-IN
Teacher introduces the Project Idea.
Topic: Energy or _____
Material: Magazines or _____
Comprehension Skill: Cause and
effect or _____

SEARCH & RECORD
Group Size: 3 or 4 or _____
Project Idea: Make a poster using
magazine pictures to show how to
conserve energy or _____.

SHARING
Explain to the class how each picture
represents wasting or saving energy or
_____.
  Papers are dated and filed.

Recreational Reading

All students read books for approximately
30 minutes.

CONVERSATIONS
The teacher also reads silently. The
teacher has some short conversations with
readers. When appropriate, the main
focus of these conversations is on making
inferences.

CLIPBOARD NOTES
Teacher notes students' selections of
books and whether students seem to be
calling words without getting meanings.

READ-ALOUD BOOK
Cinderella by Barbara Karlin or
_____

Writing

Theme: Energy or _____

MINI-LESSON
Teacher leads discussion of details to
include in factual pieces: who, what,
where, when, and why or _____.

COMPOSING
Continue earlier draft or _____.

SHARING
Individuals share drafts with class or
_____.
  Papers are dated and filed.

Word Study

CHART DEVELOPMENT
Spelling Emphasis: *re* or _____
Other Emphasis:
- paragraphs or _____
- literature or _____
  On the chart, the teacher writes a
paragraph of sentences volunteered by
students using:
- *re* words
- literature vocabulary
- _____

WRITING
On their papers, students write their
favorite words from the chart or other
words, phrases, or sentences that would
be appropriate for the chart.

SPELLING
Partners call out words for each other to
spell aloud.
  Papers are dated and filed.

HOMEWORK
Write a poem using as many words as
possible that contain the letters *re*.

Lesson **82**

Research

LEAD-IN
Teacher introduces the Project Idea.
Topic: Energy or _____
Material: Encyclopedias or _____
Comprehension Skill: Reference skills or _____

SEARCH & RECORD
Group Size: Partners or _____
Project Idea: Find facts related to energy. Record most important information you find or _____.

SHARING
Volunteers tell the class the most interesting information they found or
_____.
  Papers are dated and filed.

Recreational Reading

All students read books for approximately 30 minutes.

CONVERSATIONS
The teacher also reads silently. The teacher has some short conversations with readers. When appropriate, the main focus of these conversations is on making inferences.

CLIPBOARD NOTES
Teacher notes students' selections of books and whether students seem to be calling words without getting meanings.

READ-ALOUD BOOK
_____

Writing

Theme: Energy or _____

MINI-LESSON
Students review lists of books they have read or _____.

COMPOSING
Write journal entry about a book recently read or _____.

SHARING
Response groups share entries about books or _____.
  Papers are dated and filed.

Word Study

CHART DEVELOPMENT
Spelling Emphasis: *it* or _____
Other Emphasis:
- paragraphs or _____
- art or _____
  On the chart, the teacher writes a paragraph of sentences volunteered by students using:
- *it* words
- art vocabulary
- _____

WRITING
On their papers, students write their favorite words from the chart and other words, phrases, or sentences that would be appropriate for the chart.

SPELLING
Partners call out words for each other to spell aloud.
  Papers are dated and filed.

HOMEWORK
Describe your last art project using as many words as possible that contain the letters *it*.

Lesson 83

Research

LEAD-IN
Teacher introduces the Project Idea.
Topic: Energy or _____
Material: Magazines or _____
Comprehension Skill: Sequence of events or _____

SEARCH & RECORD
Group Size: 3 or 4 or _____
Project Idea: Cut out pictures about energy. Arrange them in an order that tells a story about energy. Glue them to poster or _____.

SHARING
Tell your story to another group. Display posters or _____.
Papers are dated and filed.

Recreational Reading

All students read books for approximately 30 minutes.

CONVERSATIONS
The teacher also reads silently. The teacher has some short conversations with readers. When appropriate, the main focus of these conversations is on making inferences.

CLIPBOARD NOTES
Teacher notes students' selections of books and whether students seem to be calling words without getting meanings.

READ-ALOUD BOOK
How to Eat Fried Worms by Thomas Rockwell* or _____

Writing

Theme: Energy or _____

MINI-LESSON
Discussion of how to write plan for doing a science fair project or _____.

COMPOSING
Write plan for science fair project, including purpose, supplies, procedures, and ideas for presentation or _____

SHARING
Partners discuss ideas or _____.
Papers are dated and filed.

Word Study

CHART DEVELOPMENT
Spelling Emphasis: *ck* or _____

Other Emphasis:
- paragraphs or _____
- music or _____
On the chart, the teacher writes a paragraph of sentences volunteered by students using:
- *ck* words
- music vocabulary
- _____

WRITING
On their papers, students write their favorite words from the chart or other words, phrases, or sentences that would be appropriate for the chart.

SPELLING
Partners call out words for each other to spell aloud.
Papers are dated and filed.

HOMEWORK
Listen to a favorite song. Write words from the song that contain the letters *ck*. What other words can you think of that have *ck*?

Research

LEAD-IN
Teacher introduces the Project Idea.
Topic: Energy or _____
Material: Magazines or _____
Comprehension Skill: Comparison or _____

SEARCH & RECORD
Group Size: Partners or _____
Project Idea: Cut out pictures of two kinds of transportation that use energy. Write lists of ways they are alike and ways they are different or _____.

SHARING
Show your comparisons to another team or _____.
   Papers are dated and filed.

Recreational Reading

All students read books for approximately 30 minutes.

CONVERSATIONS
The teacher also reads silently. The teacher has some short conversations with readers. When appropriate, the main focus of these conversations is on making inferences.

CLIPBOARD NOTES
Teacher notes students' selections of books and whether students seem to be calling words without getting meanings.

READ-ALOUD BOOK
_____

Writing

Theme: Energy or _____

MINI-LESSON
Discussion of techniques for keeping notes and recording data or _____

COMPOSING
Write drafts of ways to record information for science fair project or _____.

SHARING
Partners share note-taking plans or _____.
   Papers are dated and filed.

Word Study

CHART DEVELOPMENT
Spelling Emphasis: *on* or _____

Other Emphasis:
■ paragraphs or _____
■ ecology or _____
   On the chart, the teacher writes a paragraph of sentences volunteered by students using:
■ *on* words
■ ecology vocabulary
■ _____

WRITING
On their papers, students write their favorite words from the chart or other words, phrases, or sentences that would be appropriate for the chart.

SPELLING
Partners call out words for each other to spell aloud.
   Papers are dated and filed.

HOMEWORK
In 5 minutes, write as many words as you can that contain the letters *on*.

Lesson 85

Research

LEAD-IN
Teacher introduces the Project Idea.
Topic: Energy or _____
Material: Students choose or

_____

Comprehension Skill: Main idea or

_____

SEARCH & RECORD
Group Size: Individuals or partners or

_____

Project Idea: Search for new and
important information you didn't know
about energy. Write notes about what you
find out or _____.

SHARING
Volunteers tell class what they learned or

_____.
Papers are dated and filed.

Recreational Reading

All students read books for approximately
30 minutes.

CONVERSATIONS
The teacher also reads silently. The
teacher has some short conversations with
readers. When appropriate, the main
focus of these conversations is on making
inferences.

CLIPBOARD NOTES
Teacher notes students' selections of
books and whether students seem to be
calling words without getting meanings.

READ-ALOUD BOOK

_____

Writing

Theme: Energy or _____

MINI-LESSON
Demonstration of making notes of
observations during science projects or

_____.

COMPOSING
Write observation notes of actual project
or of classroom phenomena or _____.

SHARING
Response groups share observation notes
or _____.
Papers are dated and filed.

Word Study

CHART DEVELOPMENT
Spelling Emphasis: *en* or

_____

Other Emphasis:
- paragraphs or _____
- mathematics or _____
  On the chart, the teacher writes a
paragraph of sentences volunteered by
students using:
- *en* words
- mathematics vocabulary
- _____

WRITING
On their papers, students write their
favorite words from the chart or other
words, phrases, or sentences that would
be appropriate for the chart.

SPELLING
Partners call out words for each other to
spell aloud.
Papers are dated and filed.

HOMEWORK
Look in your math book and find words
containing the letters *en*. Write them on a
piece of paper.

Research

LEAD-IN
Teacher introduces the Project Idea.
Topic: Transportation or _____
Material: Newspapers or _____
Comprehension Skill: Main idea or
_____

SEARCH & RECORD
Group Size: Partners or _____
Project Idea: Cut out pictures of
different kinds of transportation. Glue on
poster and write captions to tell the main
thing about each picture or _____

SHARING
Display posters or _____.
   Papers are dated and filed.

Recreational Reading

All students read books for approximately
30 minutes.

CONVERSATIONS
The teacher also reads silently. The
teacher has some short conversations with
readers. When appropriate, the main
focus of these conversations is on making
inferences.

CLIPBOARD NOTES
Teacher notes students' selections of
books and whether students seem to be
calling words without getting meanings.

READ-ALOUD BOOK
Princess Furball by Charlotte Huck or
_____

Writing

Theme: Energy or _____

MINI-LESSON
Teacher leads discussion of importance of
including events in correct sequence,
especially when describing procedures or
_____.

COMPOSING
Continue writing about science fair
project or other classroom observation or
_____.

SHARING
Partners check sequence of events or

   Papers are dated and filed.

Word Study

CHART DEVELOPMENT
Spelling Emphasis: *gh* or
_____

Other Emphasis:
■ paragraphs or _____
■ transportation or _____
   On the chart, the teacher writes a
paragraph of sentences volunteered by
students using:
■ *gh* words
■ transportation vocabulary
■ _____

WRITING
On their papers, students write their
favorite words from the chart or other
words, phrases, or sentences that would
be appropriate for the chart.

SPELLING
Partners call out words for each other to
spell aloud.
   Papers are dated and filed.

HOMEWORK
Look in your science book for words
containing the letters *gh*. Write them on
a piece of paper.

185

Lesson 87

Research

LEAD-IN
Teacher introduces the Project Idea.
Topic: Transportation or _____
Material: Social studies books or
_____

Comprehension Skill: Cause and
effect or _____

SEARCH & RECORD
Group Size: Partners or _____
Project Idea: Write a list of different
climates and lands. Describe the most
useful transportation for each or
_____.

SHARING
Tell another team why your transportation plans are most appropriate for each
place or _____.
Papers are dated and filed.

Recreational Reading

All students read books for approximately
30 minutes.

CONVERSATIONS
The teacher also reads silently. The
teacher has some short conversations with
readers. When appropriate, the main
focus of these conversations is on making
inferences.

CLIPBOARD NOTES
Teacher notes students' selections of
books and whether students seem to be
calling words without getting meanings.

READ-ALOUD BOOK
_____

Writing

Theme: Energy or _____

MINI-LESSON
Teacher leads discussion of ways to help
writers identify incomplete or omitted
information in reports or _____.

COMPOSING
Continue science fair report or
_____.

SHARING
Response groups look for omissions in
each other's reports or _____.
Papers are dated and filed.

Word Study

CHART DEVELOPMENT
Spelling Emphasis: *cy* or _____
Other Emphasis:
- paragraphs or _____
- transportation or _____
  On the chart, the teacher writes a
paragraph of sentences volunteered by
students using:
- *cy* words
- transportation vocabulary
- _____

WRITING
On their papers, students write their
favorite words from the chart or other
words, phrases, sentences that would be
appropriate for the chart.

SPELLING
Partners call out words for each other to
spell aloud.
Papers are dated and filed.

HOMEWORK
Write about what you learned about
transportation today.

Lesson 88

Research

LEAD-IN
Teacher introduces the Project Idea.
Topic: Transportation or _____
Material: Maps or _____
Comprehension Skill: Sequence of events or _____

SEARCH & RECORD
Group Size: Partners or _____
Project Idea: Use a map to write an itinerary for a trip that would require travel in boats, airplanes, and cars, or _____.

SHARING
Show your trip to another team. Starting at the beginning of the trip, point out where you'd need to take different kinds of transportation or _____.
Papers are dated and filed.

Recreational Reading

All students read books for approximately 30 minutes.

CONVERSATIONS
The teacher also reads silently. The teacher has some short conversations with readers. When appropriate, the main focus of these conversations is on making inferences.

CLIPBOARD NOTES
Teacher notes students' selections of books and whether students seem to be calling words without getting meanings.

READ-ALOUD BOOK
A Frog Prince by Alix Berenzy or _____

Writing

Theme: Energy or _____

MINI-LESSON
Teacher demonstrates use of charts, graphs, and illustrations in scientific reports or _____.

COMPOSING
Add appropriate charts, graphs, or illustrations to your science report or _____.

SHARING
Response groups examine writers' use of charts, graphs, and illustrations or _____.
Papers are dated and filed.

Word Study

CHART DEVELOPMENT
Spelling Emphasis: *es* or _____
Other Emphasis:
- paragraphs or _____
- transportation or _____
On the chart, the teacher writes a paragraph of sentences volunteered by students using:
- *es* words
- transportation vocabulary
- _____

WRITING
On their papers, students write their favorite words from the chart or other words, phrases, sentences that would be appropriate for the chart.

SPELLING
Partners call out words for each other to spell aloud.
Papers are dated and filed.

HOMEWORK
Write a list of words that need *es* to make them plural.

Lesson 89

Research

LEAD-IN
Teacher introduces the Project Idea.
Topic: Transportation or _____
Material: Newspapers or _____
Comprehension Skill: Cause and effect or _____

SEARCH & RECORD
Group Size: 3 or 4 or _____
Project Idea: Search for stories and pictures about transportation. Write notes about why they're in the news or _____.

SHARING
Volunteers show the class what they found and why it was in the news or _____.

Papers are dated and filed.

Recreational Reading

All students read books for approximately 30 minutes.

CONVERSATIONS
The teacher also reads silently. The teacher has some short conversations with readers. When appropriate, the main focus of these conversations is on making inferences.

CLIPBOARD NOTES
Teacher notes students' selections of books and whether students seem to be calling words without getting meanings.

READ-ALOUD BOOK
_____

Writing

Theme: Energy or _____

MINI-LESSON
Teacher presents editing tip for finishing science reports: correct spelling in all charts, graphs, and illustrations or _____.

COMPOSING
Final editing and rewriting of science report or _____.

SHARING
Partners help edit or _____.
Papers are dated and filed.

Word Study

CHART DEVELOPMENT
Spelling Emphasis: *rt* or _____
Other Emphasis:
■ paragraphs or _____
■ transportation or _____
On the chart, the teacher writes a paragraph of sentences volunteered by students using:
■ *rt* words
■ transportation vocabulary
■ _____

WRITING
On their papers, students write their favorite words from the chart or other words, phrases, or sentences that would be appropriate for the chart.

SPELLING
Partners call out words for each other to spell aloud.
Papers are dated and filed.

HOMEWORK
The horse-drawn cart was one means of transportation used in America. What others have been used over the years? Draw pictures of them.

Research

LEAD-IN
Teacher introduces the Project Idea.
Topic: Transportation or _____
Material: Magazines or _____
Comprehension Skill: Classification
or _____.

SEARCH & RECORD
Group Size: 3 or 4 or _____
Project Idea: Cut out pictures
involving transportation. Organize them
in a way that makes sense to your group.
Paste them on a poster and write labels
for the categories or _____.

SHARING
Display the posters or _____.
  Papers are dated and filed.

Recreational Reading

All students read books for approximately
30 minutes.

CONVERSATIONS
The teacher also reads silently. The
teacher has some short conversations with
readers. When appropriate, the main
focus of these conversations is on making
inferences.

CLIPBOARD NOTES
Teacher notes students' selections of
books and whether students seem to be
calling words without getting meanings.

READ-ALOUD BOOK
_____

Writing

Theme: Energy or _____

MINI-LESSON
Teacher explains how science projects and
reports will be presented to class or
_____.

COMPOSING
Prepare report for presentation to class or
_____.

SHARING
Writers present work to class or
_____.
  Papers are dated and filed.

Word Study

CHART DEVELOPMENT
Spelling Emphasis: *ud* or
_____

Other Emphasis:
■ paragraphs or _____
■ transportation or _____
  On the chart, the teacher writes a
paragraph of sentences volunteered by
students using:
■ *ud* words
■ transportation vocabulary
■ _____

WRITING
On their papers, students write their
favorite words from the chart or other
words, phrases, or sentences that would
be appropriate for the chart.

SPELLING
Partners call out words for each other to
spell aloud.
  Papers are dated and filed.

HOMEWORK
Write about a kind of transportation you
think will be ordinary in the future.

Lesson **91**

Research

LEAD-IN
Teacher introduces the Project Idea.
Topic: Transportation or _____
Material: Maps or _____
Comprehension Skill: Cause and effect or _____

SEARCH & RECORD
Group Size: Individuals or partners or _____

Project Idea: List places on the map where you would like to go and tell why you'd like to go there. List the kinds of transportation you'd need to take to get to each one from your home or _____.

SHARING
Show other people your travel plans or _____.
Papers are dated and filed.

Recreational Reading

All students read books for approximately 30 minutes.

CONVERSATIONS
The teacher also reads silently. The teacher has some short conversations with readers. When appropriate, the main focus of these conversations is on each student's ability to predict upcoming events in a story.

CLIPBOARD NOTES
Teacher notes students' selections of books and whether students ever talk about what they think is going to happen in a story.

READ-ALOUD BOOK
Jimmy's Boa and the Big Splash Birthday Bash by Trinka Noble or _____

Writing

The overall theme for the next 15 days is Friends or _____. One or more of the other modules will reflect this theme.
Theme: Friends or _____

MINI-LESSON
Brainstorm ideas about friends and why they are important or _____.

COMPOSING
Write list of important things about friends and why they are important or _____.

SHARING
Everyone shares one thing from his or her list or _____.
Papers are dated and filed.

Word Study

CHART DEVELOPMENT
Spelling Emphasis: *ro* or _____
Other Emphasis:
■ paragraphs or _____
■ friends or _____
On the chart, the teacher writes two paragraphs of sentences volunteered by students using:
■ *ro* words
■ friends vocabulary
■ _____

WRITING
On their papers, students write their favorite words from the chart or other words, phrases, or sentences that would be appropriate for the chart.

SPELLING
Partners call out words for each other to spell aloud.
Papers are dated and filed.

HOMEWORK
Rotten Rose just would not grow. Finish the story using as many *ro* words as you can.

Research

LEAD-IN
Teacher introduces the Project Idea.
Topic: Transportation or _____
Material: Advertisements or _____

Comprehension Skill: Cause and effect or _____

SEARCH & RECORD
Group Size: Partners or _____
Project Idea: Cut out ads for 3 automobiles you would like to buy. Write some facts about each and why you like them or _____.

SHARING
Tell other people about your choices or _____.
   Papers are dated and filed.

Recreational Reading

All students read books for approximately 30 minutes.

CONVERSATIONS
The teacher also reads silently. The teacher has some short conversations with readers. When appropriate, the main focus of these conversations is on each student's ability to predict upcoming events in a story.

CLIPBOARD NOTES
Teacher notes students' selections of books and whether students ever talk about what they think is going to happen in a story.

READ-ALOUD BOOK
_____

Writing

Theme: Friends or _____

MINI-LESSON
Brainstorm recommendations for being a good friend or _____.

COMPOSING
Write list of recommendations for being a good friend or _____.

SHARING
Partners share ideas of how to be a good friend or _____.
   Papers are dated and filed.

Word Study

CHART DEVELOPMENT
Spelling Emphasis: *ox* or _____

Other Emphasis:
■ paragraphs or _____
■ friends or _____
   On the chart, the teacher writes two paragraphs of sentences volunteered by students using:
■ *ox* words
■ friends vocabulary
■ _____

WRITING
On their papers, students write their favorite words from the chart or other words, phrases, or sentences that would be appropriate for the chart.

SPELLING
Partners call out words for each other to spell aloud.
   Papers are dated and filed.

HOMEWORK
Write some sentences using the *ox* words you thought of at school.

Lesson 93

Research

LEAD-IN
Teacher introduces the Project Idea.
Topic: Transportation or _____
Material: Encyclopedias or _____
Comprehension Skill: Reference skills or _____

SEARCH & RECORD
Group Size: Partners or _____
Project Idea: Locate information about a kind of transportation. Search for facts about its history; find out when it was invented or _____.

SHARING
Make a class timeline showing the invention dates of the kinds of transportation that everyone studied or _____.
Papers are dated and filed.

Recreational Reading

All students read books for approximately 30 minutes.

CONVERSATIONS
The teacher also reads silently. The teacher has some short conversations with readers. When appropriate, the main focus of these conversations is on each student's ability to predict upcoming events in a story.

CLIPBOARD NOTES
Teacher notes students' selections of books and whether students ever talk about what they think is going to happen in a story.

READ-ALOUD BOOK
_____

Writing

Theme: Friends or _____

MINI-LESSON
Students study brainstorming lists to find an idea for writing a piece about friends or _____.

COMPOSING
Begin first draft of piece about friends or _____.

SHARING
Volunteers tell class their ideas for a piece about friends or _____.
Papers are dated and filed.

Word Study

CHART DEVELOPMENT
Spelling Emphasis: *ke* or _____

Other Emphasis:
■ paragraphs or _____
■ friends or _____
On the chart, the teacher writes two paragraphs of sentences volunteered by students using:
■ *ke* words
■ friends vocabulary
■ _____

WRITING
On their papers, students write their favorite words from the chart or other words, phrases, or sentences that would be appropriate for the chart.

SPELLING
Partners call out words for each other to spell aloud.
Papers are dated and filed.

HOMEWORK
Look for *ke* words in a library book. Write them on a piece of paper.

Research

LEAD-IN
Teacher introduces the Project Idea.
Topic: Transportation or _____
Material: Social studies book or _____

Comprehension Skill: Cause and effect or _____

SEARCH & RECORD
Group Size: Partners or _____
Project Idea: Find information about a city and list ways transportation helps people there or _____.

SHARING
Show another team what you found. Compare your city to the other team's city or _____
 Papers are dated and filed.

Recreational Reading

All students read books for approximately 30 minutes.

CONVERSATIONS
The teacher also reads silently. The teacher has some short conversations with readers. When appropriate, the main focus of these conversations is on each student's ability to predict upcoming events in a story.

CLIPBOARD NOTES
Teacher notes students' selections of books and whether students ever talk about what they think is going to happen in a story.

READ-ALOUD BOOK
Where the Sidewalk Ends by Shel Silverstein** or _____

Writing

Theme: Friends or _____

MINI-LESSON
Teacher reads factual information (from health textbook, perhaps) about how people need friends or _____.

COMPOSING
Write facts about how people need friends. Continue first draft or _____.

SHARING
Partners share ideas or _____.
 Papers are dated and filed.

Word Study

CHART DEVELOPMENT
Spelling Emphasis: *tu* or _____
Other Emphasis:
 ■ paragraphs or _____
 ■ friends or _____
 On the chart, the teacher writes two paragraphs of sentences volunteered by students using:
 ■ *tu* words
 ■ friends vocabulary
 ■ _____

WRITING
On their papers, students write their favorite words from the chart or other words, phrases, or sentences that would be appropriate for the chart.

SPELLING
Partners call out words for each other to spell aloud.
 Papers are dated and filed.

HOMEWORK
Write a list of valentine messages for your friends.

Lesson 95

Research

LEAD-IN
Teacher introduces the Project Idea.
Topic: Transportation or _____
Material: Students choose or _____

Comprehension Skill: Main idea or _____

SEARCH & RECORD
Group Size: Individuals or partners or _____

Project Idea: Draw a picture to show the most important things you have learned about transportation. Search for more information if you need it. Write a caption for your picture or _____.

SHARING
Display the pictures or _____.
   Papers are dated and filed.

Recreational Reading

All students read books for approximately 30 minutes.

CONVERSATIONS
The teacher also reads silently. The teacher has some short conversations with readers. When appropriate, the main focus of these conversations is on each student's ability to predict upcoming events in a story.

CLIPBOARD NOTES
Teacher notes students' selections of books and whether students ever talk about what they think is going to happen in a story.

READ-ALOUD BOOK
_____

Writing

Theme: Friends or _____

MINI-LESSON
Teacher reads a poem about friends or _____.

COMPOSING
Write a poem about friends or _____.

SHARING
Volunteers read poems to class or _____.
   Papers are dated and filed.

Word Study

CHART DEVELOPMENT
Spelling Emphasis: *om* or _____

Other Emphasis:
- paragraphs or _____
- friends or _____
   On the chart, the teacher writes two paragraphs of sentences volunteered by students using:
- *om* words
- friends vocabulary
- _____

WRITING
On their papers, students write their favorite words from the chart or other words, phrases, or sentences that would be appropriate for the chart.

SPELLING
Partners call out words for each other to spell aloud.
   Papers are dated and filed.

HOMEWORK
Make a list of people you know who like to eat tomatoes. Make a list of people who don't like tomatoes.

Lesson 96

Research

LEAD-IN
Teacher introduces the Project Idea.
Topic: Music or _____
Material: Assorted music textbooks or _____

Comprehension Skill: Main idea or _____

SEARCH & RECORD
Group Size: Partners or _____
Project Idea: Search for songs that have lyrics about friends. Write a list of titles and page numbers or _____.

SHARING
Show another team the best song you found or _____.
Papers are dated and filed.

Recreational Reading

All students read books for approximately 30 minutes.

CONVERSATIONS
The teacher also reads silently. The teacher has some short conversations with readers. When appropriate, the main focus of these conversations is each student's ability to predict upcoming events in a story.

CLIPBOARD NOTES
Teacher notes students' selections of books and whether students ever talk about what they think is going to happen in a story.

READ-ALOUD BOOK
_____

Writing

Theme: Friends or _____

MINI-LESSON
Teacher uses sample poem to identify various parts of speech and how they are used in some form of poetry or _____.

COMPOSING
Work on friendship poem or _____.

SHARING
Partners help each other identify necessary parts of speech in poems or _____.
Papers are dated and filed.

Word Study

CHART DEVELOPMENT
Spelling Emphasis: *in* or _____
Other Emphasis:
■ paragraphs or _____
■ music or _____
On the chart, the teacher writes two paragraphs of sentences volunteered by students using:
■ *in* words
■ music vocabulary
■ _____

WRITING
On their papers, students write their favorite words from the chart or other words, phrases, or sentences that would be appropriate for the chart.

SPELLING
Partners call out words for each other to spell aloud.
Papers are dated and filed.

HOMEWORK
Write about your favorite song. Circle words that contain the letters *in*.

Lesson 97

Research

LEAD-IN
Teacher introduces the Project Idea.
Topic: Music or _____
Material: Music books or _____
Comprehension Skill: Details or
_____

SEARCH & RECORD
Group Size: Partners or _____
Project Idea: Refer to notes taken in
previous lesson. Write a list of the words
that tell about friends in the songs you
located yesterday or _____.

SHARING
Show another team what you found or
_____.
  Papers are dated and filed.

Recreational Reading

All students read books for approximately
30 minutes.

CONVERSATIONS
The teacher also reads silently. The
teacher has some short conversations with
readers. When appropriate, the main
focus of these conversations is on each
student's ability to predict upcoming
events in a story.

CLIPBOARD NOTES
Teacher notes students' selections of
books and whether students ever talk
about what they think is going to happen
in a story.

READ-ALOUD BOOK
Jumanji by Chris Van Allsburg or
_____

Writing

Theme: Friends or _____

MINI-LESSON
Students review their lists of books read
or _____.

COMPOSING
Write about the friends that are in the
books you've read lately or _____.

SHARING
Volunteers share with class or
_____.
  Papers are dated and filed.

Word Study

CHART DEVELOPMENT
Spelling Emphasis: *sc* or _____
Other Emphasis:
■ paragraphs or _____
■ music or _____
  On the chart, the teacher writes two
paragraphs of sentences volunteered by
students using:
■ *sc* words
■ music vocabulary
■ _____

WRITING
On their papers, students write their
favorite words from the chart or other
words, phrases, or sentences that would
be appropriate for the chart.

SPELLING
Partners call out words for each other to
spell aloud.
  Papers are dated and filed.

HOMEWORK
How does your school differ from the
schools that pioneers attended? Write
about schools and illustrate with a school
scene.

Research

LEAD-IN
Teacher introduces the Project Idea.
Topic: Music or _____
Material: Newspapers or _____
Comprehension Skill: Main idea or _____

SEARCH & RECORD
Group Size: 3 or 4 or _____
Project Idea: Create a song about friends with words cut out of the newspaper or _____.

SHARING
Groups sing their songs or _____.
Papers are dated and filed.

Recreational Reading

All students read books for approximately 30 minutes.

CONVERSATIONS
The teacher also reads silently. The teacher has some short conversations with readers. When appropriate, the main focus of these conversations is on each student's ability to predict upcoming events in a story.

CLIPBOARD NOTES
Teacher notes students' selections of books and whether students ever talk about what they think is going to happen in a story.

READ-ALOUD BOOK
_____

Writing

Theme: Friends or _____

MINI-LESSON
Teacher displays poetry book. Students begin planning poetry books of their own or _____.

COMPOSING
Write notes about what to include in poetry book or _____.

SHARING
Response group share ideas for poetry book or _____.
Papers are dated and filed.

Word Study

CHART DEVELOPMENT
Spelling Emphasis: *pr* or _____

Other Emphasis:
■ paragraphs or _____
■ music or _____
   On the chart, the teacher writes two paragraphs of sentences volunteered by students using:
■ *pr* words
■ music vocabulary
■ _____

WRITING
On their papers, students write their favorite words from the chart or other words, phrases, or sentences that would be appropriate for the chart.

SPELLING
Partners call out words for each other to spell aloud.
Papers are dated and filed.

HOMEWORK
Write directions for playing a musical instrument.

197

Lesson **99**

Research

LEAD-IN
Teacher introduces the Project Idea.
Topic: Music or _____
Material: Magazines or _____
Comprehension Skill:
Characterization or _____

SEARCH & RECORD
Group Size: Individuals or _____
Project Idea: Create a song about a product advertised in the magazine. Choose something a friend would like as a birthday present or _____.

SHARING
Sing song for a friend or _____.
Papers are dated and filed.

Recreational Reading

All students read books for approximately 30 minutes.

CONVERSATIONS
The teacher also reads silently. The teacher has some short conversations with readers. When appropriate, the main focus of these conversations is on each student's ability to predict upcoming events in a story.

CLIPBOARD NOTES
Teacher notes students' selections of books and whether students ever talk about what they think is going to happen in a story.

READ-ALOUD BOOK
_____

Writing

Theme: Friends or _____

MINI-LESSON
Discussion of additional poetry techniques, such as personification or simile or _____.

COMPOSING
Continue drafts of poems for poetry book or _____.

SHARING
Share with partner or _____.
Papers are dated and filed.

Word Study

CHART DEVELOPMENT
Spelling Emphasis: *ph* or
_____
Other Emphasis:
- paragraphs or _____
- music or _____
  On the chart, the teacher writes two paragraphs of sentences volunteered by students using:
- *ph* words
- music vocabulary
- _____

WRITING
On their papers, students write their favorite words from the chart or other words, phrases, or sentences that would be appropriate for the chart.

SPELLING
Partners call out words for each other to spell aloud.
Papers are dated and filed.

HOMEWORK
Look in the *Yellow Pages* of the telephone book to find places that sell musical instruments. Write their names on a piece of paper.

Research

LEAD-IN
Teacher introduces the Project Idea.
Topic: Music or _____
Material: Music books or _____
Comprehension Skill: Classification or _____

SEARCH & RECORD
Group Size: 3 or 4 or _____
Project Idea: Make a list of the group's favorite songs in the music book. Write the list again, dividing the list into categories or _____.

SHARING
Show another group your categories or _____.
    Papers are dated and filed.

Recreational Reading

All students read books for approximately 30 minutes.

CONVERSATIONS
The teacher also reads silently. The teacher has some short conversations with readers. When appropriate, the main focus of these conversations is each student's ability to predict upcoming events in a story.

CLIPBOARD NOTES
Teacher notes students' selections of books and whether students ever talk about what they think is going to happen in a story.

READ-ALOUD BOOK
The Mouse and the Motorcycle by Beverly Cleary or _____

Writing

Theme: Friends or _____

MINI-LESSON
Teacher leads discussion of ideas for organizing poetry books. Discuss ideas for 100th Day of School or _____.

COMPOSING
Continue work on poems for poetry book. Write about 100th Day or _____.

SHARING
Volunteers share a piece they plan to include in poetry book or _____.
    Papers are dated and filed.

Word Study

CHART DEVELOPMENT
Spelling Emphasis: *wr* or
_____
Other Emphasis:
■ paragraphs or _____
■ music or _____
    On the chart, the teacher writes two paragraphs of sentences volunteered by students using:
■ *wr* words
■ music vocabulary
■

WRITING
On their papers, students write their favorite words from the chart or other words, phrases, or sentences that would be appropriate for the chart.

SPELLING
Partners call out words for each other to spell aloud.
    Papers are dated and filed.

HOMEWORK
What does a songwriter do? Write about his or her job.

Lesson 101

Research

LEAD-IN
Teacher introduces the Project Idea.
Topic: Music or _____
Material: Poetry books (or basals that include poetry) or _____
Comprehension Skill: Classification or _____

SEARCH & RECORD
Group Size: Partners or _____
Project Idea: List titles of poems that would make good songs and those that would not or _____.

SHARING
Explain to another team why you included a song in a particular category or _____.
Papers are dated and filed.

Recreational Reading

All students read books for approximately 30 minutes.

CONVERSATIONS
The teacher also reads silently. The teacher has some short conversations with readers. When appropriate, the main focus of these conversations is on each student's reading habits outside of school.

CLIPBOARD NOTES
Teacher notes students' selections of books and whether students talk about home reading.

READ-ALOUD BOOK
_____

Writing

Theme: Friends or _____

MINI-LESSON
Teacher leads discussion of choosing titles for poems or _____.

COMPOSING
Continue work on drafts of poems. List ideas for titles of poems or _____.

SHARING
Response groups share title ideas or _____.
Papers are dated and filed.

Word Study

CHART DEVELOPMENT
Spelling Emphasis: *tl* or _____
Other Emphasis:
■ paragraphs or _____
■ mathematics or _____
On the chart, the teacher writes two paragraphs of sentences volunteered by students using:
■ *tl* words
■ mathematics vocabulary
■ _____

WRITING
On their papers, students write their favorite words from the chart or other words, phrases, or sentences that would be appropriate for the chart.

SPELLING
Partners call out words for each other to spell aloud.
Papers are dated and filed.

HOMEWORK
Write a paragraph explaining something new you have learned to do in mathematics.

Lesson 102

Research

LEAD-IN
Teacher introduces the Project Idea.
Topic: Music or _____
Material: Music books or _____
Comprehension Skill: Questions and answers or _____

SEARCH & RECORD
Group Size: Partners or _____
Project Idea: Write questions that your partner can answer by looking in the music book or _____.

SHARING
Trade questions with your partner. Find the answers to each other's questions in the music book or _____.
Papers are dated and filed.

Recreational Reading

All students read books for approximately 30 minutes.

CONVERSATIONS
The teacher also reads silently. The teacher has some short conversations with readers. When appropriate, the main focus of these conversations is on each student's reading habits outside of school.

CLIPBOARD NOTES
Teacher notes students' selections of books and whether students talk about home reading.

READ-ALOUD BOOK
_____

Writing

Theme: Friends or _____

MINI-LESSON
Teacher leads discussion about what makes poems good or _____.

COMPOSING
Continue drafts of poems or _____.

SHARING
Response groups help writers choose their best poems or _____.
Papers are dated and filed.

Word Study

CHART DEVELOPMENT
Spelling Emphasis: *ef* or _____
Other Emphasis:
■ paragraphs or _____
■ science or _____
On the chart, the teacher writes two paragraphs of sentences volunteered by students using:
■ *ef* words
■ science vocabulary
■ _____

WRITING
On their papers, students write their favorite words from the chart or other words, phrases, or sentences that would be appropriate for the chart.

SPELLING
Partners call out words for each other to spell aloud.
Papers are dated and filed.

HOMEWORK
Look in your science book to find words containing the letters *ef*. Write words and page numbers on a piece of paper.

Lesson 103

Research

LEAD-IN
Teacher introduces the Project Idea.
Topic: Music or _____
Material: Music books or _____
Comprehension Skill: Sequence or _____

SEARCH & RECORD
Group Size: Partners or _____
Project Idea: List titles of songs and the dates they were published. Rearrange the list in chronological order according to when the songs were published or _____.

SHARING
Everyone contributes one title and date to a class timeline of music history or _____.
  Papers are dated and filed.

Recreational Reading

All students read books for approximately 30 minutes.

CONVERSATIONS
The teacher also reads silently. The teacher has some short conversations with readers. When appropriate, the main focus of these conversations is on each student's reading habits outside of school.

CLIPBOARD NOTES
Teacher notes students' selections of books and whether students talk about home reading.

READ-ALOUD BOOK
Alexander and the Terrible, Horrible, No Good, Very Bad Day by Judith Viorst or _____

Writing

Theme: Friends or _____

MINI-LESSON
Teacher uses poetry books to demonstrate ideas for illustrating student poetry books or _____.

COMPOSING
Work on illustrations for poetry book or _____.

SHARING
Partners share illustrations for poetry books or _____.
  Papers are dated and filed.

Word Study

CHART DEVELOPMENT
Spelling Emphasis: *ri* or _____
Other Emphasis:
■ paragraphs or _____
■ geography or _____
  On the chart, the teacher writes two paragraphs of sentences volunteered by students using:
■ *ri* words
■ geography vocabulary
■ _____

WRITING
On their papers, students write their favorite words from the chart or other words, phrases, or sentences that would be appropriate for the chart.

SPELLING
Partners call out words for each other to spell aloud.
  Papers are dated and filed.

HOMEWORK
Look at a map and find words that contain the letters *ri*. Write them on a piece of paper.

Lesson **104**

Research

LEAD-IN
Teacher introduces the Project Idea.
Topic: Music or _____
Material: Music books or _____
Comprehension Skill: Comparison and contrast or _____

SEARCH & RECORD
Group Size: Partners or _____
Project Idea: Choose two songs and list the ways they are alike and the ways they are different or _____.

SHARING
Show another team your chart or _____.
   Papers are dated and filed.

Recreational Reading

All students read books for approximately 30 minutes.

CONVERSATIONS
The teacher also reads silently. The teacher has some short conversations with readers. When appropriate, the main focus of these conversations is on each student's reading habits outside of school.

CLIPBOARD NOTES
Teacher notes students' selections of books and whether students talk about home reading.

READ-ALOUD BOOK
_____

Writing

Theme: Friends or _____

MINI-LESSON
Teacher demonstrates how to make table of contents or _____.

COMPOSING
Write table of contents for poetry book or _____.

SHARING
Partners share progress on final copies of poetry books or _____.
   Papers are dated and filed.

Word Study

CHART DEVELOPMENT
Spelling Emphasis: *ja* or _____
Other Emphasis:
- paragraphs or _____
- sports or _____
   On the chart, the teacher writes two paragraphs of sentences volunteered by students using:
- *ja* words
- sports vocabulary
- _____

WRITING
On their papers, students write their favorite words from the chart or other words, phrases, or sentences that would be appropriate for the chart.

SPELLING
Partners call out words for each other to spell aloud.
   Papers are dated and filed.

HOMEWORK
Write about your favorite sport. What must you do to play it well?

Lesson **105**

Research

LEAD-IN
Teacher introduces the Project Idea.
Topic: Music or _____
Material: Students choose or
_____

Comprehension Skill: Summary or
_____

SEARCH & RECORD
Group Size: Individuals or _____
Project Idea: Locate information that
is new to you about music. Write a
summary of what you have learned about
music or _____.

SHARING
Make class display of summaries and/or
songs prepared during the study of music
or _____.
 Papers are dated and filed.

Recreational Reading

All students read books for approximately
30 minutes.

CONVERSATIONS
The teacher also reads silently. The
teacher has some short conversations with
readers. When appropriate, the main
focus of these conversations is on each
student's reading habits outside of school.

CLIPBOARD NOTES
Teacher notes students' selections of
books and whether students talk about
home reading.

READ-ALOUD BOOK
_____

Writing

Theme: Friends or _____

MINI-LESSON
Teacher explains system for checking out
student poetry books or _____

COMPOSING
Complete poetry book and prepare it for
class library or _____.

SHARING
Students enjoy each other's completed
books or _____.
 Papers are dated and filed.

Word Study

CHART DEVELOPMENT
Spelling Emphasis: _wh_ or
_____

Other Emphasis:
■ paragraphs or _____
■ health or _____
 On the chart, the teacher writes two
paragraphs of sentences volunteered by
students using:
■ _wh_ words
■ health vocabulary
■ _____

WRITING
On their papers, students write their
favorite words from the chart or other
words, phrases, or sentences that would
be appropriate for the chart.

SPELLING
Partners call out words for each other to
spell aloud.
 Papers are dated and filed.

HOMEWORK
Look for words in your health book that
contain _wh_. Write a list and make up
some sentences using the words.

Research

LEAD-IN
Teacher introduces the Project Idea.
Topic: Famous Americans or
_____

Material: Encyclopedias or _____
Comprehension Skill: Cause and
effect or _____

SEARCH & RECORD
Group Size: Partners or _____
Project Idea: Write a list of famous
people you find in the encyclopedia.
Beside each, write a reason he or she
became famous or _____.

SHARING
Share your findings with another team or
_____

Papers are dated and filed.

Recreational Reading

All students read books for approximately
30 minutes.

CONVERSATIONS
The teacher also reads silently. The
teacher has some short conversations with
readers. When appropriate, the main
focus of these conversations is on each
student's reading habits outside of school.

CLIPBOARD NOTES
Teacher notes students' selections of
books and whether students talk about
home reading.

READ-ALOUD BOOK
Ragtime Tumpie by Alan Schroeder or

Writing

The overall theme for the next 15 days is
Communication or _____. One or
more of the other modules will reflect this
theme.
Theme: Communication or _____

MINI-LESSON
Brainstorm ideas to talk about or
_____.

COMPOSING
Write list of ideas to talk about or
_____.

SHARING
Everyone names one thing from list or
_____.

Papers are dated and filed.

Word Study

CHART DEVELOPMENT
Spelling Emphasis: *gy* or
_____

Other Emphasis:
■ paragraphs or _____
■ famous Americans or _____
On the chart, the teacher writes two
paragraphs of sentences volunteered by
students using:
■ *gy* words
■ vocabulary about famous Americans
■ _____

WRITING
On their papers, students write their
favorite words from the chart or other
words, phrases, or sentences that would
be appropriate for the chart.

SPELLING
Partners call out words for each other to
spell aloud.
Papers are dated and filed.

HOMEWORK
Write about a gymnasium where you
have been. Have any famous people
been there?

Lesson **107**

Research

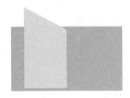

LEAD-IN
Teacher introduces the Project Idea.
Topic: Famous Americans or _____

Material: Encyclopedias or _____
Comprehension Skill: Details or _____

SEARCH & RECORD
Group Size: Partners or _____
Project Idea: Make a list of famous Americans in the encyclopedia. Write some facts about each or _____.

SHARING
Everyone tells the class about one famous person or _____.
   Papers are dated and filed.

Recreational Reading

All students read books for approximately 30 minutes.

CONVERSATIONS
The teacher also reads silently. The teacher has some short conversations with readers. When appropriate, the main focus of these conversations is on each student's reading habits outside of school.

CLIPBOARD NOTES
Teacher notes students' selections of books and whether students talk about home reading.

READ-ALOUD BOOK
_____

Writing

Theme: Communication or _____

MINI-LESSON
Teacher demonstrates how dialogue can show characters' feelings or _____.

COMPOSING
Write dialogue that shows a particular feeling or _____.

SHARING
Partners try to determine what feeling each other's dialogue is intended to show or _____.
   Papers are dated and filed.

Word Study

CHART DEVELOPMENT
Spelling Emphasis: *ob* or _____

Other Emphasis:
■ paragraphs or _____
■ famous Americans or _____
   On the chart, the teacher writes two paragraphs of sentences volunteered by students using:
■ *ob* words
■ vocabulary about famous Americans
■ _____

WRITING
On their papers, students write their favorite words from the chart or other words, phrases, or sentences that would be appropriate for the chart.

SPELLING
Partners call out words for each other to spell aloud.
   Papers are dated and filed.

HOMEWORK
Make a list of the jobs some famous Americans had. Write each person's name next to his or her job.

Research

LEAD-IN
Teacher introduces the Project Idea.
Topic: Famous Americans or
_____

Material: Encyclopedias or _____
Comprehension Skill: Details or
_____

SEARCH & RECORD
Group Size: Partners or _____
Project Idea: Make a chart listing the names of famous Americans, some people they knew, and some things they probably discussed with each other or
_____.

SHARING
Show another team what you recorded or
_____.

Papers are dated and filed.

Recreational Reading

All students read books for approximately 30 minutes.

CONVERSATIONS
The teacher also reads silently. The teacher has some short conversations with readers. When appropriate, the main focus of these conversations is on each student's reading habits outside of school.

CLIPBOARD NOTES
Teacher notes students' selections of books and whether students talk about home reading.

READ-ALOUD BOOK
_____

Writing

Theme: Communication or _____

MINI-LESSON
Teacher demonstrates punctuation of dialogue or _____.

COMPOSING
Write and punctuate dialogue or
_____.

SHARING
Partners read each other's dialogue or
_____.

Papers are dated and filed.

Word Study

CHART DEVELOPMENT
Spelling Emphasis: *da* or _____

Other Emphasis:
■ paragraphs or _____
■ famous Americans or _____
   On the chart, the teacher writes two paragraphs of sentences volunteered by students using:
■ *da* words
■ vocabulary about famous Americans
■ _____

WRITING
On their papers, students write their favorite words from the chart or other words, phrases, or sentences that would be appropriate for the chart.

SPELLING
Partners call out words for each other to spell aloud.
   Papers are dated and filed.

HOMEWORK
Write a list of famous Americans and the places where they lived.

Lesson **109**

Research

LEAD-IN
Teacher introduces the Project Idea.
Topic: Famous Americans or

_____

Material: Encyclopedias or _____
Comprehension Skill: Comparison
and contrast or _____

SEARCH & RECORD
Group Size: Partners or _____
Project Idea: Choose one famous
American. Write a list of ways he or she
is like you and of ways he or she is
different or _____.

SHARING
Show another team what you decided or

_____.

   Papers are dated and filed.

Recreational Reading

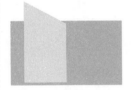

All students read books for approximately
30 minutes.

CONVERSATIONS
The teacher also reads silently. The
teacher has some short conversations with
readers. When appropriate, the main
focus of these conversations is on each
student's reading habits outside of school.

CLIPBOARD NOTES
Teacher notes students' selections of
books and whether students talk about
home reading.

READ-ALOUD BOOK
Owl Moon by Jane Yolen or _____

Writing

Theme: Communication or _____

MINI-LESSON
Teacher reads excerpt of dialogue from a
novel or _____.

COMPOSING
Write dialogue that could be a reply to
what the teacher read or _____.

SHARING
Volunteers read dialogue to class or

_____.

   Papers are dated and filed.

Word Study

CHART DEVELOPMENT
Spelling Emphasis: *gr* or

_____

Other Emphasis:
■ paragraphs or _____
■ famous Americans or _____
   On the chart, the teacher writes two
paragraphs of sentences volunteered by
students using:
■ *gr* words
■ vocabulary about famous Americans
■ _____

WRITING
On their papers students write their
favorite words from the chart or other
words, phrases, or sentences that would
be appropriate for the chart.

SPELLING
Partners call out words for each other to
spell aloud.
   Papers are dated and filed.

HOMEWORK
Choose one famous American you have
studied. Write about what made that
person great.

Lesson **110**

Research

LEAD-IN
Teacher introduces the Project Idea.
Topic: Famous Americans or _____

Material: Encyclopedias and library books or _____
Comprehension Skill: Main idea and details or _____

SEARCH & RECORD
Group Size: 3 or 4 or _____
Project Idea: Make some information cards, like baseball cards, about several famous Americans or _____.

SHARING
Show another team the cards you made or _____.

Papers are dated and filed.

Recreational Reading

All students read books for approximately 30 minutes.

CONVERSATIONS
The teacher also reads silently. The teacher has some short conversations with readers. When appropriate, the main focus of these conversations is on each student's reading habits outside of school.

CLIPBOARD NOTES
Teacher notes students' selections of books and whether students talk about home reading.

READ-ALOUD BOOK
_____

Writing

Theme: Communication or _____

MINI-LESSON
Teacher reads excerpt from a play or _____.

COMPOSING
Write lines for a play or _____.

SHARING
Response group share ideas for plays or _____.

Papers are dated and filed.

Word Study

CHART DEVELOPMENT
Spelling Emphasis: *th* or _____
Other Emphasis:
■ paragraphs or _____
■ famous Americans or _____
   On the chart, the teacher writes two paragraphs of sentences volunteered by students using:
■ *th* words
■ vocabulary about famous Americans
■ _____

WRITING
On their papers, students write their favorite words from the chart or other words, phrases, or sentences that would be appropriate for the chart.

SPELLING
Partners call out words for each other to spell aloud.
   Papers are dated and filed.

HOMEWORK
Write a list of the *th* words you find in newspaper articles about famous people. Write the names of the famous people you find as well.

Lesson 111

Research

LEAD-IN
Teacher introduces the Project Idea.
Topic: Famous Americans or _____

Material: Cards made in Lesson 110 or _____

Comprehension Skill: Classification or _____

SEARCH & RECORD
Group Size: Combine two groups from Lesson 110 or _____
Project Idea: Compile all cards made by the group. Group the cards that go together or _____

SHARING
Display groups of cards for others to see or _____.
  Papers are dated and filed.

Recreational Reading

All students read books for approximately 30 minutes.

CONVERSATIONS
The teacher also reads silently. The teacher has some short conversations with readers. When appropriate, the main focus of these conversations is on each student's decisions to abandon or finish books.

CLIPBOARD NOTES
Teacher notes students' selections of books and whether students abandon or finish books they chose.

READ-ALOUD BOOK
_____

Writing

Theme: Communication or _____

MINI-LESSON
Teacher demonstrates use of quotation marks in writing dialogue. Compare to punctuation of lines in a play or _____.

COMPOSING
Continue a previous piece or _____.

SHARING
Check quotation marks with a partner or _____.
  Papers are dated and filed.

Word Study

CHART DEVELOPMENT
Spelling Emphasis: *ru* or _____

Other Emphasis:
- paragraphs or _____
- ecology or _____
  On the chart, the teacher writes two paragraphs of sentences volunteered by students using:
- *ru* words
- ecology vocabulary
- _____

WRITING
On their papers, students write their favorite words from the chart or other words, phrases, or sentences that would be appropriate for the chart.

SPELLING
Partners call out words for each other to spell aloud.
  Papers are dated and filed.

HOMEWORK
Use the following words in a story: run, truth, ruin, rule, rumble, rust, rut, rush, rub.

Research

LEAD-IN
Teacher introduces the Project Idea.
Topic: Famous Americans or
_____

Material: Cards made in Lesson 110 or
_____

Comprehension Skill: Questions
and answers or _____

SEARCH & RECORD
Group Size: Partners or _____
Project Idea: Study partner's
information cards. Write some questions
you'd like answered or _____.

SHARING
Partners try to answer each others
questions about the famous Americans or
_____.
  Papers are dated and filed.

Recreational Reading

All students read books for approximately
30 minutes.

CONVERSATIONS
The teacher also reads silently. The
teacher has some short conversations with
readers. When appropriate, the main
focus of these conversations is on each
student's decisions to abandon or finish
books.

CLIPBOARD NOTES
Teacher notes students' selections of
books and whether students abandon or
finish books they chose.

READ-ALOUD BOOK
The Wednesday Surprise by Eve Bunting
or _____

Writing

Theme: Communication or _____

MINI-LESSON
Students review lists of books they have
read or _____.

COMPOSING
Write about the ways characters talk to
each other in some books you've read
lately or _____.

SHARING
Volunteers share their observations about
characters' conversations or _____.
  Papers are dated and filed.

Word Study

CHART DEVELOPMENT
Spelling Emphasis: *de* or
_____

Other Emphasis:
■ paragraphs or _____
■ mathematics or _____
  On the chart, the teacher writes two
paragraphs of sentences volunteered by
students using:
■ *de* words
■ mathematics vocabulary
■ _____

WRITING
On their papers, students write their
favorite words from the chart or other
words, phrases, or sentences that would
be appropriate for the chart.

SPELLING
Partners call out words for each other to
spell aloud.
  Papers are dated and filed.

HOMEWORK
Write some story problems using *de* words
from your list.

Lesson **113**

Research

LEAD-IN
Teacher introduces the Project Idea.
Topic: Famous Americans or
_____

Material: Cards made in Lesson 110 or _____

Comprehension Skill: Sequence or _____

SEARCH & RECORD
Group Size: 3 or 4 or _____
Project Idea: Compile everyone's cards. Arrange in chronological order according to the year of each famous American's birth or _____.

SHARING
Each group reports which of their Americans was born earliest and which was born latest or _____.
　Papers are dated and filed.

Recreational Reading

All students read books for approximately 30 minutes.

CONVERSATIONS
The teacher also reads silently. The teacher has some short conversations with readers. When appropriate, the main focus of these conversations is on each student's decisions to abandon or finish books.

CLIPBOARD NOTES
Teacher notes students' selections of books and whether students abandon or finish books they chose.

READ-ALOUD BOOK
_____

Writing

Theme: Communication or _____

MINI-LESSON
Teacher leads discussion about working with groups to write script of play or _____.

COMPOSING
Groups form to begin draft of play or _____.

SHARING
Spokesperson for each group reports topic of play or _____.
　Papers are dated and filed.

Word Study

CHART DEVELOPMENT
Spelling Emphasis: *ft* or _____
Other Emphasis:
■ paragraphs or _____
■ science or _____
　On the chart, the teacher writes two paragraphs of sentences volunteered by students using:
■ *ft* words
■ science vocabulary
■ _____

WRITING
On their papers, students write their favorite words from the chart or other words, phrases, or sentences that would be appropriate for the chart.

SPELLING
Partners call out words for each other to spell aloud.
　Papers are dated and filed.

HOMEWORK
Look in your science book and find words containing the letters *ft*. Write some of them on a piece of paper.

Research

LEAD-IN
Teacher introduces the Project Idea.
Topic: Famous Americans or _____

Material: Cards made in Lesson 110 or _____

Comprehension Skill: Comparison and contrast or _____

SEARCH & RECORD
Group Size: Partners or _____
Project Idea: Choose pairs of Americans described on your cards. Write a list of ways they are alike and of ways they are different or _____.

SHARING
Each team tells the class about one of its pairs or _____.
  Papers are dated and filed.

Recreational Reading

All students read books for approximately 30 minutes.

CONVERSATIONS
The teacher also reads silently. The teacher has some short conversations with readers. When appropriate, the main focus of these conversations is on each student's decisions to abandon or finish books.

CLIPBOARD NOTES
Teacher notes students' selections of books and whether students abandon or finish books they chose.

READ-ALOUD BOOK
_____

Writing

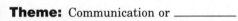

Theme: Communication or _____

MINI-LESSON
Teacher leads discussion of more ideas for developing scripts for plays or _____.

COMPOSING
Groups continue drafts of plays or _____.

SHARING
Groups read through their scripts or _____.
  Papers are dated and filed.

Word Study

CHART DEVELOPMENT
Spelling Emphasis: _rd_ or _____

Other Emphasis:
■ paragraphs or _____
■ geography or _____
  On the chart, the teacher writes two paragraphs of sentences volunteered by students using:
■ _rd_ words
■ geography vocabulary
■ _____

WRITING
On their papers, students write their favorite words from the chart or other words, phrases, or sentences that would be appropriate for the chart.

SPELLING
Partners call out words for each other to spell aloud.
  Papers are dated and filed.

HOMEWORK
Make a postcard of one of your favorite places. Write a message to a friend about that place.

Lesson **115**

Research

LEAD-IN
Teacher introduces the Project Idea.
Topic: Famous Americans or _____

Material: Students choose or _____

Comprehension Skill: Summary or _____

SEARCH & RECORD
Group Size: Individuals or _____
Project Idea: Read about famous Americans you haven't had a chance to study. Write the main things you learn or _____.

SHARING
Volunteers tell the class the most interesting things learned or _____.
   Papers are dated and filed.

Recreational Reading

All students read books for approximately 30 minutes.

CONVERSATIONS
The teacher also reads silently. The teacher has some short conversations with readers. When appropriate, the main focus of these conversations is on each student's decisions to abandon or finish books.

CLIPBOARD NOTES
Teacher notes students' selections of books and whether students abandon or finish books they chose.

READ-ALOUD BOOK
Song and Dance Man by Karen Ackerman or _____

Writing

Theme: Communication or _____

MINI-LESSON
Teacher leads discussion of how a script for a puppet show would differ from that for a play or _____.

COMPOSING
Groups decide whether to revise script for a puppet show or continue with script for a play or _____.

SHARING
Spokesperson reports to class about status of group's script or _____.
   Papers are dated and filed.

Word Study

CHART DEVELOPMENT
Spelling Emphasis: *kn* or _____

Other Emphasis:
■ paragraphs or _____
■ education or _____
   On the chart, the teacher writes two paragraphs of sentences volunteered by students using:
■ *kn* words
■ education vocabulary
■ _____

WRITING
On their papers, students write their favorite words from the chart or other words, phrases, or sentences that would be appropriate for the chart.

SPELLING
Partners call out words for each other to spell aloud.
   Papers are dated and filed.

HOMEWORK
Make a list of the kinds of knowledge you need to do well in third grade. Use some *kn* words.

Research

LEAD-IN
Teacher introduces the Project Idea.
Topic: Plants or _____
Material: Library books or _____
Comprehension Skill: Alphabetical order or _____

SEARCH & RECORD
Group Size: Partners or _____
Project Idea: Write a list of different kinds of plants. Write the list again in alphabetical order or _____.

SHARING
Show another team your list or _____.
    Papers are dated and filed.

Recreational Reading

All students read books for approximately 30 minutes.

CONVERSATIONS
The teacher also reads silently. The teacher has some short conversations with readers. When appropriate, the main focus of these conversations is on each student's decisions to abandon or finish books.

CLIPBOARD NOTES
Teacher notes students' selections of books and whether students abandon or finish books they chose.

READ-ALOUD BOOK
_____

Writing

Theme: Communication or _____

MINI-LESSON
Teacher shares examples of stage directions from scripts of plays or _____.

COMPOSING
Continue work on script. Add stage directions or _____.

SHARING
Groups read scripts and follow stage directions or _____.
    Papers are dated and filed.

Word Study

CHART DEVELOPMENT
Spelling Emphasis: *ve* or _____
Other Emphasis:
- paragraphs or _____.
- plants or _____
    On the chart, the teacher writes two paragraphs of sentences volunteered by students using:
- *ve* words
- plant vocabulary
- _____

WRITING
On their papers, students write their favorite words from the chart or other words, phrases, or sentences that would be appropriate for the chart.

SPELLING
Partners call out words for each other to spell aloud.
    Papers are dated and filed.

HOMEWORK
Write a list of vegetables. Organize the things on your list in some way.

Lesson 117

Research

LEAD-IN
Teacher introduces the Project Idea.
Topic: Plants or _____
Material: Science textbooks and library books or _____
Comprehension Skill: Details or _____

SEARCH & RECORD
Group Size: Partners or _____
Project Idea: Write a list of plants and one detail about each or _____.

SHARING
Volunteers tell the class one interesting detail they learned or _____.
    Papers are dated and filed.

Recreational Reading

All students read books for approximately 30 minutes.

CONVERSATIONS
The teacher also reads silently. The teacher has some short conversations with readers. When appropriate, the main focus of these conversations is on each student's decisions to abandon or finish books.

CLIPBOARD NOTES
Teacher notes students' selections of books and whether students abandon or finish books they chose.

READ-ALOUD BOOK
_____

Writing

Theme: Communication or _____

MINI-LESSON
One response group demonstrates reading its script for the class, stopping to discuss revisions or _____.

COMPOSING
Work on revisions of script with group or _____.

SHARING
Response groups read through revised scripts or _____.
    Papers are dated and filed.

Word Study

CHART DEVELOPMENT
Spelling Emphasis: *sh* or _____

Other Emphasis:
- paragraphs or _____
- plants or _____
    On the chart, the teacher writes two paragraphs of sentences volunteered by students using:
- *sh* words
- plant vocabulary
- _____

WRITING
On their papers, students write their favorite words from the chart or other words, phrases, or sentences that would be appropriate for the chart.

SPELLING
Partners call out words for each other to spell aloud.
    Papers are dated and filed.

HOMEWORK
Write a poem about plants.

Lesson **118**

Research

LEAD-IN
Teacher introduces the Project Idea.
Topic: Plants or _____
Material: Science textbooks and library books or _____
Comprehension Skill: Organizing information or _____

SEARCH & RECORD
Group Size: 3 or 4 or _____
Project Idea: Make a chart with headings for name of plant, leaf, flower, and fruit. Name several plants and describe their leaves, flowers, or fruits or _____.

SHARING
Display charts or _____.
  Papers are dated and filed.

Recreational Reading

All students read books for approximately 30 minutes.

CONVERSATIONS
The teacher also reads silently. The teacher has some short conversations with readers. When appropriate, the main focus of these conversations is on each student's decisions to abandon or finish books.

CLIPBOARD NOTES
Teacher notes students' selections of books and whether students abandon or finish books they chose.

READ-ALOUD BOOK
The Wall by Eve Bunting or _____

Writing

Theme: Communication or _____

MINI-LESSON
Teacher leads discussion of ways to conclude plays or _____.

COMPOSING
Continue work on script. Write alternative endings or _____.

SHARING
Response groups read various endings and choose favorite or _____.
  Papers are dated and filed.

Word Study

CHART DEVELOPMENT
Spelling Emphasis: *ch* or _____

Other Emphasis:
■ paragraphs or _____
■ plants or _____
  On the chart, the teacher writes two paragraphs of sentences volunteered by students using:
■ *ch* words
■ plant vocabulary
■ _____

WRITING
On their papers, students write their favorite words from the chart or other words, phrases, or sentences that would be appropriate for the chart.

SPELLING
Partners call out words for each other to spell aloud.
  Papers are dated and filed.

HOMEWORK
Find information in your science book about plants. Write a list of all words that have *ch*.

217

Lesson **119**

Research

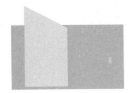

LEAD-IN
Teacher introduces the Project Idea.
Topic: Plants or _____
Material: Magazines or _____
Comprehension Skill: Cause and effect or _____

SEARCH & RECORD
Group Size: Partners or _____
Project Idea: Make a poster with magazine pictures to tell how plants are used. Write captions or _____.

SHARING
Display posters or _____.
   Papers are dated and filed.

Recreational Reading

All students read books for approximately 30 minutes.

CONVERSATIONS
The teacher also reads silently. The teacher has some short conversations with readers. When appropriate, the main focus of these conversations is on each student's decisions to abandon or finish books.

CLIPBOARD NOTES
Teacher notes students' selections of books and whether students abandon or finish books they chose.

READ-ALOUD BOOK
Sing a Song of Popcorn by Beatrice de Regniers** or _____

Writing

Theme: Communication or _____

MINI-LESSON
Teacher leads discussion of suggestions for effective acting, especially the use of clear and audible speech or _____.

COMPOSING
Group rehearses play or puppet show or _____.

SHARING
Group discusses goals for improving performance or _____.
   Papers are dated and filed.

Word Study

CHART DEVELOPMENT
Spelling Emphasis: *be* or
_____
Other Emphasis:
■ paragraphs or _____
■ plants or _____
   On the chart, the teacher writes two paragraphs of sentences volunteered by students using:
■ *be* words
■ plant vocabulary
■ _____

WRITING
On their papers, students write their favorite words from the chart or other words, phrases, or sentences that would be appropriate for the chart.

SPELLING
Partners call out words for each other to spell aloud.
   Papers are dated and filed.

HOMEWORK
Write about what happens after you plant a bean seed.

Research

LEAD-IN
Teacher introduces the Project Idea.
Topic: Plants or _____
Material: Instructions about plant care or _____
Comprehension Skill: Questions and answers or _____

SEARCH & RECORD
Group Size: Partners or _____
Project Idea: Write questions you'll need to answer to plant, grow, and care for a plant. Look for answers in the instructions or _____.

SHARING
Partners call out questions to each other to see if they can remember the answers they recorded or _____.
Papers are dated and filed.

Recreational Reading

All students read books for approximately 30 minutes.

CONVERSATIONS
The teacher also reads silently. The teacher has some short conversations with readers. When appropriate, the main focus of these conversations is on each student's decisions to abandon or finish books.

CLIPBOARD NOTES
Teacher notes students' selections of books and whether students abandon or finish books they chose.

READ-ALOUD BOOK
_____

Writing

Theme: Communication or _____

MINI-LESSON
Teacher leads discussion of appropriate audience behavior at plays and puppet shows or _____.

COMPOSING
Groups present plays and puppet shows or _____.

SHARING
Volunteers praise best accomplishments of plays and puppet shows or _____.
Papers are dated and filed.

Word Study

CHART DEVELOPMENT
Spelling Emphasis: *bo* or _____

Other Emphasis:
- paragraphs or _____
- plants or _____
  On the chart, the teacher writes two paragraphs of sentences volunteered by students using:
- *bo* words
- plant vocabulary
- _____

WRITING
On their papers, students write their favorite words from the chart and other words, phrases, or sentences that would be appropriate for the chart.

SPELLING
Partners call out words for each other to spell aloud.
Papers are dated and filed.

HOMEWORK
Write about why people need plants.

Lesson 121

Research

LEAD-IN
Teacher introduces the Project Idea.
Topic: Plants or _____
Material: Magazines or _____
Comprehension Skill: Classification or _____

SEARCH & RECORD
Group Size: 3 or 4 or _____
Project Idea: Cut out pictures of foods that come from plants. Arrange the pictures in categories the group chooses. Paste on poster or _____.

SHARING
Display posters or _____.
Papers are dated and filed.

Recreational Reading

All students read books for approximately 30 minutes.

CONVERSATIONS
The teacher also reads silently. The teacher has some short conversations with readers. When appropriate, the main focus of these conversations is on each student's ability to describe main characters in a story.

CLIPBOARD NOTES
Teacher notes students' selections of books and whether students prefer certain types of characters.

READ-ALOUD BOOK
The Indian in the Cupboard by Lynne Banks* or _____

Writing

The overall theme for the next 15 days is Changes or _____. One or more of the other modules will reflect this theme.
Theme: Changes or _____

MINI-LESSON
Brainstorm about things that change or _____.

COMPOSING
Write a list of things that change or _____.

SHARING
Volunteers share one thing from their lists of things that change or _____.
Papers are dated and filed.

Word Study

CHART DEVELOPMENT
Spelling Emphasis: *ell* or _____

Other Emphasis:
- paragraphs or _____
- health or _____
  On the chart, the teacher writes 2 or 3 paragraphs of sentences volunteered by students using:
- *ell* words
- health vocabulary
- _____

WRITING
On their papers, students write their favorite words from the chart or other words, phrases, or sentences that would be appropriate for the chart.

SPELLING
Partners call out words for each other to spell aloud.
Papers are dated and filed.

HOMEWORK
Write about some of the things you do to keep well.

Research

LEAD-IN
Teacher introduces the Project Idea.
Topic: Plants or _____
Material: Magazines or _____
Comprehension Skill: Sequence or
_____

SEARCH & RECORD
Group Size: 3 or 4 or _____
Project Idea: Cut out pictures of
plants. Arrange them in order to show
how plants change. Paste pictures on
poster or _____.

SHARING
Display posters or _____.
    Papers are dated and filed.

Recreational Reading

All students read books for approximately
30 minutes.

CONVERSATIONS
The teacher also reads silently. The
teacher has some short conversations with
readers. When appropriate, the main
focus of these conversations is on each
student's ability to describe main
characters in a story.

CLIPBOARD NOTES
Teacher notes students' selections of
books and whether students prefer certain
types of characters.

READ-ALOUD BOOK
_____

Writing

Theme: Changes or _____

MINI-LESSON
Brainstorm ways that people change or
_____.

COMPOSING
Write list of ways that people change or
_____.

SHARING
Partners share lists or _____.
    Papers are dated and filed.

Word Study

CHART DEVELOPMENT
Spelling Emphasis: *chi* or
_____
Other Emphasis:
■ paragraphs or _____
■ business or _____
    On the chart, the teacher writes 2 or 3
paragraphs of sentences volunteered by
students using:
■ *chi* words
■ business vocabulary
■ _____

WRITING
On their papers, students write their
favorite words from the chart and other
words, phrases, or sentences that would
be appropriate for the chart.

SPELLING
Partners call out words for each other to
spell aloud.
    Papers are dated and filed.

HOMEWORK
Write about the machines that are used
in a school.

Lesson 123

Research

LEAD-IN
Teacher introduces the Project Idea.
Topic: Plants or _____
Material: Magazines or _____
Comprehension Skill: Classification
or _____

SEARCH & RECORD
Group Size: 3 or 4 or _____
Project Idea: Cut out pictures of
plants. Arrange them in categories
according to the seasons. Paste pictures
on poster or _____.

SHARING
Display posters or _____.
    Papers are dated and filed.

Recreational Reading

All students read books for approximately
30 minutes.

CONVERSATIONS
The teacher also reads silently. The
teacher has some short conversations with
readers. When appropriate, the main
focus of these conversations is on each
student's ability to describe main
characters in a story.

CLIPBOARD NOTES
Teacher notes students' selections of
books and whether students prefer certain
types of characters.

READ-ALOUD BOOK
_____

Writing

Theme: Changes or _____

MINI-LESSON
Students name things they can observe in
and from the classroom or _____.

COMPOSING
Choose one thing to observe. Write notes
about observations or _____

SHARING
Response groups read observation notes to
each other or _____.
    Papers are dated and filed.

Word Study

CHART DEVELOPMENT
Spelling Emphasis: *jus* or

_____
Other Emphasis:
■ paragraphs or _____
■ world news or _____
    On the chart, the teacher writes 2 or 3
paragraphs of sentences volunteered by
students using:
■ *jus* words
■ news vocabulary
■ _____

WRITING
On their papers, students write their
favorite words from the chart and other
words, phrases, or sentences that would
be appropriate for the chart.

SPELLING
Partners call out words for each other to
spell aloud.
    Papers are dated and filed.

HOMEWORK
Write about the places that were
mentioned in today's news.

Lesson **124**

Research

LEAD-IN
Teacher introduces the Project Idea.
Topic: Plants or _____
Material: Science textbooks or _____

Comprehension Skill: Comparison or _____

SEARCH & RECORD
Group Size: Partners or _____
Project Idea: Choose 2 plants that are discussed in the science textbook. List facts about each and the ways they are alike or different or _____.

SHARING
Share conclusions with another team or _____.
Papers are dated and filed.

Recreational Reading

All students read books for approximately 30 minutes.

CONVERSATIONS
The teacher also reads silently. The teacher has some short conversations with readers. When appropriate, the main focus of these conversations is on each student's ability to describe main characters in a story.

CLIPBOARD NOTES
Teacher notes students' selections of books and whether students prefer certain types of characters.

READ-ALOUD BOOK
The Magic Fan by Keith Baker or _____

Writing

Theme: Changes or _____

MINI-LESSON
Teacher reads factual information about something that changes, perhaps a plant or _____

COMPOSING
Write important information about something that changes or _____.

SHARING
Partners check each other's writing for information about changes or _____.
Papers are dated and filed.

Word Study

CHART DEVELOPMENT
Spelling Emphasis: *opp* or _____

Other Emphasis:
- paragraphs or _____
- local news or _____
On the chart, the teacher writes 2 or 3 paragraphs of sentences volunteered by students using:
- *opp* words
- news vocabulary
- _____

WRITING
On their papers, students write their favorite words from the chart and other words, phrases, or sentences that would be appropriate for the chart.

SPELLING
Partners call out words for each other to spell aloud.
Papers are dated and filed.

HOMEWORK
Write a list of words that are opposites, or antonyms.

Lesson 125

Research

LEAD-IN
Teacher introduces the Project Idea.
Topic: Plants or _____
Material: Students choose or _____

Comprehension Skill: Summary or _____

SEARCH & RECORD
Group Size: Individuals or _____
Project Idea: Search for information that you don't already know about plants. Write a summary of what you find or _____.

SHARING
Volunteers tell class one interesting thing they each discovered or _____.
Papers are dated and filed.

Recreational Reading

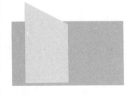

All students read books for approximately 30 minutes.

CONVERSATIONS
The teacher also reads silently. The teacher has some short conversations with readers. When appropriate, the main focus of these conversations is on each student's ability to describe main characters in a story.

CLIPBOARD NOTES
Teacher notes students' selections of books and whether students prefer certain types of characters.

READ-ALOUD BOOK
_____

Writing

Theme: Changes or _____

MINI-LESSON
Teacher reads poem about change, perhaps about plants changing with the seasons or _____.

COMPOSING
Write poem about change, perhaps using information from Lesson 124 in poetic form or _____.

SHARING
Volunteers read poems to class or _____.
Papers are dated and filed.

Word Study

CHART DEVELOPMENT
Spelling Emphasis: *les* or _____

Other Emphasis:
- paragraphs or _____
- sports or _____
  On the chart, the teacher writes 2 or 3 paragraphs of sentences volunteered by students using:
- *les* words
- sports vocabulary
- _____

WRITING
On their papers, students write their favorite words from the chart and other words, phrases, or sentences that would be appropriate for the chart.

SPELLING
Partners call out words for each other to spell aloud.
Papers are dated and filed.

HOMEWORK
Your teacher giggles and chuckles upon hearing your silly poems. Write some poems using *les* words.

Research

LEAD-IN
Teacher introduces the Project Idea.
Topic: Weather or _____
Material: Science textbook or

_____

Comprehension Skill: Skimming or

_____

SEARCH & RECORD
Group Size: Partners or _____
Project Idea: Write a list of words
associated with weather or _____.

SHARING
Volunteers give suggestions for making a
class weather word list or _____.
    Papers are dated and filed.

Recreational Reading

All students read books for approximately
30 minutes.

CONVERSATIONS
The teacher also reads silently. The
teacher has some short conversations with
readers. When appropriate, the main
focus of these conversations is on each
student's ability to describe main
characters in a story.

CLIPBOARD NOTES
Teacher notes students' selections of
books and whether students prefer certain
types of characters.

READ-ALOUD BOOK

_____

Writing

Theme: Changes or _____

MINI-LESSON
Teacher leads discussion of information
that needs to be included in factual
writing: who, what, where, when, and
why or _____.

COMPOSING
Write about something that changes.
Include details or _____.

SHARING
Partners proofread each other's drafts for
details or _____.
    Papers are dated and filed.

Word Study

CHART DEVELOPMENT
Spelling Emphasis: *kno* or

_____

Other Emphasis:
■ paragraphs or _____
■ weather or _____
    On the chart, the teacher writes 2 or 3
paragraphs of sentences volunteered by
students using:
■ *kno* words
■ weather vocabulary
■ _____

WRITING
On their papers, students write their
favorite words from the chart and other
words, phrases, or sentences that would
be appropriate for the chart.

SPELLING
Partners call out words for each other to
spell aloud.
    Papers are dated and filed.

HOMEWORK
Write sentences telling what you know
about weather.

Lesson 127

Research

LEAD-IN
Teacher introduces the Project Idea.
Topic: Weather or _____
Material: Science textbooks or
_____

Comprehension Skill: Skimming or
_____

SEARCH & RECORD
Group Size: Partners or _____
Project Idea: Search science textbook
for names of instruments used in
measuring and reporting weather. List
their names and what they do or
_____.

SHARING
Share findings with another team or
_____.
   Papers are dated and filed.

Recreational Reading

All students read books for approximately
30 minutes.

CONVERSATIONS
The teacher also reads silently. The
teacher has some short conversations with
readers. When appropriate, the main
focus of these conversations is on each
student's ability to describe main
characters in a story.

CLIPBOARD NOTES
Teacher notes students' selections of
books and whether students prefer certain
types of characters.

READ-ALOUD BOOK
Big Al by Andrew Clements or
_____

Writing

Theme: Changes or _____

MINI-LESSON
Students review lists of books read
recently or _____.

COMPOSING
Write about the way things changed in a
book you read recently or _____.

SHARING
Volunteers share book discussion with
class or _____.
   Papers are dated and filed.

Word Study

CHART DEVELOPMENT
Spelling Emphasis: *ott* or
_____

Other Emphasis:
■ paragraphs or _____
■ weather or _____
   On the chart, the teacher writes 2 or 3
paragraphs of sentences volunteered by
students using:
■ *ott* words
■ weather vocabulary
■ _____

WRITING
On their papers, students write their
favorite words from the chart and other
words, phrases, or sentences that would
be appropriate for the chart.

SPELLING
Partners call out words for each other to
spell aloud.
   Papers are dated and filed.

HOMEWORK
Look in your science book for important
words about weather. Write them on a
piece of paper.

Research

LEAD-IN
Teacher introduces the Project Idea.
Topic: Weather or _____
Material: Newspapers or _____
Comprehension Skill: Cause and effect or _____

SEARCH & RECORD
Group Size: Partners or _____
Project Idea: Make a chart of weather information from the newspaper. Report findings according to cause and effect: It rained 2 inches (cause), and the streets flooded (effect) or _____.

SHARING
Volunteers suggest findings for a class cause-and-effect chart or _____.
   Papers are dated and filed.

Recreational Reading

All students read books for approximately 30 minutes.

CONVERSATIONS
The teacher also reads silently. The teacher has some short conversations with readers. When appropriate, the main focus of these conversations is on each student's ability to describe main characters in a story.

CLIPBOARD NOTES
Teacher notes students' selections of books and whether students prefer certain types of characters.

READ-ALOUD BOOK
_____

Writing

Theme: Changes or _____

MINI-LESSON
Teacher points out variety of articles in newspaper. Class will publish a paper in Lesson 135 or _____.

COMPOSING
Students choose a type of article to write. Topic ideas come from drafts about changes or _____.

SHARING
Everyone tells what type of article he or she will prepare for the paper or _____.
   Papers are dated and filed.

Word Study

CHART DEVELOPMENT
Spelling Emphasis: *ten* or
_____
Other Emphasis:
■ paragraphs or _____
■ weather or _____
   On the chart, the teacher writes 2 or 3 paragraphs of sentences volunteered by students using:
■ *ten* words
■ weather vocabulary
■ _____

WRITING
On their papers, students write their favorite words from the chart and other words, phrases, or sentences that would be appropriate for the chart.

SPELLING
Partners call out words for each other to spell aloud.
   Papers are dated and filed.

HOMEWORK
Write a weather forecast for the next five days. Use *ten* words if possible.

Lesson **129**

Research

LEAD-IN
Teacher introduces the Project Idea.
Topic: Weather or _____
Material: Newspaper weather reports or _____
Comprehension Skill: Details or _____

SEARCH & RECORD
Group Size: Partners or _____
Project Idea: Take notes about the weather in some different places or _____ .

SHARING
Report findings to another team or _____ .

  Papers are dated and filed.

Recreational Reading

All students read books for approximately 30 minutes.

CONVERSATIONS
The teacher also reads silently. The teacher has some short conversations with readers. When appropriate, the main focus of these conversations is on each student's ability to describe main characters in a story.

CLIPBOARD NOTES
Teacher notes students' selections of books and whether students prefer certain types of characters.

READ-ALOUD BOOK
_____

Writing

Theme: Changes or _____

MINI-LESSON
Teacher leads discussion about writing leads for news articles or _____ .

COMPOSING
Continue draft or _____ .

SHARING
Volunteers share leads of articles or _____ .

  Papers are dated and filed.

Word Study

CHART DEVELOPMENT
Spelling Emphasis: *rab* or _____

Other Emphasis:
■ paragraphs or _____
■ weather or _____
  On the chart, the teacher writes 2 or 3 paragraphs of sentences volunteered by students using:
■ *rab* words
■ weather vocabulary
■ _____

WRITING
On their papers, students write their favorite words from the chart and other words, phrases, or sentences that would be appropriate for the chart.

SPELLING
Partners call out words for each other to spell aloud.
  Papers are dated and filed.

HOMEWORK
Write a list of things you like to do when the weather is drab and dreary. Use *rab* words if you can.

Research

LEAD-IN
Teacher introduces the Project Idea.
Topic: Weather or _____
Material: Newspaper weather reports
or _____
Comprehension Skill: Comparison
or _____

SEARCH & RECORD
Group Size: Partners or _____
Project Idea: Write a list of places
that have similar weather and a list of
some that have different weather or
_____

SHARING
Share findings with another team or
_____.
Papers are dated and filed.

Recreational Reading

All students read books for approximately
30 minutes.

CONVERSATIONS
The teacher also reads silently. The
teacher has some short conversations with
readers. When appropriate, the main
focus of these conversations is on each
student's ability to describe main
characters in a story.

CLIPBOARD NOTES
Teacher notes students' selections of
books and whether students prefer certain
types of characters.

READ-ALOUD BOOK
Wilfrid Gordon McDonald Partridge by
Mem Fox or _____

Writing

Theme: Changes or _____

MINI-LESSON
Teacher reviews inclusion of details in
newspaper: who, what, when, where, why
or _____.

COMPOSING
Continue draft or _____.

SHARING
Partners proofread for details or
_____.
Papers are dated and filed.

Word Study

CHART DEVELOPMENT
Spelling Emphasis: *plu* or
_____

Other Emphasis:
- paragraphs or _____
- weather or _____
  On the chart, the teacher writes 2 or 3
paragraphs of sentences volunteered by
students using:
- *plu* words
- weather vocabulary
- _____

WRITING
On their papers, students write their
favorite words from the chart or other
words, phrases, or sentences that would
be appropriate for the chart.

SPELLING
Partners call out words for each other to
spell aloud.
Papers are dated and filed.

HOMEWORK
Look at the weather report in the
newspaper. Write a list of words that
have *plu*.

229

Lesson 131

Research

LEAD-IN
Teacher introduces the Project Idea.
Topic: Weather or _____
Material: Library books and textbooks
or _____
Comprehension Skill: Main idea
and details or _____

SEARCH & RECORD
Group Size: 2 or 3 or _____
Project Idea: Choose a weather topic.
Read to learn new information about your
topic. Write notes about what you learn
or _____.

SHARING
Volunteers tell the class an interesting
fact or _____.
Papers are dated and filed.

Recreational Reading

All students read books for approximately
30 minutes.

CONVERSATIONS
The teacher also reads silently. The
teacher has some short conversations with
readers. When appropriate, the main
focus of these conversations is on each
student's ability to explain events in a
story.

CLIPBOARD NOTES
Teacher notes students' selections of
books and whether students explain
reasons for events when they discuss
books with friends.

READ-ALOUD BOOK
_____

Writing

Theme: Changes or _____

MINI-LESSON
Teacher demonstrates dividing articles
into paragraphs or _____.

COMPOSING
Continue draft or _____.

SHARING
Partners proofread for effective
paragraphing or _____.
Papers are dated and filed.

Word Study

CHART DEVELOPMENT
Spelling Emphasis: *qui* or
_____

Other Emphasis:
- paragraphs or _____
- music or _____
  On the chart, the teacher writes 2 or 3
paragraphs of sentences volunteered by
students using:
- *qui* words
- music vocabulary
- _____

WRITING
On their papers, students write their
favorite words from the chart or other
words, phrases, or sentences that would
be appropriate for the chart.

SPELLING
Partners call out words for each other to
spell aloud.
Papers are dated and filed.

HOMEWORK
Write about the kinds of music that make
you quiet and the kinds that make you
move quickly.

Research

LEAD-IN
Teacher introduces the Project Idea.
Topic: Weather or _____
Material: Library books or _____
Comprehension Skill: Questions and answers or _____

SEARCH & RECORD
Group Size: 2 or 3 or _____
Project Idea: Continue reading about chosen weather topic. Write questions that you can answer with the information you learn from reading. Write each question on a separate notecard or

_____.

SHARING
Call out questions and recite answers or
_____.
Papers are dated and filed.

Recreational Reading

All students read books for approximately 30 minutes.

CONVERSATIONS
The teacher also reads silently. The teacher has some short conversations with readers. When appropriate, the main focus of these conversations is on each student's ability to explain events in a story.

CLIPBOARD NOTES
Teacher notes students' selections of books and whether students explain reasons for events when they discuss books with friends.

READ-ALOUD BOOK
_____

Writing

Theme: Changes or _____

MINI-LESSON
Response groups discuss ways to help fellow writers divide work into paragraphs or _____.

COMPOSING
Continue draft or _____.

SHARING
Response groups share drafts, giving attention to dividing work into paragraphs or _____.
Papers are dated and filed.

Word Study

CHART DEVELOPMENT
Spelling Emphasis: *str* or
_____

Other Emphasis:
- paragraphs or _____
- communications or _____
  On the chart, the teacher writes 2 or 3 paragraphs of sentences volunteered by students using:
- *str* words
- communications vocabulary
- _____

WRITING
On their papers, students write their favorite words from the chart or other words, phrases, or sentences that would be appropriate for the chart.

SPELLING
Partners call out words for each other to spell aloud.
Papers are dated and filed.

HOMEWORK
Look in the telephone book for places that sell string guitars. Write the information you need for finding these stores on a piece of paper.

231

Lesson **133**

Research

LEAD-IN
Teacher introduces the Project Idea.
Topic: Weather or _____
Material: Cards from Lesson 132 or

_____

Comprehension Skill: Classification
or _____

SEARCH & RECORD
Group Size: 2 or 3 or _____
Project Idea: Sort cards into groups
that belong together or _____.

SHARING
Show another group your stacks of cards
and explain how you decided to arrange
them or _____.
  Papers are dated and filed.

Recreational Reading

All students read books for approximately
30 minutes.

CONVERSATIONS
The teacher also reads silently. The
teacher has some short conversations with
readers. When appropriate, the main
focus of these conversations is on each
student's ability to explain events in a
story.

CLIPBOARD NOTES
Teacher notes students' selections of
books and whether students explain
reasons for events when they discuss
books with friends.

READ-ALOUD BOOK
*The People Could Fly, American Black
Folk Tales* by Virginia Hamilton** or
_____

Writing

Theme: Changes or _____

MINI-LESSON
Teacher leads discussion about preparing
illustrations, graphs, maps, etc., to
accompany newspaper articles or

_____.

COMPOSING
Continue draft. Add illustrations, graphs,
maps, etc., or _____.

SHARING
Response groups share and check
appropriateness of illustrations or
_____.
  Papers are dated and filed.

Word Study

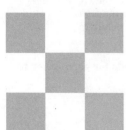

CHART DEVELOPMENT
Spelling Emphasis: *twi* or _____

Other Emphasis:
■ paragraphs or _____
■ mathematics or _____
  On the chart, the teacher writes 2 or 3
paragraphs of sentences volunteered by
students using:
■ *twi* words
■ mathematics vocabulary
■ _____

WRITING
On their papers, students write their
favorite words from the chart and other
words, phrases, or sentences that would
be appropriate for the chart.

SPELLING
Partners call out words for each other to
spell aloud.
  Papers are dated and filed.

HOMEWORK
Interview people who know something
about twisters, or tornadoes. Make a
graph to report what you learn.

Lesson **134**

Research

LEAD-IN
Teacher introduces the Project Idea.
Topic: Weather or _____
Material: Magazines or _____
Comprehension Skill: Main idea
and details or _____

SEARCH & RECORD
Group Size: Partners or _____
Project Idea: Cut out pictures that
illustrate different kinds of weather.
Write captions for them or _____.

SHARING
Display pictures and captions or
_____
   Papers are dated and filed.

Recreational Reading

All students read books for approximately
30 minutes.

CONVERSATIONS
The teacher also reads silently. The
teacher has some short conversations with
readers. When appropriate, the main
focus of these conversations is on each
student's ability to explain events in a
story. .

CLIPBOARD NOTES
Teacher notes students' selections of
books and whether students explain
reasons for events when they discuss
books with friends.

READ-ALOUD BOOK
_____

Writing

Theme: Changes or _____

MINI-LESSON
Teacher leads discussion of how to
compose good titles for news articles or
_____.

COMPOSING
Edit piece for newspaper. Check title or
_____.

SHARING
Partners help edit and check title or
_____.
   Papers are dated and filed.

Word Study

CHART DEVELOPMENT
Spelling Emphasis: *est* or
_____

Other Emphasis:
- paragraphs or _____
- science or _____
   On the chart, the teacher writes 2 or 3
paragraphs of sentences volunteered by
students using:
- *est* words
- science vocabulary
- _____

WRITING
On their papers, students write their
favorite words from the chart and other
words, phrases, or sentences that would
be appropriate for the chart.

SPELLING
Partners call out words for each other to
spell aloud.
   Papers are dated and filed.

HOMEWORK
Look in your science book for words
containing the letters *est*. Write them on
a piece of paper.

Lesson 135

Research

LEAD-IN
Teacher introduces the Project Idea.
Topic: Weather or _____
Material: Students choose or
_____

Comprehension Skill: Summary or
_____

SEARCH & RECORD
Group Size: Individuals or _____
Project Idea: Read about a new
weather topic. Write a summary of what
you find out or _____.

SHARING
Volunteers tell the class something
interesting they learned or _____.
Papers are dated and filed.

Recreational Reading

All students read books for approximately
30 minutes.

CONVERSATIONS
The teacher also reads silently. The
teacher has some short conversations with
readers. When appropriate, the main
focus of these conversations is on each
student's ability to explain events in a
story.

CLIPBOARD NOTES
Teacher notes students' selections of
books and whether students explain
reasons for events when they discuss
books with friends.

READ-ALOUD BOOK
_____

Writing

Theme: Changes or _____

MINI-LESSON
Teacher gives instructions for final
assembly of newspaper or _____.

COMPOSING
Complete piece for newspaper or
_____.

SHARING
Read class newspaper or _____.
Papers are dated and filed.

Word Study

CHART DEVELOPMENT
Spelling Emphasis: *stu* or
_____

Other Emphasis:
■ paragraphs or _____
■ geography or _____
   On the chart, the teacher writes 2 or 3
paragraphs of sentences volunteered by
students using:
■ *stu* words
■ geography vocabulary
■ _____

WRITING
On their papers, students write their
favorite words from the chart and other
words, phrases, or sentences that would
be appropriate for the chart.

SPELLING
Partners call out words for each other to
spell aloud.
   Papers are dated and filed.

HOMEWORK
Write a story using the following words:
student, stuck, study, studio, stuff,
stumble, stump, stunt.

Research

LEAD-IN
Teacher introduces the Project Idea.
Topic: Cities or _____
Material: Maps or _____
Comprehension Skill: Alphabetizing
or _____

SEARCH & RECORD
Group Size: Partners or _____
Project Idea: Make a list of cities on
the map. Write the list in alphabetical
order or _____.

SHARING
Teacher lists volunteered city names in
alphabetical order or _____.
   Papers are dated and filed.

Recreational Reading

All students read books for approximately
30 minutes.

CONVERSATIONS
The teacher also reads silently. The
teacher has some short conversations with
readers. When appropriate, the main
focus of these conversations is on each
student's ability to explain events in a
story.

CLIPBOARD NOTES
Teacher notes students' selections of
books and whether students explain
reasons for events when they discuss
books with friends.

READ-ALOUD BOOK
Wings, A Tale of Two Chickens by James
Marshall or _____

Writing

The overall theme for the next 15 days is
Cities or_____. One or more of the
other modules will reflect this theme.
Theme: Cities or _____

MINI-LESSON
Brainstorm list of cities or _____.

COMPOSING
Write list of cities or _____.

SHARING
Volunteers name cities not mentioned
during the mini-lesson or _____.
   Papers are dated and filed.

Word Study

CHART DEVELOPMENT
Spelling Emphasis: *tro* or
_____

Other Emphasis:
■ paragraphs or _____
■ health or _____
   On the chart, the teacher writes 2 or 3
paragraphs of sentences volunteered by
students using:
■ *tro* words
■ health vocabulary
■ _____

WRITING
On their papers, students write their
favorite words from the chart and other
words, phrases, or sentences that would
be appropriate for the chart.

SPELLING
Partners call out words for each other to
spell aloud.
   Papers are dated and filed.

HOMEWORK
Create a health poster that would win a
trophy.

235

Lesson **137**

Research

LEAD-IN
Teacher introduces the Project Idea.
Topic: Cities or _____
Material: Maps or _____
Comprehension Skill: Sequencing
or _____

SEARCH & RECORD
Group Size: Partners or _____
Project Idea: Choose a city and list
other cities on the map according to their
distance from the first city, from closest to
most distant or _____.

SHARING
Show another team your list of cities or
_____.
Papers are dated and filed.

Recreational Reading

All students read books for approximately
30 minutes.

CONVERSATIONS
The teacher also reads silently. The
teacher has some short conversations with
readers. When appropriate, the main
focus of these conversations is on each
student's ability to explain events in a
story.

CLIPBOARD NOTES
Teacher notes students' selections of
books and whether students explain
reasons for events when they discuss
books with friends.

READ-ALOUD BOOK
_____

Writing

Theme: Cities or _____

MINI-LESSON
Brainstorm list of things found in a city
or _____.

COMPOSING
Write list of things found in a city or
_____.

SHARING
Partners compare lists or _____.
Papers are dated and filed.

Word Study

CHART DEVELOPMENT
Spelling Emphasis: *mot* or
_____

Other Emphasis:
■ paragraphs or _____
■ art or _____
On the chart, the teacher writes 2 or 3
paragraphs of sentences volunteered by
students using:
■ *mot* words
■ art vocabulary
■ _____

WRITING
On their papers, students write their
favorite words from the chart and other
words, phrases, or sentences that would
be appropriate for the chart.

SPELLING
Partners call out words for each other to
spell aloud.
Papers are dated and filed.

HOMEWORK
Describe an art project you could do for
your mother. What kinds of art does she
like?

Research

LEAD-IN
Teacher introduces the Project Idea.
Topic: Cities or _____
Material: Newspapers or _____
Comprehension Skill: Skimming or _____

SEARCH & RECORD
Group Size: Partners or _____
Project Idea: Search for names of cities. Record those that are on your lists from Lessons 136 and 137. Write the reason for each city's mention in the newspaper or _____.

SHARING
Compare your list to another team's or _____.
    Papers are dated and filed.

Recreational Reading

All students read books for approximately 30 minutes.

CONVERSATIONS
The teacher also reads silently. The teacher has some short conversations with readers. When appropriate, the main focus of these conversations is on each student's ability to explain events in a story.

CLIPBOARD NOTES
Teacher notes students' selections of books and whether students explain reasons for events when they discuss books with friends.

READ-ALOUD BOOK
_____

Writing

Theme: Cities or _____

MINI-LESSON
Students study lists written for Lessons 136 and 137 to find best topics for further writing or _____.

COMPOSING
Begin draft or _____.

SHARING
Everyone tells topics chosen for pieces about cities or _____.
    Papers are dated and filed.

Word Study

CHART DEVELOPMENT
Spelling Emphasis: *ing* or _____

Other Emphasis:
■ paragraphs or _____
■ education or _____
    On the chart, the teacher writes 2 or 3 paragraphs of sentences volunteered by students using:
■ *ing* words
■ education vocabulary
■ _____

WRITING
On their papers, students write their favorite words from the chart and other words, phrases, or sentences that would be appropriate for the chart.

SPELLING
Partners call out words for each other to spell aloud.
    Papers are dated and filed.

HOMEWORK
Write a list of things you are learning in school.

Lesson 139

Research

LEAD-IN
Teacher introduces the Project Idea.
Topic: Cities or _____
Material: Social studies textbooks or _____

Comprehension Skill: Details or _____

SEARCH & RECORD
Group Size: Partners or _____
Project Idea: Choose one city that is described in the textbook. Write a list of facts about the city or _____.

SHARING
Show another team your findings or _____.
Papers are dated and filed.

Recreational Reading

All students read books for approximately 30 minutes.

CONVERSATIONS
The teacher also reads silently. The teacher has some short conversations with readers. When appropriate, the main focus of these conversations is on each student's ability to explain events in a story.

CLIPBOARD NOTES
Teacher notes students' selections of books and whether students explain reasons for events when they discuss books with friends.

READ-ALOUD BOOK
Shoes from Grandpa by Mem Fox or _____

Writing

Theme: Cities or _____

MINI-LESSON
Teacher reads factual information about cities or _____.

COMPOSING
Students write facts about cities or _____.

SHARING
Partners share drafts and check for facts or _____.
Papers are dated and filed.

Word Study

CHART DEVELOPMENT
Spelling Emphasis: *cks* or _____

Other Emphasis:
- paragraphs or _____
- local news or _____
  On the chart, the teacher writes 2 or 3 paragraphs of sentences volunteered by students using:
- *cks* words
- local news vocabulary
- _____

WRITING
On their papers, students write their favorite words from the chart and other words, phrases, or sentences that would be appropriate for the chart.

SPELLING
Partners call out words for each other to spell aloud.
Papers are dated and filed.

HOMEWORK
Look in the newspaper for important words about news events in your town. Also look for words with the letters *cks*. Write them all on a piece of paper.

Research

LEAD-IN
Teacher introduces the Project Idea.
Topic: Cities or _____
Material: Encyclopedia or _____
Comprehension Skill: Organizing information or _____

SEARCH & RECORD
Group Size: Partners or _____
Project Idea: Search for information about a city in the encyclopedia. Organize your findings into a chart. For example, you might make a column to list the jobs people have in the city or _____.

SHARING
Show another team your chart or _____.
Papers are dated and filed.

Recreational Reading

All students read books for approximately 30 minutes.

CONVERSATIONS
The teacher also reads silently. The teacher has some short conversations with readers. When appropriate, the main focus of these conversations is on each student's ability to explain events in a story.

CLIPBOARD NOTES
Teacher notes students' selections of books and whether students explain reasons for events when they discuss books with friends.

READ-ALOUD BOOK
_____

Writing

Theme: Cities or _____

MINI-LESSON
Teacher reads a poem about life in a city or _____.

COMPOSING
Students write poems about cities, perhaps using facts from earlier drafts or _____.

SHARING
Volunteers read poems to class or _____.
Papers are dated and filed.

Word Study

CHART DEVELOPMENT
Spelling Emphasis: *ter* or
_____
Other Emphasis:
■ paragraphs or _____
■ business or _____
   On the chart, the teacher writes 2 or 3 paragraphs of sentences volunteered by students using:
■ *ter* words
■ business vocabulary
■ _____

WRITING
On their papers, students write their favorite words from the chart or other words, phrases, or sentences that would be appropriate for the chart.

SPELLING
Partners call out words for each other to spell aloud.
   Papers are dated and filed.

HOMEWORK
Write a list of suggestions for better business in your town.

239

Lesson **141**

Research

LEAD-IN
Teacher introduces the Project Idea.
Topic: Cities or _____
Material: Encyclopedias or _____
Comprehension Skill: Classification
or _____

SEARCH & RECORD
Group Size: Partners or _____
Project Idea: Write question and
answer cards about a city. Use
information from encyclopedia or
_____.

SHARING
Read questions to another team. Can they
guess the city? or _____.
  Papers are dated and filed.

Recreational Reading

All students read books for approximately
30 minutes.

CONVERSATIONS
The teacher also reads silently. The
teacher has some short conversations with
readers. When appropriate, the main
focus of these conversations is on each
student's favorite books.

CLIPBOARD NOTES
Teacher notes students' selections of
books and whether students talk with
friends about favorite books.

READ-ALOUD BOOK
_____

Writing

Theme: Cities or _____

MINI-LESSON
Teacher demonstrates use of commas to
separate items in a series or _____.

COMPOSING
Continue draft or _____.

SHARING
Partners proofread, paying special
attention to punctuation or _____.
  Papers are dated and filed.

Word Study

CHART DEVELOPMENT
Spelling Emphasis: *tch* or _____

Other Emphasis:
■ paragraphs or _____
■ geography or _____
  On the chart, the teacher writes 2 or 3
paragraphs of sentences volunteered by
students using:
■ *tch* words
■ geography vocabulary
■ _____

WRITING
On their papers, students write their
favorite words from the chart or other
words, phrases, or sentences that would
be appropriate for the chart.

SPELLING
Partners call out words for each other to
spell aloud.
  Papers are dated and filed.

HOMEWORK
Write an activity in which another
student will match cities with their
states.

Research

LEAD-IN
Teacher introduces the Project Idea.
Topic: Cities or _____
Material: Brochures or _____
Comprehension Skill: Questions and answers or _____

SEARCH & RECORD
Group Size: Partners or _____
Project Idea: Write questions about a city that are answered in a brochure about that city or _____.

SHARING
Call out questions to your partner. Look for answers in the brochure or _____.
   Papers are dated and filed.

Recreational Reading

All students read books for approximately 30 minutes.

CONVERSATIONS
The teacher also reads silently. The teacher has some short conversations with readers. When appropriate, the main focus of these conversations is on each student's favorite books.

CLIPBOARD NOTES
Teacher notes students' selections of books and whether students talk with friends about favorite books.

READ-ALOUD BOOK
The True Story of the Three Little Pigs by Jon Scieszka or _____

Writing

Theme: Cities or _____

MINI-LESSON
Students review lists of books they have read recently or _____.

COMPOSING
Write about a book you have read recently. Mention the setting of the book or _____.

SHARING
Partners compare settings of books they have read or _____.
   Papers are dated and filed.

Word Study

CHART DEVELOPMENT
Spelling Emphasis: *ser* or _____

Other Emphasis:
■ paragraphs or _____
■ law or _____
   On the chart, the teacher writes 2 or 3 paragraphs of sentences volunteered by students using:
■ *ser* words
■ law vocabulary
■ _____

WRITING
On their papers, students write their favorite words from the chart or other words, phrases, or sentences that would be appropriate for the chart.

SPELLING
Partners call out words for each other to spell aloud.
   Papers are dated and filed.

HOMEWORK
Draw signs containing the letters *ser* that relate to the law.

Lesson 143

Research

LEAD-IN
Teacher introduces the Project Idea.
Topic: Cities or _____
Material: Brochures or _____
Comprehension Skill: Cause and effect or _____

SEARCH & RECORD
Group Size: Partners or _____
Project Idea: Based on information in the brochures, list cities you would like to visit, beginning with the ones you like best. Beside each, write the reason you'd like to visit, or _____.

SHARING
Compare your list with another team's or _____.
Papers are dated and filed.

Recreational Reading

All students read books for approximately 30 minutes.

CONVERSATIONS
The teacher also reads silently. The teacher has some short conversations with readers. When appropriate, the main focus of these conversations is on each student's favorite books.

CLIPBOARD NOTES
Teacher notes students' selections of books and whether students talk with friends about favorite books.

READ-ALOUD BOOK
_____

Writing

Theme: Cities or _____

MINI-LESSON
Teacher introduces publishing opportunity: class will assemble an exhibit about cities in Lesson 150. Brainstorm list of artifacts to include or _____.

COMPOSING
Write list of artifacts you can contribute. Begin drafts of write-ups to accompany them or _____

SHARING
Everyone shares an item he or she plans to contribute to the exhibit or _____.
Papers are dated and filed.

Word Study

CHART DEVELOPMENT
Spelling Emphasis: *ara* or
_____

Other Emphasis:
■ paragraphs or _____
■ medicine or _____
On the chart, the teacher writes paragraphs of sentences volunteered by students using:
■ *ara* words
■ medicine vocabulary
■ _____

WRITING
On their papers, students write their favorite words from the chart or other words, phrases, or sentences that would be appropriate for the chart.

SPELLING
Partners call out words for each other to spell aloud.
Papers are dated and filed.

HOMEWORK
Write a paragraph about important things to remember about taking medicine.

Lesson 144

Research

LEAD-IN
Teacher introduces the Project Idea.
Topic: Cities or _____
Material: Encyclopedias or _____
Comprehension Skill: Comparison
or _____

SEARCH & RECORD
Group Size: Partners or _____
Project Idea: Choose one city in the
United States and one in another country.
List the ways they are similar and ways
they are different or _____.

SHARING
Share your findings with another team or
_____.
　Papers are dated and filed.

Recreational Reading

All students read books for approximately
30 minutes.

CONVERSATIONS
The teacher also reads silently. The
teacher has some short conversations with
readers. When appropriate, the main
focus of these conversations is on each
student's favorite books.

CLIPBOARD NOTES
Teacher notes students' selections of
books and whether students talk with
friends about favorite books.

READ-ALOUD BOOK
_____

Writing

Theme: Cities or _____

MINI-LESSON
Teacher leads discussion of types of
writing needed for exhibit: poetry,
narrative history, explanations, etc., or
_____

COMPOSING
Work on draft of pieces for exhibit or
_____.

SHARING
Partners discuss plans for exhibit pieces
or _____.
　Papers are dated and filed.

Word Study

CHART DEVELOPMENT
Spelling Emphasis: *dge* or
_____

Other Emphasis:
- 4 paragraphs or _____
- mathematics or _____
　On the chart, the teacher writes
paragraphs of sentences volunteered by
students using:
- *dge* words
- mathematics vocabulary
- _____

WRITING
On their papers, students write their
favorite words from the chart or other
words, phrases, or sentences that would
be appropriate for the chart.

SPELLING
Partners call out words for each other to
spell aloud.
　Papers are dated and filed.

HOMEWORK
Write directions for doing something you
have learned in mathematics.

Lesson **145**

Research

LEAD-IN
Teacher introduces the Project Idea.
Topic: Cities or _____
Material: Students choose or
_____

Comprehension Skill: Summary or
_____

SEARCH & RECORD
Group Size: Individuals or _____
Project Idea: Search for information
about a city that you haven't studied.
Write notes about the most interesting
information or _____.

SHARING
Summarize your information for your
partner or _____.
Papers are dated and filed.

Recreational Reading

All students read books for approximately
30 minutes.

CONVERSATIONS
The teacher also reads silently. The
teacher has some short conversations with
readers. When appropriate, the main
focus of these conversations is on each
student's favorite books.

CLIPBOARD NOTES
Teacher notes students' selections of
books and whether students talk with
friends about favorite books.

READ-ALOUD BOOK
Owls in the Family by Farley Mowat* or
_____

Writing

Theme: Cities or _____

MINI-LESSON
Students announce their contributions to
the exhibit. Teacher records list. Class
analyzes list to make certain that all the
important ideas are covered or
_____.

COMPOSING
Continue draft or _____.

SHARING
Partners proofread for good sequence of
ideas in exhibit labels or _____.
Papers are dated and filed.

Word Study

CHART DEVELOPMENT
Spelling Emphasis: *fre* or _____

Other Emphasis:
■ 4 paragraphs or _____
■ literature or _____
On the chart, the teacher writes
paragraphs of sentences volunteered by
students using:
■ *fre* words
■ literature vocabulary
■ _____

WRITING
On their papers, students write their
favorite words from the chart or other
words, phrases, or sentences that would
be appropriate for the chart.

SPELLING
Partners call out words for each other to
spell aloud.
Papers are dated and filed.

HOMEWORK
Write about your favorite book. Use some
words containing the letters *fre* if you
can.

Lesson **146**

Research

LEAD-IN
Teacher introduces the Project Idea.
Topic: Our state or _____
Material: Maps of state or _____
Comprehension Skill: Map reading or _____

SEARCH & RECORD
Group Size: Partners or _____
Project Idea: Write a list of cities in our state. Circle the state capital or _____.

SHARING
Volunteers read one city each from their lists. Teacher may record class list or _____.

Papers are dated and filed.

Recreational Reading

All students read books for approximately 30 minutes.

CONVERSATIONS
The teacher also reads silently. The teacher has some short conversations with readers. When appropriate, the main focus of these conversations is on each student's favorite books.

CLIPBOARD NOTES
Teacher notes students' selections of books and whether students talk with friends about favorite books.

READ-ALOUD BOOK
_____

Writing

Theme: Cities or _____

MINI-LESSON
Teacher leads review of importance of including main idea and supporting details in exhibit labels or _____.

COMPOSING
Continue draft or _____.

SHARING
Partners check each other's drafts for main ideas and supporting details or _____.

Papers are dated and filed.

Word Study

CHART DEVELOPMENT
Spelling Emphasis: *ght* or _____

Other Emphasis:
- 4 paragraphs or _____
- our state or _____
  On the chart, the teacher writes paragraphs of sentences volunteered by students using:
- *ght* words
- vocabulary about our state
- _____

WRITING
On their papers, students write their favorite words from the chart or other words, phrases, or sentences that would be appropriate for the chart.

SPELLING
Partners call out words for each other to spell aloud.
Papers are dated and filed.

HOMEWORK
Write some sentences telling facts about our state.

Lesson **147**

Research

LEAD-IN
Teacher introduces the Project Idea.
Topic: Our state or _____
Material: Newspapers or _____
Comprehension Skill: Main idea and details or _____

SEARCH & RECORD
Group Size: 3 or 4 or _____
Project Idea: Search for events that happened in our state and make a list or _____.

SHARING
Each group reports one event to the class or _____.
Papers are dated and filed.

Recreational Reading

All students read books for approximately 30 minutes.

CONVERSATIONS
The teacher also reads silently. The teacher has some short conversations with readers. When appropriate, the main focus of these conversations is on each student's favorite book.

CLIPBOARD NOTES
Teacher notes students' selections of books and whether students talk with friends about favorite books.

READ-ALOUD BOOK
_____

Writing

Theme: Cities or _____

MINI-LESSON
Response group demonstrates how to help fellow writers make sure all necessary information is included or _____.

COMPOSING
Continue draft or _____.

SHARING
Response groups help each other make sure all necessary information is included in drafts or _____.
Papers are dated and filed.

Word Study

CHART DEVELOPMENT
Spelling Emphasis: *les* or _____

Other Emphasis:
- 4 paragraphs or _____
- our state or _____
  On the chart, the teacher writes paragraphs of sentences volunteered by students using:
- *les* words
- vocabulary about our state
- _____

WRITING
On their papers, students write their favorite words from the chart or other words, phrases, or sentences that would be appropriate for the chart.

SPELLING
Partners call out words for each other to spell aloud.
Papers are dated and filed.

HOMEWORK
Write a list of places you would like to visit in our state. Give one reason you'd like to visit each.

Research

LEAD-IN
Teacher introduces the Project Idea.
Topic: Our state or _____
Material: Newspapers or _____
Comprehension Skill: Main idea
and details or _____

SEARCH & RECORD
Group Size: 3 or 4 or _____
Project Idea: Make a list of state
leaders in the news. Write one fact about
each and explain why he or she is in the
news or _____.

SHARING
Volunteers tell the class about one person
in the news or _____.
Papers are dated and filed.

Recreational Reading

All students read books for approximately
30 minutes.

CONVERSATIONS
The teacher also reads silently. The
teacher has some short conversations with
readers. When appropriate, the main
focus of these conversations is on each
student's favorite books.

CLIPBOARD NOTES
Teacher notes students' selections of
books and whether students talk with
friends about favorite books.

READ-ALOUD BOOK
The Way to Start a Day by Byrd Baylor or
_____

Writing

Theme: Cities or _____

MINI-LESSON
Teacher leads discussion of other types of
writing for exhibit: diagrams, charts, etc.
or _____.

COMPOSING
Continue draft. Add diagrams, charts, etc.
if needed or _____.

SHARING
Response groups share progress on drafts,
diagrams, charts, etc. or _____.
Papers are dated and filed.

Word Study

CHART DEVELOPMENT
Spelling Emphasis: *fer* or
_____

Other Emphasis:
■ 4 paragraphs or _____
■ our state or _____
On the chart, the teacher writes
paragraphs of sentences volunteered by
students using:
■ *fer* words
■ vocabulary about our state
■ _____

WRITING
On their papers, students write their
favorite words from the chart or other
words, phrases, or sentences that would
be appropriate for the chart.

SPELLING
Partners call out words for each other to
spell aloud.
Papers are dated and filed.

HOMEWORK
Write a list of kinds of jobs people in our
state might have. Write a list of kinds of
jobs they would not have.

Lesson 149

Research

LEAD-IN
Teacher introduces the Project Idea.
Topic: Our state or _____
Material: Magazines or _____
Comprehension Skill: Main idea or
_____

SEARCH & RECORD
Group Size: 3 or 4 or _____
Project Idea: Cut out pictures of
places that could be in our state. Write a
caption to go with each or _____.

SHARING
Display pictures and captions or
_____.
   Papers are dated and filed.

Recreational Reading

All students read books for approximately
30 minutes.

CONVERSATIONS
The teacher also reads silently. The
teacher has some short conversations with
readers. When appropriate, the main
focus of these conversations is on each
student's favorite books.

CLIPBOARD NOTES
Teacher notes students' selections of
books and whether students talk with
friends about favorite books.

READ-ALOUD BOOK
_____

Writing

Theme: Cities or _____

MINI-LESSON
Teacher demonstrates use of maps for
checking spelling and capitalization of
words in exhibit or _____.

COMPOSING
Edit pieces for exhibit or _____.

SHARING
Partners edit or _____.
   Papers are dated and filed.

Word Study

CHART DEVELOPMENT
Spelling Emphasis: *ble* or
_____

Other Emphasis:
■ 4 paragraphs or _____
■ our state or _____
   On the chart, the teacher writes
paragraphs of sentences volunteered by
students using:
■ *ble* words
■ vocabulary about our state
■ _____

WRITING
On their papers, students write their
favorite words from the chart or other
words, phrases, or sentences that would
be appropriate for the chart.

SPELLING
Partners call out words for each other to
spell aloud.
   Papers are dated and filed.

HOMEWORK
Write a list of the most important words
about our state that a student must know
how to spell. Study them.

Research

LEAD-IN
Teacher introduces the Project Idea.
Topic: Our state or _____
Material: Newspapers or _____
Comprehension Skill: Classification
or _____

SEARCH & RECORD
Group Size: Partners or _____
Project Idea: Search for pictures,
stories, and advertisements that represent
what people in our state do for a living.
Write a list of your findings. Organize the
list into groups of similar jobs or

_____

SHARING
Show another team your findings or
_____.
    Papers are dated and filed.

Recreational Reading

All students read books for approximately
30 minutes.

CONVERSATIONS
The teacher also reads silently. The
teacher has some short conversations with
readers. When appropriate, the main
focus of these conversations is on each
student's favorite books.

CLIPBOARD NOTES
Teacher notes students' selections of
books and whether students talk with
friends about favorite books.

READ-ALOUD BOOK
_____

Writing

Theme: Cities or _____

MINI-LESSON
Teacher gives instructions for assembly of
exhibit or _____.

COMPOSING
Complete final piece for exhibit or
_____.

SHARING
Tour the exhibit you have made or
_____.
    Papers are dated and filed.

Word Study

CHART DEVELOPMENT
Spelling Emphasis: *che* or

Other Emphasis:
■ 4 paragraphs or _____
■ our state or _____
    On the chart, the teacher writes
paragraphs of sentences volunteered by
students using:
■ *che* words
■ vocabulary about our state
■ _____

WRITING
On their papers, students write their
favorite words from the chart or other
words, phrases, or sentences that would
be appropriate for the chart.

SPELLING
Partners call out words for each other to
spell aloud.
    Papers are dated and filed.

HOMEWORK
Write sentences to tell facts about the
things you have learned this week about
our state.

Lesson 151

Research

LEAD-IN
Teacher introduces the Project Idea.
Topic: Our state or _____.
Material: Grocery ads in newspaper or _____

Comprehension Skill: Classification or _____

SEARCH & RECORD
Group Size: Partners or _____
Project Idea: List items in the grocery ads that were produced in our state. Use your textbook or encyclopedias to get additional information. Organize the list into categories or _____.

SHARING
Volunteers tell the class what they found or _____.
Papers are dated and filed.

Recreational Reading

All students read books for approximately 30 minutes.

CONVERSATIONS
The teacher also reads silently. The teacher has some short conversations with readers. When appropriate, the main focus of these conversations is on the way students get ideas for their writing from the books they read.

CLIPBOARD NOTES
Teacher notes students' selections of books and how students get ideas for writing from books they read.

READ-ALOUD BOOK
The Magic Schoolbus Inside the Earth by Joanna Cole or _____

Writing

The overall theme for the next 15 days is Nutrition or _____. One or more of the other modules will reflect this theme.
Theme: Nutrition or _____

MINI-LESSON
Brainstorm list of kinds of food or _____.

COMPOSING
Write list of kinds of food or _____.

SHARING
Everyone names a different kind of food or _____.
Papers are dated and filed.

Word Study

CHART DEVELOPMENT
Spelling Emphasis: *low* or _____

Other Emphasis:
- 4 paragraphs or _____
- nutrition or _____
On the chart, the teacher writes paragraphs of sentences volunteered by students using:
- *low* words
- nutrition vocabulary
- _____

WRITING
On their papers, students write their favorite words from the chart or other words, phrases, or sentences that would be appropriate for the chart.

SPELLING
Partners call out words for each other to spell aloud.
Papers are dated and filed.

HOMEWORK
Make a list of your favorite foods. Put check marks next to the ones you think are nutritious.

Research

LEAD-IN
Teacher introduces the Project Idea.
Topic: Our state or _____.
Material: Magazines or _____.
Comprehension Skill: Organization of information or _____.

SEARCH & RECORD
Group Size: 3 or 4 or _____.
Project Idea: Cut out words and phrases that can be used to describe our state. Organize the words and glue them on a poster or _____.

SHARING
Display posters or _____.
   Papers are dated and filed.

Recreational Reading

All students read books for approximately 30 minutes.

CONVERSATIONS
The teacher also reads silently. The teacher has some short conversations with readers. When appropriate, the main focus of these conversations is on the way students get ideas for their writing from the books they read.

CLIPBOARD NOTES
Teacher notes students' selections of books and how students get ideas for writing from books they read.

READ-ALOUD BOOK
_____

Writing

Theme: Nutrition or _____.

MINI-LESSON
Students review lists of foods or _____.

COMPOSING
Write list of recommendations of food to eat or _____.

SHARING
Partners share lists or _____.
   Papers are dated and filed.

Word Study

CHART DEVELOPMENT
Spelling Emphasis: *ded* or _____.

Other Emphasis:
■ 4 paragraphs or _____.
■ nutrition or _____.
   On the chart, the teacher writes paragraphs of sentences volunteered by students using:
■ *ded* words
■ nutrition vocabulary
■ _____

WRITING
On their papers, students write their favorite words from the chart or other words, phrases, or sentences that would be appropriate for the chart.

SPELLING
Partners call out words for each other to spell aloud.
   Papers are dated and filed.

HOMEWORK
Read labels on some canned foods. Write a list of ingredients that are added to the foods that are named on the labels.

251

Lesson **153**

Research

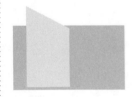

LEAD-IN
Teacher introduces the Project Idea.
Topic: Our state or _____
Material: Newspapers or _____
Comprehension Skill: Comparison
or _____

SEARCH & RECORD
Group Size: Partners or _____
Project Idea: Find information in the
newspaper about another state. Make a
list of ways it is like our state and ways
it is different. Use textbooks and
encyclopedias to get additional
information or _____.

SHARING
Volunteers tell the class about the states
they compared or _____.
    Papers are dated and filed.

Recreational Reading

All students read books for approximately
30 minutes.

CONVERSATIONS
The teacher also reads silently. The
teacher has some short conversations with
readers. When appropriate, the main
focus of these conversations is on the way
students get ideas for their writing from
the books they read.

CLIPBOARD NOTES
Teacher notes students' selections of
books and how students get ideas for
writing from books they read.

READ-ALOUD BOOK
_____

Writing

Theme: Nutrition or _____

MINI-LESSON
Students review lists written for Lessons
151 and 152 or _____.

COMPOSING
Write more about a topic on your lists or
_____.

SHARING
Partners share or _____.
    Papers are dated and filed.

Word Study

CHART DEVELOPMENT
Spelling Emphasis: *wri* or

Other Emphasis:
■ 4 paragraphs or _____
■ nutrition or _____
    On the chart, the teacher writes
paragraphs of sentences volunteered by
students using:
■ *wri* words
■ nutrition vocabulary
■ _____

WRITING
On their papers, students write their
favorite words from the chart or other
words, phrases, or sentences that would
be appropriate for the chart.

SPELLING
Partners call out words for each other to
spell aloud.
    Papers are dated and filed.

HOMEWORK
Write a paragraph for a health book that
will by read by other third-graders. Use
some words that contain the letters *wri*.

Lesson **154**

Research

LEAD-IN
Teacher introduces the Project Idea.
Topic: Our state or _____
Material: Maps of state or _____
Comprehension Skill: Map reading
or _____

SEARCH & RECORD
Group Size: 3 or 4 or _____
Project Idea: Search for names of
rivers, mountains, lakes, and other
geographical features on the state map.
Write lists or _____.

SHARING
Show another group what you found or
_____
  Papers are dated and filed.

Recreational Reading

All students read books for approximately
30 minutes.

CONVERSATIONS
The teacher also reads silently. The
teacher has some short conversations with
readers. When appropriate, the main
focus of these conversations is on the way
students get ideas for their writing from
the books they read.

CLIPBOARD NOTES
Teacher notes students' selections of
books and how students get ideas for
writing from books they read.

READ-ALOUD BOOK
The Tenth Good Thing about Barney by
Judith Viorst or _____

Writing

Theme: Nutrition or _____

MINI-LESSON
Teacher reads factual information about
nutrition or _____.

COMPOSING
Write facts about nutrition or _____.

SHARING
Partners read each other's drafts; check
for facts or _____.
  Papers are dated and filed.

Word Study

CHART DEVELOPMENT
Spelling Emphasis: *cha* or
_____

Other Emphasis:
■ 4 paragraphs or _____
■ nutrition or _____
  On the chart, the teacher writes
paragraphs of sentences volunteered by
students using:
■ *cha* words
■ nutrition vocabulary
■ _____

WRITING
On their papers, students write their
favorite words from the chart or other
words, phrases, or sentences that would
be appropriate for the chart.

SPELLING
Partners call out words for each other to
spell aloud.
  Papers are dated and filed.

HOMEWORK
If you were the owner of a fast-food
restaurant, what would you do to
encourage people to buy nutritious foods?
Write your ideas for changing their
eating habits.

Lesson **155**

Research

LEAD-IN
Teacher introduces the Project Idea.
Topic: Our state or _____
Material: Students choose or
_____

Comprehension Skill: Summary or
_____

SEARCH & RECORD
Group Size: Individuals or _____
Project Idea: Read more about our state. Write a summary of the most interesting things you learn or
_____.

SHARING
Volunteers tell the class their most interesting findings or _____.
Papers are dated and filed.

Recreational Reading

All students read books for approximately 30 minutes.

CONVERSATIONS
The teacher also reads silently. The teacher has some short conversations with readers. When appropriate, the main focus of these conversations is on the way students get ideas for their writing from the books they read.

CLIPBOARD NOTES
Teacher notes students' selections of books and how students get ideas for writing from books they read.

READ-ALOUD BOOK
_____

Writing

Theme: Nutrition or _____

MINI-LESSON
Teacher reviews acrostic poetry format or
_____.

COMPOSING
Write acrostic poem that includes facts about nutrition or _____.

SHARING
Response groups share poetry or
_____.
Papers are dated and filed.

Word Study

CHART DEVELOPMENT
Spelling Emphasis: *tio* or
_____

Other Emphasis:
- 4 paragraphs or _____
- nutrition or _____
On the chart, the teacher writes paragraphs of sentences volunteered by students using:
- *tio* words
- nutrition vocabulary
- _____

WRITING
On their papers, students write their favorite words from the chart or other words, phrases, or sentences that would be appropriate for the chart.

SPELLING
Partners call out words for each other to spell aloud.
Papers are dated and filed.

HOMEWORK
Look in the newspaper for words containing the letters *tio*. Write them on a piece of paper.

Research

LEAD-IN
Teacher introduces the Project Idea.
Topic: Human body or _____
Material: Magazines or _____
Comprehension Skill: Inference or
_____

SEARCH & RECORD
Group Size: 3 or 4 or _____
Project Idea: Cut out pictures of
people doing things. Write a caption for
each that gives advice for keeping healthy
or _____.

SHARING
Share pictures and captions or
_____.
  Papers are dated and filed.

Recreational Reading

All students read books for approximately
30 minutes.

CONVERSATIONS
The teacher also reads silently. The
teacher has some short conversations with
readers. When appropriate, the main
focus of these conversations is on the way
students get ideas for their writing from
the books they read.

CLIPBOARD NOTES
Teacher notes students' selections of
books and how students get ideas for
writing from books they read.

READ-ALOUD BOOK
_____

Writing

Theme: Nutrition or _____

MINI-LESSON
Teacher demonstrates correct spellings of
words that he or she has noticed many
students misspelling or _____.

COMPOSING
Continue draft or _____.

SHARING
Partners proofread for spelling mistakes
or _____.
  Papers are dated and filed.

Word Study

CHART DEVELOPMENT
Spelling Emphasis: *tai* or
_____

Other Emphasis:
■ 4 paragraphs or _____
■ human body or _____
  On the chart, the teacher writes
paragraphs of sentences volunteered by
students using:
■ *tai* words
■ vocabulary about the human body
■ _____

WRITING
On their papers, students write their
favorite words from the chart or other
words, phrases, or sentences that would
be appropriate for the chart.

SPELLING
Partners call out words for each other to
spell aloud.
  Papers are dated and filed.

HOMEWORK
Write a list of parts of the human body
that you have read about.

Lesson **157**

Research

LEAD-IN
Teacher introduces the Project Idea.
Topic: Human body or _____
Material: Science and health textbooks
or _____
Comprehension Skill: Main idea
and details or _____

SEARCH & RECORD
Group Size: Partners or _____
Project Idea: Search for information
about keeping various parts of the body
healthy. Record what you find in a chart
or _____.

SHARING
Volunteers share their findings, and the
teacher records information in a class
chart or _____.
   Papers are dated and filed.

Recreational Reading

All students read books for approximately
30 minutes.

CONVERSATIONS
The teacher also reads silently. The
teacher has some short conversations with
readers. When appropriate, the main
focus of these conversations is on the way
students get ideas for their writing from
the books they read.

CLIPBOARD NOTES
Teacher notes students' selections of
books and how students get ideas for
writing from books they read.

READ-ALOUD BOOK
Stringbean's Trip to the Shining Sea by
Vera Williams and Jennifer Williams or
_____

Writing

Theme: Nutrition or _____

MINI-LESSON
Students review lists of books they have
read recently or _____.

COMPOSING
Write about a book you've read recently.
Write about how characters exhibit good

nutrition habits, if that is included in the
book, or _____.

SHARING
Share book discussions with partner or
_____.
   Papers are dated and filed.

Word Study

CHART DEVELOPMENT
Spelling Emphasis: *orm* or
_____

Other Emphasis:
- 4 paragraphs or _____
- human body or _____
   On the chart, the teacher writes
paragraphs of sentences volunteered by
students using:
- *orm* words
- vocabulary about the human body
- _____

WRITING
On their papers, students write their
favorite words from the chart or other
words, phrases, or sentences that would
be appropriate for the chart.

SPELLING
Partners call out words for each other to
spell aloud.
   Papers are dated and filed.

HOMEWORK
Make a form that you can use to tell
what you know about caring for the
human body. The form might have
questions with spaces for answers.

Research

LEAD-IN
Teacher introduces the Project Idea.
Topic: Human body or _____
Material: Grocery ads from newspapers
or _____
Comprehension Skill: Inference or
_____

SEARCH & RECORD
Group Size: 3 or 4 or _____
Project Idea: Cut out things a person
needs to be healthy. Organize them and
glue them on a poster or _____.

SHARING
Display posters or _____.
Papers are dated and filed.

Recreational Reading

All students read books for approximately
30 minutes.

CONVERSATIONS
The teacher also reads silently. The
teacher has some short conversations with
readers. When appropriate, the main
focus of these conversations is on the way
students get ideas for their writing from
the books they read.

CLIPBOARD NOTES
Teacher notes students' selections of
books and how students get ideas for
writing from books they read.

READ-ALOUD BOOK
_____

Writing

Theme: Nutrition or _____

MINI-LESSON
Teacher announces publication
opportunity: class will post public service
posters about nutrition in school cafeteria
in Lesson 165. Brainstorm examples or
_____.

COMPOSING
Write drafts of ideas for posters or
_____.

SHARING
Response groups explain poster ideas or
_____.
Papers are dated and filed.

Word Study

CHART DEVELOPMENT
Spelling Emphasis: *ese* or
_____

Other Emphasis:
- 4 paragraphs or _____
- human body or _____
  On the chart, the teacher writes
paragraphs of sentences volunteered by
students using:
- *ese* words
- vocabulary about the human body
- _____

WRITING
On their papers, students write their
favorite words from the chart or other
words, phrases, or sentences that would
be appropriate for the chart.

SPELLING
Partners call out words for each other to
spell aloud.
Papers are dated and filed.

HOMEWORK
Look in the newspaper for words
containing the letters *ese*. Write them on
a piece of paper. Beside each word, write
a reason that it might relate to the
human body.

Lesson **159**

Research

LEAD-IN
Teacher introduces the Project Idea.
Topic: Human body or _____
Material: Newspaper or _____
Comprehension Skill: Inference or
_____

SEARCH & RECORD
Group Size: 3 or 4 or _____
Project Idea: Cut out pictures and words that refer to things that harm the human body. Organize the items you choose, paste them on a poster, and write captions about how they harm the body or
_____.

SHARING
Display posters or _____.
  Papers are dated and filed.

Recreational Reading

All students read books for approximately 30 minutes.

CONVERSATIONS
The teacher also reads silently. The teacher has some short conversations with readers. When appropriate, the main focus of these conversations is on the way students get ideas for their writing from the books they read.

CLIPBOARD NOTES
Teacher notes students' selections of books and how students get ideas for writing from books they read.

READ-ALOUD BOOK
_____

Writing

Theme: Nutrition or _____

MINI-LESSON
Teacher leads discussion of ideas for making effective posters or _____.

COMPOSING
Continue draft of poster ideas or
_____.

SHARING
Everyone tells class topic for his or her poster or _____.
  Papers are dated and filed.

Word Study

CHART DEVELOPMENT
Spelling Emphasis: *cre* or
_____

Other Emphasis:
- 4 paragraphs or _____
- human body or _____
  On the chart, the teacher writes paragraphs of sentences volunteered by students using:
- *cre* words
- vocabulary about the human body
- _____

WRITING
On their papers, students write their favorite words from the chart or other words, phrases, or sentences that would be appropriate for the chart.

SPELLING
Partners call out words for each other to spell aloud.
  Papers are dated and filed.

HOMEWORK
Write a list of ways human beings are different from other creatures.

Lesson 160

Research

LEAD-IN
Teacher introduces the Project Idea.
Topic: Human body or _____
Material: Magazines or _____
Comprehension Skill: Classification or _____

SEARCH & RECORD
Group Size: 3 or 4 or _____
Project Idea: Cut out things that affect the body. Organize them into groups of helpful and harmful things. Glue on poster or _____.

SHARING
Display posters or _____.
Papers are dated and filed.

Recreational Reading

All students read books for approximately 30 minutes.

CONVERSATIONS
The teacher also reads silently. The teacher has some short conversations with readers. When appropriate, the main focus of these conversations is on the way students get ideas for their writing from the books they read.

CLIPBOARD NOTES
Teacher notes students' selections of books and how students get ideas for writing from books they read.

READ-ALOUD BOOK
Sideways Stories from Wayside School by Louis Sachar* or _____

Writing

Theme: Nutrition or _____

MINI-LESSON
Teacher leads discussion of ways to make main idea of poster stand out or _____.

COMPOSING
Continue draft or _____.

SHARING
Response group members tell each other the main ideas of their posters or _____.
Papers are dated and filed.

Word Study

CHART DEVELOPMENT
Spelling Emphasis: _nes_ or _____

Other Emphasis:
■ 4 paragraphs or _____
■ human body or _____
 On the chart, the teacher writes paragraphs of sentences volunteered by students using:
■ _nes_ words
■ vocabulary about the human body
■ _____

WRITING
On their papers, students write their favorite words from the chart or other words, phrases, or sentences that would be appropriate for the chart.

SPELLING
Partners call out words for each other to spell aloud.
 Papers are dated and filed.

HOMEWORK
Write sentences about illnesses. Explain how you can catch them and how you get well.

Lesson **161**

Research

LEAD-IN
Teacher introduces the Project Idea.
Topic: Human body or _____
Material: Science and health textbooks
or _____
Comprehension Skill: Questions
and answers or _____

SEARCH & RECORD
Group Size: Partners or _____
Project Idea: Find information about
different systems in the body. Write
questions that you can answer or
_____.

SHARING
Partners call out questions to each other
and give answers orally or _____.
Papers are dated and filed.

Recreational Reading

All students read books for approximately
30 minutes.

CONVERSATIONS
The teacher also reads silently. The
teacher has some short conversations with
readers. When appropriate, the main
focus of these conversations is on the way
students discuss their favorite books.

CLIPBOARD NOTES
Teacher notes students' selections of
books and how students tell each other
about their favorites.

READ-ALOUD BOOK
_____

Writing

Theme: Nutrition or _____

MINI-LESSON
Teacher reviews concepts of main idea
and supporting details in poster
information or _____.

COMPOSING
Continue draft or _____.

SHARING
Partners locate main idea and supporting
details in each other's drafts or
_____.
Papers are dated and filed.

Word Study

CHART DEVELOPMENT
Spelling Emphasis: *tion* or
_____
Other Emphasis:
■ dialogue or _____
■ geography or _____
On the chart, the teacher writes
dialogue of sentences volunteered by
students using:
■ *tion* words
■ geography vocabulary
■ _____

WRITING
On their papers, students write their
favorite words from the chart and other
words, phrases, or sentences that would
be appropriate for the chart.

SPELLING
Partners call out words for each other to
spell aloud.
Papers are dated and filed.

HOMEWORK
Write words containing the letters *tion*
that relate to mountains.

Lesson 162

Research

LEAD-IN
Teacher introduces the Project Idea.
Topic: Human body or _____
Material: Textbooks or _____
Comprehension Skill: Main idea and details or _____

SEARCH & RECORD
Group Size: 3 or 4 or _____

Project Idea: Find information about a system of the human body. Write facts that you learn or _____.

SHARING
Teach another group some of your facts or _____.
  Papers are dated and filed.

Recreational Reading

All students read books for approximately 30 minutes.

CONVERSATIONS
The teacher also reads silently. The teacher has some short conversations with readers. When appropriate, the main focus of these conversations is on the way students discuss their favorite books.

CLIPBOARD NOTES
Teacher notes students' selections of books and how students tell each other about their favorites.

READ-ALOUD BOOK
_____

Writing

Theme: Nutrition or _____

MINI-LESSON
Response group demonstrates how to help a writer arrange the ideas for his or her poster in the best order or _____.

COMPOSING
Continue draft or _____.

SHARING
Response groups help each other arrange ideas on posters in best order or _____.
  Papers are dated and filed.

Word Study

CHART DEVELOPMENT
Spelling Emphasis: *crea* or _____

Other Emphasis:
■ dialogue or _____
■ health or _____
  On the chart, the teacher writes dialogue of sentences volunteered by students using:
■ *crea* words
■ health vocabulary
■ _____

WRITING
On their papers, students write their favorite words from the chart and other words, phrases, or sentences that would be appropriate for the chart.

SPELLING
Partners call out words for each other to spell aloud.
  Papers are dated and filed.

HOMEWORK
Write about the following foods and tell whether they are good for you: cream, cream cheese, cream of tartar, cream puffs.

Lesson **163**

Research

LEAD-IN
Teacher introduces the Project Idea.
Topic: Human body or _____
Material: Magazines or _____
Comprehension Skill: Inference or
_____

SEARCH & RECORD
Group Size: 3 or 4 or _____
Project Idea: Cut out pictures that show ways to exercise. Paste them on poster and write captions to explain how to exercise or _____.

SHARING
Display posters or _____.
Papers are dated and filed.

Recreational Reading

All students read books for approximately 30 minutes.

CONVERSATIONS
The teacher also reads silently. The teacher has some short conversations with readers. When appropriate, the main focus of these conversations is on the way students discuss their favorite books.

CLIPBOARD NOTES
Teacher notes students' selections of books and how students tell each other about their favorites.

READ-ALOUD BOOK
The News about Dinosaurs by Patricia Lauber or _____

Writing

Theme: Nutrition or _____

MINI-LESSON
Teacher leads discussion about using appropriate lettering and colors to accent main idea of poster or _____.

COMPOSING
Continue draft or _____.

SHARING
Share plans for lettering and colors with partner or _____.
Papers are dated and filed.

Word Study

CHART DEVELOPMENT
Spelling Emphasis: *each* or
_____
Other Emphasis:
■ dialogue or _____
■ history or _____
On the chart, the teacher writes dialogue of sentences volunteered by students using:
■ *each* words
■ history vocabulary
■ _____

WRITING
On their papers, students write their favorite words from the chart and other words, phrases, or sentences that would be appropriate for the chart.

SPELLING
Partners call out words for each other to spell aloud.
Papers are dated and filed.

HOMEWORK
Write a conversation two famous people from history might have had with each other.

Research

LEAD-IN
Teacher introduces the Project Idea.
Topic: Human body or _____
Material: Magazines or _____
Comprehension Skill: Inference or _____

SEARCH & RECORD
Group Size: 3 or 4 or _____
Project Idea: Cut out pictures that show how to keep clean and dress properly for the weather. Write captions for them or _____.

SHARING
Display pictures and captions or _____.
 Papers are dated and filed.

Recreational Reading

All students read books for approximately 30 minutes.

CONVERSATIONS
The teacher also reads silently. The teacher has some short conversations with readers. When appropriate, the main focus of these conversations is on the way students discuss their favorite books.

CLIPBOARD NOTES
Teacher notes students' selections of books and how students tell each other about their favorites.

READ-ALOUD BOOK
_____

Writing

Theme: Nutrition or _____

MINI-LESSON
Teacher reviews rules for capital letters that will be needed on posters or _____.

COMPOSING
Edit poster draft or _____.

SHARING
Partners help edit or _____.
 Papers are dated and filed.

Word Study

CHART DEVELOPMENT
Spelling Emphasis: *thin* or _____

Other Emphasis:

- dialogue or _____
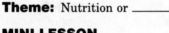
- education or _____
 On the chart, the teacher writes dialogue of sentences volunteered by students using:
- *thin* words
- education vocabulary
- _____

WRITING
On their papers, students write their favorite words from the chart and other words, phrases, or sentences that would be appropriate for the chart.

SPELLING
Partners call out words for each other to spell aloud.
 Papers are dated and filed.

HOMEWORK
Write a conversation that two teachers might have at the end of the day.

Lesson **165**

Research

LEAD-IN
Teacher introduces the Project Idea.
Topic: Human body or _____
Material: Students choose or

_____

Comprehension Skill: Summary or

_____

SEARCH & RECORD
Group Size: Individuals or _____
Project Idea: Find information about
the human body that you haven't studied
yet. Write a summary of what you find
out or _____.

SHARING
Volunteers teach class what they learned
or _____.
   Papers are dated and filed.

Recreational Reading

All students read books for approximately
30 minutes.

CONVERSATIONS
The teacher also reads silently. The
teacher has some short conversations with
readers. When appropriate, the main
focus of these conversations is on the way
students discuss their favorite books.

CLIPBOARD NOTES
Teacher notes students' selections of
books and how students tell each other
about their favorites.

READ-ALOUD BOOK

_____

Writing

Theme: Nutrition or _____

MINI-LESSON
Teacher gives instructions for displaying
completed posters or _____.

COMPOSING
Complete poster or _____.

SHARING
Read posters on exhibit or _____.
   Papers are dated and filed.

Word Study

CHART DEVELOPMENT
Spelling Emphasis: *able* or

_____

Other Emphasis:
- dialogue or _____
- art or _____
   On the chart, the teacher writes
dialogue of sentences volunteered by
students using:
- *able* words
- art vocabulary
- _____

WRITING
On their papers, students write their
favorite words from the chart and other
words, phrases, or sentences that would
be appropriate for the chart.

SPELLING
Partners call out words for each other to
spell aloud.
   Papers are dated and filed.

HOMEWORK
Write a conversation between 2 artists
about the materials they use for their work.

Research

LEAD-IN
Teacher introduces the Project Idea.
Topic: Art or _____
Material: Prints and art books or
_____

Comprehension Skill: Main idea or
_____

SEARCH & RECORD
Group Size: Partners or _____
Project Idea: Choose pictures you
like. Write captions to go with them or
_____.

SHARING
Show another team your favorite picture
or _____.
Papers are dated and filed.

Recreational Reading

All students read books for approximately
30 minutes.

CONVERSATIONS
The teacher also reads silently. The
teacher has some short conversations with
readers. When appropriate, the main
focus of these conversations is on the way
students discuss their favorite books.

CLIPBOARD NOTES
Teacher notes students' selections of
books and how students tell each other
about their favorites.

READ-ALOUD BOOK
The Island of the Skog by Steven Kellogg
or _____

Writing

The overall theme for the next 15 days is
Art or _____. One or more of the
other modules will reflect this theme.
Theme: Art or _____

MINI-LESSON
Brainstorm list of kinds of art or
_____.

COMPOSING
Write list of kinds of art or _____.

SHARING
Volunteers name kinds of art not
mentioned in mini-lesson or _____.
Papers are dated and filed.

Word Study

CHART DEVELOPMENT
Spelling Emphasis: *ness* or
_____
Other Emphasis:
■ dialogue or _____
■ mathematics or _____
On the chart, the teacher writes
dialogue of sentences volunteered by
students using:
■ *ness* words
■ mathematics vocabulary
■ _____

WRITING
On their papers, students write their
favorite words from the chart and other
words, phrases, or sentences that would
be appropriate for the chart.

SPELLING
Partners call out words for each other to
spell aloud.
Papers are dated and filed.

HOMEWORK
Write a conversation between you and a
friend about how to do division problems.

Lesson 167

Research

LEAD-IN
Teacher introduces the Project Idea.
Topic: Art or _____
Material: Prints and art books or
_____

Comprehension Skill: Main idea
and details or _____

SEARCH & RECORD
Group Size: Partners or _____
Project Idea: Choose paintings of
people that you like. Write lists of details
about the people or _____.

SHARING
Show another team your favorite
painting. Point out the details you
discovered or _____.
Papers are dated and filed.

Recreational Reading

All students read books for approximately
30 minutes.

CONVERSATIONS
The teacher also reads silently. The
teacher has some short conversations with
readers. When appropriate, the main
focus of these conversations is on the way
students discuss their favorite books.

CLIPBOARD NOTES
Teacher notes students' selections of
books and how students tell each other
about their favorites.

READ-ALOUD BOOK
The Not-Just-Anybody Family by Betsy
Byars* or _____

Writing

Theme: Art or _____

MINI-LESSON
Brainstorm list of things we know how to
do in art or _____.

COMPOSING
Write list of things you can do in art or
_____.

SHARING
Partners discuss lists or _____.
Papers are dated and filed.

Word Study

CHART DEVELOPMENT
Spelling Emphasis: *ings* or
_____

Other Emphasis:
■ dialogue or _____
■ business or _____
On the chart, the teacher writes
dialogue of sentences volunteered by
students using:
■ *ings* words
■ business vocabulary
■ _____

WRITING
On their papers, students write their
favorite words from the chart and other
words, phrases, or sentences that would
be appropriate for the chart.

SPELLING
Partners call out words for each other to
spell aloud.
Papers are dated and filed.

HOMEWORK
Look in the telephone book for businesses
whose names contain the letters *ings*.
Write them on a piece of paper.

Lesson **168**

Research

LEAD-IN
Teacher introduces the Project Idea.
Topic: Art or _____
Material: Magazines or _____
Comprehension Skill: Comparison or _____

SEARCH & RECORD
Group Size: Partners or _____
Project Idea: Cut out pictures that remind you of the paintings you've studied. Cut out pictures that are very different or _____.

SHARING
Show another team the pictures that remind you of paintings and explain how they do or _____.
Papers are dated and filed.

Recreational Reading

All students read books for approximately 30 minutes.

CONVERSATIONS
The teacher also reads silently. The teacher has some short conversations with readers. When appropriate, the main focus of these conversations is on the way students discuss their favorite books.

CLIPBOARD NOTES
Teacher notes students' selections of books and how students tell each other about their favorites.

READ-ALOUD BOOK
_____

Writing

Theme: Art or _____

MINI-LESSON
Students study lists written for Lessons 166 and 167 or _____.

COMPOSING
Write a story about art using some ideas from your lists or _____.

SHARING
Partners discuss story ideas or _____.
Papers are dated and filed.

Word Study

CHART DEVELOPMENT
Spelling Emphasis: *chlo* or _____

Other Emphasis:
■ dialogue or _____
■ world news or _____
On the chart, the teacher writes dialogue of sentences volunteered by students using:
■ *chlo* words
■ world news vocabulary
■ _____

WRITING
On their papers, students write their favorite words from the chart and other words, phrases, or sentences that would be appropriate for the chart.

SPELLING
Partners call out words for each other to spell aloud.
Papers are dated and filed.

HOMEWORK
Write an imaginary conversation between 2 world leaders.

Lesson **169**

Research

LEAD-IN
Teacher introduces the Project Idea.
Topic: Art or _____
Material: Art books and prints or
_____

Comprehension Skill: Classification
or _____

SEARCH & RECORD
Group Size: 3 or 4 or _____
Project Idea: Write notes about your
favorite paintings. Classify your favorites
into categories such as animals or
_____.

SHARING
Show another group your favorite
paintings and your classifications or
_____.

Papers are dated and filed.

Recreational Reading

All students read books for approximately
30 minutes.

CONVERSATIONS
The teacher also reads silently. The
teacher has some short conversations with
readers. When appropriate, the main
focus of these conversations is on the way
students discuss their favorite books.

CLIPBOARD NOTES
Teacher notes students' selections of
books and how students tell each other
about their favorites.

READ-ALOUD BOOK
_____

Writing

Theme: Art or _____

MINI-LESSON
Teacher reads factual information about
art or _____.

COMPOSING
Continue draft of story. Include some
factual information or _____.

SHARING
Response groups share story drafts or
_____.

Papers are dated and filed.

Word Study

CHART DEVELOPMENT
Spelling Emphasis: *read* or
_____

Other Emphasis:
■ dialogue or _____
■ medicine or _____
   On the chart, the teacher writes
dialogue of sentences volunteered by
students using:
■ *read* words
■ medicine vocabulary
■ _____

WRITING
On their papers, students write their
favorite words from the chart and other
words, phrases, or sentences that would
be appropriate for the chart.

SPELLING
Partners call out words for each other to
spell aloud.
   Papers are dated and filed.

HOMEWORK
Write words containing *read* that relate
to a doctor.

Lesson **170**

Research

LEAD-IN
Teacher introduces the Project Idea.
Topic: Art or _____
Material: Art books and prints or _____

Comprehension Skill: Classification or _____

SEARCH & RECORD
Group Size: Partners or _____
Project Idea: Choose a favorite painting. Make a list of all the small things in it and a list of all the large things or _____

SHARING
Show another team what you found or _____.
Papers are dated and filed.

Recreational Reading

All students read books for approximately 30 minutes.

CONVERSATIONS
The teacher also reads silently. The teacher has some short conversations with readers. When appropriate, the main focus of these conversations is on the way students discuss their favorite books.

CLIPBOARD NOTES
Teacher notes students' selections of books and how students tell each other about their favorites.

READ-ALOUD BOOK
Visiting the Art Museum by Laurene Brown and Marc Browne or _____

Writing

Theme: Art or _____

MINI-LESSON
Brainstorm ways to write poems about art or _____.

COMPOSING
Write poem about art or _____.

SHARING
Volunteers read drafts of poems or _____.
Papers are dated and filed.

Word Study

CHART DEVELOPMENT
Spelling Emphasis: *ence* or _____

Other Emphasis:
■ dialogue or _____
■ sports or _____
  On the chart, the teacher writes dialogue of sentences volunteered by students using:
■ *ence* words
■ sports vocabulary
■ _____

WRITING
On their papers, students write their favorite words from the chart or other words, phrases, or sentences that would be appropriate for the chart.

SPELLING
Partners call out words for each other to spell aloud.
  Papers are dated and filed.

HOMEWORK
Write a conversation between the captains of two teams that are about to play a game.

269

Lesson **171**

Research

LEAD-IN
Teacher introduces the Project Idea.
Topic: Art or _____
Material: Artbooks and prints or
_____

Comprehension Skill: Inference or
_____

SEARCH & RECORD
Group Size: Partners or _____
Project Idea: Search for paintings
that show places where people live. Write
notes that explain why you think each
painting shows a home or _____.

SHARING
Volunteers show class their best examples
or _____.
   Papers are dated and filed.

Recreational Reading

All students read books for approximately
30 minutes.

CONVERSATIONS
The teacher also reads silently. The
teacher has some short conversations with
readers. When appropriate, the main
focus of these conversations is on each
student's plans for summer reading.

CLIPBOARD NOTES
Teacher notes students' selections of
books and how students tell each other
about their favorites.

READ-ALOUD BOOK
_____

Writing

Theme: Art or _____

MINI-LESSON
Teacher gives examples of correct use of
possessives or _____.

COMPOSING
Continue draft or _____.

SHARING
Partners proofread for correct use of
possessives or _____.
   Papers are dated and filed.

Word Study

CHART DEVELOPMENT
Spelling Emphasis: *graph* or _____

Other Emphasis:
- 5 paragraphs or _____
- music or _____
   On the chart, the teacher writes
paragraphs of sentences volunteered by
students using:
- *graph* words
- music vocabulary
- _____

WRITING
On their papers, students write their
favorite words from the chart or other
words, phrases, or sentences that would
be appropriate for the chart.

SPELLING
Partners call out words for each other to
spell aloud.
   Papers are dated and filed.

HOMEWORK
List the ways people have used the
following to their advantage: telegraph,
phonograph, bar graph.

Research

LEAD-IN
Teacher introduces the Project Idea.
Topic: Art or _____
Material: Art books and prints or
_____

Comprehension Skill: Alphabetical
order or _____

SEARCH & RECORD
Group Size: Partners or _____
Project Idea: Locate names of artists
and list them in alphabetical order or
_____ .

SHARING
Volunteers share names and the teacher
records an alphabetical class list of artists
or _____ .
    Papers are dated and filed.

Recreational Reading

All students read books for approximately
30 minutes.

CONVERSATIONS
The teacher also reads silently. The
teacher has some short conversations with
readers. When appropriate, the main
focus of these conversations is on each
student's plans for summer reading.

CLIPBOARD NOTES
Teacher notes students' selections of
books and how students tell each other
about their favorites.

READ-ALOUD BOOK
_____

Writing

Theme: Art or _____

MINI-LESSON
Students review lists of books they have
read over the year or _____ .

COMPOSING
Write about favorite books of the year or
_____ .

SHARING
Everyone names a favorite book. Teacher
records class list of favorites or
_____ .
    Papers are dated and filed.

Word Study

CHART DEVELOPMENT
Spelling Emphasis: _therm_ or
_____
Other Emphasis:
■ 5 paragraphs or _____
■ science or _____
    On the chart, the teacher writes
paragraphs of sentences volunteered by
students using:
■ _therm_ words
■ science vocabulary
■ _____

WRITING
On their papers, students write their
favorite words from the chart or other
words, phrases, or sentences that would
be appropriate for the chart.

SPELLING
Partners call out words for each other to
spell aloud.
    Papers are dated and filed.

HOMEWORK
Write a story about a time when a
thermometer was very important.

Lesson 173

Research

LEAD-IN
Teacher introduces the Project Idea.
Topic: Art or _____
Material: Art books and prints or
_____

Comprehension Skill: Sequence

SEARCH & RECORD
Group Size: Partners or _____
Project Idea: Search for the dates
that paintings were done. List
information about your favorite paintings
in chronological order or _____.

SHARING
Show another team your oldest painting
or _____.
  Papers are dated and filed.

Recreational Reading

All students read books for approximately
30 minutes.

CONVERSATIONS
The teacher also reads silently. The
teacher has some short conversations with
readers. When appropriate, the main
focus of these conversations is on each
student's plans for summer reading.

CLIPBOARD NOTES
Teacher notes students' selections of
books and how students tell each other
about their favorites.

READ-ALOUD BOOK
Something Big Has Been Here by Jack
Prelutsky** or _____

Writing

Theme: Art or _____

MINI-LESSON
Teacher announces publication
opportunity: students will complete
publication of picture books in lesson 180
or _____.

COMPOSING
Write notes about the kinds of pictures
and story you would like to include in
your book. Continue draft or _____.

SHARING
Partners share ideas for what to include
in books or _____.
  Papers are dated and filed.

Word Study

CHART DEVELOPMENT
Spelling Emphasis: *photo* or
_____

Other Emphasis:
■ 5 paragraphs or _____
■ literature or _____
  On the chart, the teacher writes
paragraphs of sentences volunteered by
students using:
■ *photo* words
■ literature vocabulary
■ _____

WRITING
On their papers, students write their
favorite words from the chart or other
words, phrases, or sentences that would
be appropriate for the chart.

SPELLING
Partners call out words for each other to
spell aloud.
  Papers are dated and filed.

HOMEWORK
Write a poem using as many words as
you can that contain the letters *photo*.

Lesson **174**

Research

LEAD-IN
Teacher introduces the Project Idea.
Topic: Art or _____
Material: Art books and prints or
_____

Comprehension Skill: Main idea
and details or _____

SEARCH & RECORD
Group Size: Individuals or _____
Project Idea: Choose your favorite
painting among those you have studied.
Write a list of reasons for your choice or
_____.

SHARING
Volunteers tell which paintings are their
favorites or _____
    Papers are dated and filed.

Recreational Reading

All students read books for approximately
30 minutes.

CONVERSATIONS
The teacher also reads silently. The
teacher has some short conversations with
readers. When appropriate, the main
focus of these conversations is each
student's summer reading plans.

CLIPBOARD NOTES
Teacher notes students' selections of
books and whether they talk with friends
about their favorite books.

READ-ALOUD BOOK
_____

Writing

Theme: Art or _____

MINI-LESSON
Students browse through favorite picture
books. Brainstorm characteristics of
favorite picture books or _____.

COMPOSING
Choose earlier draft to develop into
picture book or begin draft of new story
or _____.

SHARING
Partners discuss ideas or _____.
    Papers are dated and filed.

Word Study

CHART DEVELOPMENT
Spelling Emphasis: _ocean_ or _____

Other Emphasis:
■ 5 paragraphs or _____
■ communication or _____
    On the chart, the teacher writes
paragraphs of sentences volunteered by
students using:
■ _ocean_ words
■ communication vocabulary
■ _____

WRITING
On their papers, students write their
favorite words from the chart and other
words, phrases, or sentences that would
be appropriate for the chart.

SPELLING
Partners call out words for each other to
spell aloud.
    Papers are dated and filed.

HOMEWORK
Write about the way you think oceanic
animals communicate.

Lesson 175

Research

LEAD-IN
Teacher introduces the Project Idea.
Topic: Art or _____
Material: Students choose or _____

Comprehension Skill: Summary or _____

SEARCH & RECORD
Group Size: Individuals or _____
Project Idea: Search for more information about art that interests you. Write a summary of what you learn or _____.

SHARING
Volunteers tell class something interesting they learned or _____.
Papers are dated and filed.

Recreational Reading

All students read books for approximately 30 minutes.

CONVERSATIONS
The teacher also reads silently. The teacher has some short conversations with readers. When appropriate, the main focus of these conversations is each student's summer reading plans.

CLIPBOARD NOTES
Teacher notes students' selections of books and whether they talk with friends about their favorite books.

READ-ALOUD BOOK
_____

Writing

Theme: Art or _____

MINI-LESSON
Students browse through favorite picture books. Brainstorm list of characteristics of favorite illustrations or _____.

COMPOSING
Write notes about kind of illustrations your picture book will need or _____.

SHARING
Response groups discuss appropriate illustrations or _____.
Papers are dated and filed.

Word Study

CHART DEVELOPMENT
Spelling Emphasis: *divid* or _____

Other Emphasis:
- 5 paragraphs or _____
- local news or _____
On the chart, the teacher writes paragraphs of sentences volunteered by students using:
- *divid* words
- local news vocabulary
- _____

WRITING
On their papers, students write their favorite words from the chart and other words, phrases, or sentences that would be appropriate for the chart.

SPELLING
Partners call out words for each other to spell aloud.
Papers are dated and filed.

HOMEWORK
Write a summary of something that happened recently in your town. Use some words that have the letters *divid*.

Lesson **176**

Research

LEAD-IN
Teacher introduces the Project Idea.
Topic: Individual choice or _____
Material: Students choose or
_____
Comprehension Skill: Main idea and details or _____

SEARCH & RECORD
Group Size: Individuals or _____
Project Idea: Decide on something to learn more about. Read. Record facts learned or _____.

SHARING
Everyone reports the topic he or she has chosen to study. Teacher records list or
_____.
Papers are dated and filed.

Recreational Reading

All students read books for approximately 30 minutes.

CONVERSATIONS
The teacher also reads silently. The teacher has some short conversations with readers. When appropriate, the main focus of these conversations is each student's summer reading plans.

CLIPBOARD NOTES
Teacher notes students' selections of books and whether they talk with friends about their favorite books.

READ-ALOUD BOOK
Scary Stories to Tell in the Dark by Alvin Schwartz or _____

Writing

Theme: Art or _____

MINI-LESSON
Teacher reviews proper paragraphing for stories or _____.

COMPOSING
Continue draft or _____.

SHARING
Partners proofread drafts for proper paragraphing or _____.
Papers are dated and filed.

Word Study

CHART DEVELOPMENT
Spelling Emphasis: *place* or
_____

Other Emphasis:
- 5 paragraphs or _____
- geography or _____
  On the chart, the teacher writes paragraphs of sentences volunteered by students using:
- *place*
- geography vocabulary _____.
- _____

WRITING
On their papers, students write their favorite words from the chart and other words, phrases, or sentences that would be appropriate for the chart.

SPELLING
Partners call out words for each other to spell aloud.
Papers are dated and filed.

HOMEWORK
Design a placemat you would like to have. Write a paragraph to tell why you like it.

Lesson 177

Research

LEAD-IN
Teacher introduces the Project Idea.
Topic: Individual choice or _____
Material: Magazines or _____
Comprehension Skill: Association
or _____

SEARCH & RECORD
Group Size: Individuals or _____
Project Idea: Cut out pictures that go with your topic. Write captions for the pictures or _____.

SHARING
Show a partner the pictures you chose or
_____.
Papers are dated and filed.

Recreational Reading

All students read books for approximately 30 minutes.

CONVERSATIONS
The teacher also reads silently. The teacher has some short conversations with readers. When appropriate, the main focus of these conversations is each student's summer reading plans.

CLIPBOARD NOTES
Teacher notes students' selections of books and whether they talk with friends about their favorite books.

READ-ALOUD BOOK
_____

Writing

Theme: Art or _____

MINI-LESSON
Response group demonstrates how to help writers decide on parts of stories to illustrate or _____.

COMPOSING
Continue draft of picture book. Begin illustrations or _____.

SHARING
Response groups discuss the way writers are including illustrations or _____.
Papers are dated and filed.

Word Study

CHART DEVELOPMENT
Spelling Emphasis: *store* or
_____

Other Emphasis:
- 5 paragraphs or _____
- ecology or _____
On the chart, the teacher writes paragraphs of sentences volunteered by students using:
- *store* words
- ecology vocabulary
- _____

WRITING
On their papers, students write their favorite words from the chart and other words, phrases, or sentences that would be appropriate for the chart.

SPELLING
Partners call out words for each other to spell aloud.
Papers are dated and filed.

HOMEWORK
Write about some ways you can help the ecology of the earth over the summer.

Research

LEAD-IN
Teacher introduces the Project Idea.
Topic: Individual choice or _____
Material: Students choose or
_____

Comprehension Skill: Comparison
or _____

SEARCH & RECORD
Group Size: Individuals or _____
Project Idea: List ways your topic is
like others you've studied and ways it is
different or _____.

SHARING
Show a partner your comparisons or
_____.
    Papers are dated and filed.

Recreational Reading

All students read books for approximately
30 minutes.

CONVERSATIONS
The teacher also reads silently. The
teacher has some short conversations with
readers. When appropriate, the main
focus of these conversations is each
student's summer reading plans.

CLIPBOARD NOTES
Teacher notes students' selections of
books and whether they talk with friends
about their favorite books.

READ-ALOUD BOOK
_____

Writing

Theme: Art or _____

MINI-LESSON
Teacher uses picture books to
demonstrate different techniques for
arranging text on pages with illustrations
or _____.

COMPOSING
Continue draft and illustrations or
_____.

SHARING
Partners plan where to write words on
pages with illustrations or _____.
    Papers are dated and filed.

Word Study

CHART DEVELOPMENT
Spelling Emphasis: *think* or
_____
Other Emphasis:
■ 5 paragraphs or _____
■ history or _____
    On the chart, the teacher writes
paragraphs of sentences volunteered by
students using:
■ *think* words
■ history vocabulary
■ _____

WRITING
On their papers, students write their
favorite words from the chart and other
words, phrases, or sentences that would
be appropriate for the chart.

SPELLING
Partners call out words for each other to
spell aloud.
    Papers are dated and filed.

HOMEWORK
Is it thinkable that life on Mars will be
studied in school by your children?
Explain your answer.

Lesson 179

Research

LEAD-IN
Teacher introduces the Project Idea.
Topic: Individual choice or _____
Material: Students choose or

_____

Comprehension Skill: Main idea or

_____

SEARCH & RECORD
Group Size: Individuals or _____
Project Idea: Search for information
that people should know about your topic.
Write list of facts or _____.

SHARING
Teach your facts to a group of 4 or 5 other
students or _____.
   Papers are dated and filed.

Recreational Reading

All students read books for approximately
30 minutes.

CONVERSATIONS
The teacher also reads silently. The
teacher has some short conversations with
readers. When appropriate, the main
focus of these conversations is each
student's summer reading plans.

CLIPBOARD NOTES
Teacher notes students' selections of
books and whether they talk with friends
about their favorite books.

READ-ALOUD BOOK
The Talking Eggs by Robert San Souci or
_____

Writing

Theme: Art or _____

MINI-LESSON
Teacher reminds writers about proper
paragraphing or _____.

COMPOSING
Write final book or _____.

SHARING
Partners help edit or _____.
   Papers are dated and filed.

Word Study

CHART DEVELOPMENT
Spelling Emphasis: *sprou* or

_____

Other Emphasis:
■ 5 paragraphs or _____
■ science or _____
   On the chart, the teacher writes
paragraphs of sentences volunteered by
students using:
■ *sprou* words
■ science vocabulary
■ _____

WRITING
On their papers, students write their
favorite words from the chart and other
words, phrases, or sentences that would
be appropriate for the chart.

SPELLING
Partners call out words for each other to
spell aloud.
   Papers are dated and filed.

HOMEWORK
Look in your science book for words
containing *sprou* and other important
words you would like to know how to
spell. Write these words on a piece of
paper.

Research

LEAD-IN
Teacher introduces the Project Idea.
Topic: Individual choice or _____
Material: Students choose or
_____

Comprehension Skill: Main idea or
_____

SEARCH & RECORD
Group Size: Individuals or _____
Project Idea: Make a small poster to
show the most important information you
have learned or _____.

SHARING
Display posters or _____.
Papers are dated and filed.

Recreational Reading

All students read books for approximately
30 minutes.

CONVERSATIONS
The teacher also reads silently. The
teacher has some short conversations with
readers. When appropriate, the main
focus of these conversations is each
student's summer reading plans.

CLIPBOARD NOTES
Teacher notes students' selections of
books and whether they talk with friends
about their favorite books.

READ-ALOUD BOOK
_____

Writing

Theme: Art or _____

MINI-LESSON
Teacher demonstrates assembly of books
or _____.

COMPOSING
Complete and assemble books or
_____.

SHARING
Display picture books or _____.
Papers are dated and filed.

Word Study

CHART DEVELOPMENT
Spelling Emphasis: *stati* or _____

Other Emphasis:
■ 5 paragraphs or _____
■ health or _____
   On the chart, the teacher writes
paragraphs of sentences volunteered by
students using:
■ *stati* words
■ health vocabulary
■ _____

WRITING
On their papers, students write their
favorite words from the chart and other
words, phrases, or sentences that would
be appropriate for the chart.

SPELLING
Partners call out words for each other to
spell aloud.
   Papers are dated and filed.

HOMEWORK
Make plans for a healthy, happy summer.

▶ Appendix

Sources for Further Reading

Atwell, Nancie, ed. *Coming to Know: Writing to Learn in the Intermediate Grades.* Portsmouth, NH: Heinemann, 1990.

_____. *In the Middle: Writing, Reading, and Learning with Adolescents.* Portsmouth, NH: Boynton/Cook, 1987.

Calkins, Lucy McCormick. *The Art of Teaching Writing.* Portsmouth, NH: Heinemann, 1986.

Calkins, Lucy McCormick, and Harwayne, Shelly. *Living Between the Lines.* Portsmouth, NH: Heinemann, 1991.

Goodman, Ken, Yetta Goodman, and Hood, Wendy. *The Whole Language Evaluation Book.* Portsmouth, NH: Heinemann, 1989.

Graves, Donald. *Experiment with Fiction.* Portsmouth, NH: Heinemann, 1989.

_____. *Investigating Nonfiction.* Portsmouth, NH: Heinemann, 1989.

_____. *Writing: Teachers and Children at Work.* Portsmouth, NH: Heinemann, 1983.

Routman, Regie. *Transitions: From Literature to Literacy.* Portsmouth, NH: Heinemann, 1988.

Smith, Frank. *Insult to Intelligence.* Portsmouth, NH: Heinemann, 1986.

Topics for Lessons

Lesson	Research	Writing Theme	Word Study	Lesson	Research	Writing Theme	Word Study
1	animals	animals		59	public health	things to do	medicine
2	animals	animals		60	public health	space or holidays	careers
3	animals	animals	animals	61	space	space or holidays	holidays
4	animals	animals	animals	62	space	space or holidays	holidays
5	animals	animals		63	space	space or holidays	holidays
6	animals	animals		64	space	space or holidays	holidays
7	animals	animals		65	space	space or holidays	holidays
8	animals	animals		66	space	space or holidays	holiday music
9	animals	animals		67	space	holidays	holiday business
10	animals	animals					
11	school and home	animals	animals	68	space	holidays	holiday messages
12	school and home	animals	animals				
13	school and home	animals	animals	69	space	holidays	holiday food
14	school and home	animals	animals	70	space	holidays	holiday memory
15	school and home	animals	animals				
16	school and home	places	world news	71	holidays	holidays	health
17	school and home	places	sports	72	holidays	holidays	history
18	school and home	places	school	73	holidays	holidays	education
19	school and home	places	food	74	holidays	holidays	agriculture
20	school and home	places	science	75	holidays	holidays	world news
21	land forms	places	land forms	76	energy	energy	business
22	land forms	places	land forms	77	energy	energy	communication
23	land forms	places	land forms				
24	land forms	places	land forms	78	energy	energy	medicine
25	land forms	places	land forms	79	energy	energy	local news
26	land forms	places	addition	80	energy	energy	literature
27	land forms	places	mathematics	81	energy	energy	literature
28	land forms	places	subtraction	82	energy	energy	art
29	land forms	places	money	83	energy	energy	music
30	land forms	places	measuring	84	energy	energy	ecology
31	people in the news	people	art	85	energy	energy	mathematics
32	people in the news	people	literature	86	transportation	energy	transportation
33	people in the news	people	ecology	87	transportation	energy	transportation
34	people in the news	people	business	88	transportation	energy	transportation
35	people in the news	people	science	89	transportation	energy	transportation
36	people in the news	people	geography	90	transportation	energy	transportation
37	people in the news	people	health	91	transportation	friends	friends
38	people in the news	people	history	92	transportation	friends	friends
39	people in the news	people	education	93	transportation	friends	friends
40	people in the news	people	agriculture	94	transportation	friends	friends
41	government	people	government	95	transportation	friends	friends
42	government	people	government	96	music	friends	music
43	government	people	government	97	music	friends	music
44	government	people	government	98	music	friends	music
45	government	people	government	99	music	friends	music
46	government	things to do	medicine	100	music	friends	music
47	government	things to do	music	101	music	friends	mathematics
48	government	things to do	literature	102	music	friends	science
49	government	things to do	mathematics	103	music	friends	geography
50	government	things to do	art	104	music	friends	sports
51	public health	things to do	public health	105	music	friends	health
52	public health	things to do	public health	106	famous Americans	communication	famous Americans
53	public health	things to do	public health	107	famous Americans	communication	famous Americans
54	public health	things to do	public health	108	famous Americans	communication	famous Americans
55	public health	things to do	public health				
56	public health	things to do	history				
57	public health	things to do	business				
58	public health	things to do	education				

Lesson	Research	Writing Theme	Word Study	Lesson	Research	Writing Theme	Word Study
109	famous Americans	communication	famous Americans	144	cities	cities	mathematics
110	famous Americans	communication	famous Americans	145	cities	cities	literature
111	famous Americans	communication	ecology	146	our state	cities	our state
112	famous Americans	communication	mathematics	147	our state	cities	our state
113	famous Americans	communication	science	148	our state	cities	our state
114	famous Americans	communication	geography	149	our state	cities	our state
115	famous Americans	communication	education	150	our state	cities	our state
116	plants	communication	plants	151	our state	nutrition	nutrition
117	plants	communication	plants	152	our state	nutrition	nutrition
118	plants	communication	plants	153	our state	nutrition	nutrition
119	plants	communication	plants	154	our state	nutrition	nutrition
120	plants	communication	plants	155	our state	nutrition	nutrition
121	plants	changes	health	156	human body	nutrition	human body
122	plants	changes	business	157	human body	nutrition	human body
123	plants	changes	news	158	human body	nutrition	human body
124	plants	changes	news	159	human body	nutrition	human body
125	plants	changes	sports	160	human body	nutrition	human body
126	weather	changes	weather	161	human body	nutrition	geography
127	weather	changes	weather	162	human body	nutrition	health
128	weather	changes	weather	163	human body	nutrition	history
129	weather	changes	weather	164	human body	nutrition	education
130	weather	changes	weather	165	human body	nutrition	art
131	weather	changes	music	166	art	art	mathematics
132	weather	changes	communication	167	art	art	business
133	weather	changes	mathematics	168	art	art	world news
134	weather	changes	science	169	art	art	medicine
135	weather	changes	geography	170	art	art	sports
136	cities	cities	health	171	art	art	music
137	cities	cities	art	172	art	art	science
138	cities	cities	education	173	art	art	literature
139	cities	cities	local news	174	art	art	communication
140	cities	cities	business	175	art	art	local news
141	cities	cities	geography	176	individual choice	art	geography
142	cities	cities	law	177	individual choice	art	ecology
143	cities	cities	medicine	178	individual choice	art	history
				179	individual choice	art	science
				180	individual choice	art	health

Emphases in Recreational Reading

Beginning Lesson	Emphasis	Beginning Lesson	Emphasis
1	selection of books	91	predictions
11	how students select books	101	reading habits outside of school
21	decoding	111	abandoning and finishing books
31	authors	121	main characters
41	main idea; preferences	131	reasons for events
51	characters	141	favorite books; conversations with friends
61	improvement as reader; changing tastes	151	getting ideas for writing from books
71	students' criteria for selection	161	students' favorites
81	inferences	171	plans for summer reading

Skill Emphases in Lessons

Lesson	Comprehension Skill	Composing Skill	Spelling Emphasis	Other Emphasis
1	main idea	topic list	t	
2	details	list	c	
3	drawing conclusions	choose topic	f	
4	classification	facts	l	
5	collecting data	poems	b	nouns
6	cause and effect	capital letters	j	nouns
7	cause and effect	letters	d	nouns
8	comparison	journals	h	nouns
9	cause and effect	journals	m	nouns
10	drawing conclusions	revision	r	nouns
11	association of information	nouns	g	verbs
12	association of information	response groups	v	verbs
13	classification	asking for help	k	verbs
14	drawing conclusions	illustrations	p	verbs
15	collecting data	publishing	n	verbs
16	map reading	list	qu	verbs
17	cause and effect	settings	s	verbs
18	facts	choose topic	w	verbs
19	map reading	acrostic poem	x	verbs
20	classification	poem	y	verbs
21	comparison	punctuation	z	verbs
22	searching for details	writing about books	a	adjective with noun
23	classification	description	e	adjective with noun
24	cause and effect	paragraphing	i	adjective with noun
25	cause and effect	revision	o	adjective with noun
26	association	subject-verb agreement	u	adjective with noun
27	comparison	response groups	A	proper nouns
28	prediction	illustrations	B	proper nouns
29	comparison	editing	C	proper nouns
30	main idea	publishing	D	proper nouns
31	searching for information	list	E	proper nouns
32	cause and effect	list	F	proper nouns
33	comparison	choose topic	G	proper nouns
34	searching for facts	learn from writer	H	proper nouns
35	searching for facts	poem	I	proper nouns
36	drawing conclusions	capitalization	J	proper nouns
37	classification	writing about books	K	proper nouns
38	comparison	pen-pal letters	L	proper nouns
39	characterization	letter format	M	proper nouns
40	main idea	deadlines	N	proper nouns
41	association of information	verbs	O	sentences
42	details	response groups	P	sentences
43	cause and effect	letters	QU	sentences
44	questions	editing	R	sentences
45	classification	publishing	S	sentences
46	cause and effect	list	T	sentences
47	cause and effect	list	U	sentences
48	prediction	choosing topic	V	sentences
49	cause and effect	choosing topic	W	sentences
50	main idea	poem	X	sentences
51	details	writing about books	Y	sentences
52	association	run-on sentences	Z	sentences
53	cause and effect	invitations	ai	sentences
54	details	editing	au	sentences
55	main idea	advertising	ee	sentences
56	classification	sentence patterns	ea	sentences
57	details	asking writers questions	oo	sentences

Lesson	Comprehension Skill	Composing Skill	Spelling Emphasis	Other Emphasis
58	sequence of events	editing	oa	sentences
59	comparison	lettering	oi	sentences
60	main idea	publishing	ou	sentences
61	details	list	ay	sentences
62	comparison	list	ey	sentences
63	cause and effect	choose topic	aw	sentences
64	study questions	facts	ar	sentences
65	comparison	poem	er	sentences
66	comparison	capitalization	ir	sentences
67	cause and effect	writing about books	ur	sentences
68	comparison	choosing project	ew	sentences
69	cause and effect	audience	ow	sentences
70	main idea	handwriting	igh	sentences
71	comparison	editing	cc	sentences
72	classifying	publishing	ff	sentences
73	main idea	format of letters	mm	sentences
74	cause and effect	rhymes	ll	sentences
75	sequence of events	ideas for cards	ss	sentences
76	main idea	list	bb	sentences
77	cause and effect	list	dd	sentences
78	cause and effect	choose topic	gy	sentences
79	details	facts	tt	sentences
80	classification	poems	si	paragraphs
81	cause and effect	including details	re	paragraphs
82	reference skills	writing about books	it	paragraphs
83	sequence of events	writing a poem	ck	paragraphs
84	comparison	recording data	on	paragraphs
85	main idea	observation notes	en	paragraphs
86	main idea	sequence	gh	paragraphs
87	cause and effect	response groups	cy	paragraphs
88	sequence of events	charts and graphs	es	paragraphs
89	cause and effect	editing	rt	paragraphs
90	classification	publishing	ud	paragraphs
91	cause and effect	list	ro	paragraphs
92	cause and effect	list	ox	paragraphs
93	reference skills	choose topic	ke	paragraphs
94	cause and effect	facts	tu	paragraphs
95	main idea	poem	om	paragraphs
96	main idea	parts of speech	in	paragraphs
97	details	writing about books	sc	paragraphs
98	main idea	plan book	pr	paragraphs
99	characterization	personification	ph	paragraphs
100	classification	organizing books	wr	paragraphs
101	classification	titles	tl	paragraphs
102	questions and answers	response groups	ef	paragraphs
103	sequence of events	illustrations	ri	paragraphs
104	comparison	table of contents	ja	paragraphs
105	summary	publishing	wh	paragraphs
106	cause and effect	list	gy	paragraphs
107	details	dialogue	ob	paragraphs
108	details	punctuation of dialogue	da	paragraphs
109	comparison	dialogue	gr	paragraphs
110	main idea and details	plays	th	paragraphs
111	classification	punctuation of dialogue	ru	paragraphs
112	questions and answers	writing about books	de	paragraphs
113	sequence of events	collaborating	ft	paragraphs
114	comparison	scripts	rd	paragraphs
115	summary	revision	kn	paragraphs
116	alphabetical order	stage directions	ve	paragraphs
117	details	revision	sh	paragraphs
118	organizing information	conclusions	ch	paragraphs
119	cause and effect	performance	be	paragraphs

Lesson	Comprehension Skill	Composing Skill	Spelling Emphasis	Other Emphasis
120	questions and answers	performance	bo	paragraphs
121	classification	list	ell	paragraphs
122	sequence	list	chi	paragraphs
123	classification	notes	jus	paragraphs
124	comparison	facts	opp	paragraphs
125	summary	poems	les	paragraphs
126	skimming	details	kno	paragraphs
127	skimming	writing about books	ott	paragraphs
128	cause and effect	choose topic	ten	paragraphs
129	details	leads	rab	paragraphs
130	comparison	details	plu	paragraphs
131	main idea and details	paragraphing	qui	paragraphs
132	questions and answers	response group	str	paragraphs
133	classification	illustrations	twi	paragraphs
134	main idea and details	titles	est	paragraphs
135	summary	publishing	stu	paragraphs
136	alphabetizing	list	tro	paragraphs
137	sequence of events	list	mot	paragraphs
138	skimming	choose topic	ing	paragraphs
139	details	facts	cks	paragraphs
140	organizing information	poem	ter	paragraphs
141	classification	items in series	tch	paragraphs
142	questions and answers	setting in books	law	paragraphs
143	cause and effect	list	ara	paragraphs
144	comparison	choose topic and style of writing	dge	paragraphs
145	summary	sequence of ideas	fre	paragraphs
146	map reading	main idea	ght	paragraphs
147	main idea and details	response groups	les	paragraphs
148	main idea and details	diagrams and charts	fer	paragraphs
149	main idea	editing	ble	paragraphs
150	classification	publishing	che	paragraphs
151	classification	list	low	paragraphs
152	organization of information	list	ded	paragraphs
153	comparison	choose topic	wri	paragraphs
154	map reading	facts	cha	paragraphs
155	summary	acrostic poems	tio	paragraphs
156	inference	spelling	tai	paragraphs
157	main idea and details	writing about characters	orm	paragraphs
158	inference	poster ideas	ese	paragraphs
159	inference	choosing topics	cre	paragraphs
160	classification	main ideas	nes	paragraphs
161	questions and answers	main ideas	tion	dialogue
162	main idea and details	sequence	crea	dialogue
163	inference	lettering	each	dialogue
164	inference	editing	thin	dialogue
165	summary	publishing	able	dialogue
166	main idea	list	ness	dialogue
167	main idea and details	list	ings	dialogue
168	comparison	choose topic	chlo	dialogue
169	classification	facts	read	dialogue
170	classification	poems	ence	dialogue
171	inference	possessives	graph	paragraphs
172	alphabetical order	writing about books	therm	paragraphs
173	sequence	plans for picture books	photo	paragraphs
174	main idea and details	choose topic	ocean	paragraphs
175	summary	notes for illustrations	divid	paragraphs
176	main idea and details	paragraphing	place	paragraphs
177	association	illustrations	store	paragraphs
178	comparison	illustrations	think	paragraphs
179	main idea	paragraphing	sprou	paragraphs
180	main idea	publishing	stati	paragraphs

▶ Index